S0-DXE-690

**An Aggregate Theory of
International Payments Adjustment**

By the same author

International Travel: International Trade
The Economics of Business Investment Abroad

An Aggregate Theory of International Payments Adjustment

H. Peter Gray

Lexington Books
D. C. Heath and Company
Lexington, Massachusetts
Toronto   London

The Wollman Library
BARNARD COLLEGE
Columbia University

Library of Congress Cataloging in Publication Data

Gray, H   Peter.
   An aggregate theory of international payments adjustment.

   1. Balance of Payments.   I.   Title.
HG3881.G67   1974 b   382.1'7   73–7980
ISBN 0–669–85928–1

Copyright © 1974 by H. Peter Gray

All rights reserved. No part of this publication may be reproduced or transmitted in any form or by any means, electronic or mechanical, including photocopy, recording, or any information storage or retrieval system, without permission in writing from the publisher.

Printed in Great Britain

International Standard Book Number: 0–669–85928–1

Library of Congress Catalog Card Number: 73–7980

Barnard
HG
3881
.G67
1974 b

To

JEAN M. GRAY

NPB JUN 11 1975

185294

Contents

Preface

The model presented in this book is designed to liberate balance-of-payments theory from the general equilibrium framework in which it has been confined. The theory presented here is less susceptible to elegance than is the standard model but it should be more relevant for policy formulation in a real world in which disturbances come in many shapes and sizes and in which nations do not always seek compatible payments objectives. Unfortunately the experience of Max Planck does not offer much hope to would-be creators of new proofs or methodological approaches – particularly in such an inherently imprecise field as international economics. (See *Scientific Autobiography and Other Papers*, New York: Philosophical Library, 1949, pp. 30–4.) Consequently the writing of this book has been, in large part, an act of faith – perhaps a belief that however useful it may be to fill empty boxes, it is even more useful to create those boxes. The theory developed here is by no means a finished model, but it has reached the stage at which fresh insights will more quickly enable it to reach whatever potential value it may prove to have.

The ideas presented here have had a long gestation since the original insights were gained in 1964. A Ford Foundation Faculty Fellowship, awarded in 1965–6 for work on the economics of international travel, was partially diverted to what is now the core of Part II. It was published as, 'A Keynesian Framework for the International Accounts' in *Weltwirtschaftliches Archiv* (1969), and I am grateful to the editors for permission to include that material. The book would never have been completed without the award of a Rutgers University Research Council Fellowship and the concomitant permission to accept that award by Douglass College and by my colleagues who, under the rules of that fellowship, take up the burden of an absentee. The Brookings Institution provided me with guest scholar privileges from September 1971, to February 1972, and made a significant contribution to my productivity by providing me with an office between those of Walter S. Salant and Lawrence B. Krause. In this way, the Institution allowed me to learn (and to learn much) by osmosis as well as by interchange. None of these institutions is in any way responsible for the ideas expressed in this book.

The theory presented here stands on the shoulders of many giants (and one titan): the writings of Sir Roy Harrod, Harry G. Johnson, Fritz Machlup, J. E. Meade, Joan Robinson and Jan Tinbergen have all provided grist for my synthesising mill. Valuable insights were gained from the methodological approach of the Brookings forecast of the U.S. balance-of-payments in 1968, from the Reddaway team's work on foreign investment, and from Richard N. Cooper's work on interdependence. The following people have all made a contribution to the model through conversation, correspondence or comments on parts of the manuscript, and I should like to acknowledge their help: E. Ray Canterbery, Richard E. Caves, Robert V. Eagly, Peter B. Kenen, Jan Kregel, Vincent Lin, Gail E. Makinen, D. E. Moggridge, Ingo Walter and Donald Winch. If they cannot remember doing so, the reason is the length of the gestation period. There remains the debt that I owe to my wife. It is very great. She encouraged me, she refurbished and clarified the economics. She asked insightful questions and she bore with the cyclical pattern of euphoria and despondency during the many years over which the theory evolved. Dedication is less than payment in full.

Finally, let me acknowledge the contributions of Mrs Doris Cunningham and Mrs Gerri Dructor both of whom performed nobly in the production of the manuscript in an orderly and legible form.

H. PETER GRAY

Belle Mead, New Jersey

Part One
The Infrastructure

1 The Need for a New Theory of International Payments Adjustment

This book is predicated on the belief that the existing state of balance-of-payments theory does not provide national economic authorities with a sufficiently pragmatic frame of reference for international payments policy formulation. As a result the international payments mechanism has not been functioning smoothly and efficiently during recent years. Social costs – such as unemployment and the adverse side effects of stop-go macropolicies – that might have been avoided with a more effective system of international payments and adjustment, have been commonplace. The lack of pragmatism of the theory of balance of payments derives from three main shortcomings: an unwillingness to acknowledge the possibility that any self-correcting tendencies might be deliberately nullified by national authorities; a reliance upon general equilibrium analysis; and the failure to integrate into the body of the theory, transactions on capital and transfer accounts. These shortcomings have become increasingly important since about 1950 as macro-stabilisation policies have been used more and more effectively for the solution of domestic problems, as economic interdependence among the developed nations of the world has grown, and as transactions on the capital and transfer accounts have assumed increased quantitative significance.

The purpose of this book is to evolve a short-run model of international payments adjustment that will involve international capital movements and other non-current flows as integral parts of the theory. From the analytic base presented, it may be possible for nations to achieve a new approach to the solution of payments problems so that the social costs of international adjustment can be reduced.

Anne O. Krueger has, in a recent and authoritative review of the literature of balance-of-payments theory, remarked that the 'most thoroughly explored models in payments theory are those which consider only current account transactions and a means of payment. . . . To date, such models constitute the core of payments theory.'[1] Such was the dominance of this frame of reference that Krueger felt obliged to limit her review almost wholly to models of that kind. However, even when international investment is incorporated into balance-of-payments theory, the reliance upon general equilibrium analysis is maintained. Richard N. Cooper has argued, cogently, that the increased interdependence among industrial countries has increased the magnitude and frequency of disturbances with which national policymakers must cope.[2] Finally, Robert V. Roosa has observed that the traditional approach to balance-of-payments analysis has presumed an unrealistically simple structure of the determinants of international payments – the 'woefully incomplete' formula having as its 'more significant missing elements . . . capital flows, debt servicing and governmental transfers. They have not been ignored in the customary, balance-of-payments diagnosis, but they have generally been pushed aside as residuals, fitting into whatever place the trade accounts would allow.'[3]

Any theory of international payments adjustment must take as a datum the need to preserve high levels of employment. This policy requirement imposes upon a pragmatic theory a short-run horizon since policymakers will not submit to the strains imposed upon the social fabric by ponderous adjustment mechanisms. The release of the theory from its general equilibrium framework also allows for the possibility of non-zero payments balances to exist for periods of time either deliberately or through incomplete adjustment and accommodating financing of deficits.

The essential concern of economic policy-making is efficiency. Balance-of-payments policies are essentially national or aggregative

---

[1] Anne O. Krueger, 'Balance-of-Payments Theory', *Journal of Economic Literature*, VII (March 1969) p. 2.

[2] Richard N. Cooper, *The Economics of Interdependence* (New York: McGraw-Hill: for the Council on Foreign Relations, 1968) pp. 8 and 261–2. The possibility of increased frequency of disturbances is also enhanced by concern with pollution, see Ralph C. d'Arge and Allen V. Kneese, 'Environmental Quality and International Trade', *International Organization* (Spring 1972) pp. 419–65.

[3] In 'Capital Movements and Balance-of-Payments Adjustment', in *Men, Money and Policy – Essays in Honor of Karl R. Bopp*, ed. David P. Eastburn, (Philadelphia: Federal Reserve Bank of Philadelphia, 1970) pp. 171–94, also printed in the Federal Reserve Bank of Philadelphia *Business Review* (September 1970) pp. 21–38.

phenomena and their primary impact is felt in the ability to maintain high levels of output and employment in the focus country. It is a basic premise of this book that satisfactory performance as far as rates of output and employment are concerned, is prerequisite to any claim to efficient economic operation. The importance of high employment for economic efficiency is enhanced if, as seems probable, fundamental changes in the structure of the economy or any desirable social changes are more easily accomplished in a democracy in times of prosperity. Consequently the emphasis of the payments theory to be evolved is 'quantitative' rather than 'qualitative' in Tinbergen's use of those terms.[4] The theory concerns itself with the ability of a nation to attain or maintain quantitative goals without any intentional alteration of the structure of the economy. These goals are given numerical target values and are to be achieved by changing certain political parameters and instruments that are under the control of the economic authorities and that operate within the given institutional setting that constitutes the data for the economy.[5]

The emphasis on the short-run makes it desirable to distinguish very clearly between the terms 'equilibrium' and 'balance'. Equilibrium is defined in its strict sense of a combination of selected variables such that 'no inherent tendency to change prevails in the model which they constitute.'[6] Balance exists when two opposing sets of forces counteract each other for a short period of time but without any connotation of the continuity of that state of affairs. When this distinction is translated into balance-of-payments terms, equilibrium requires an equality between selected categories of international receipts and payments such that future disequilibrium does not automatically occur, while payments balance merely requires an equality between the selected categories for a short specified period.

The shift of emphasis from general equilibrium to a short-run model requires one final qualification of the content of balance-of-payments theory as the subject is to be defined here. The present

[4] Jan Tinbergen, *On the Theory of Economic Policy* (Amsterdam: North Holland Publishing Company, 1952) pp. 1–4.

[5] *Ibid.*, Ch. 2. In practice, the distinction between the two kinds of policies is never completely clear since quantitatively-oriented policies can have qualitative side-effects.

[6] Fritz Machlup is the authority on the problem of reconciling equilibrium and policy presciptions. See his 'Equilibrium and Disequilibrium: Misplaced Concreteness and Disguised Politics', *Economic Journal*, LXVIII (March 1958) pp. 1–24, and especially p. 9.

theory regards the foreign exchange market as 'one of many interrelated markets' to be analysed in a general equilibrium framework.[7]
The aggregate theory to be evolved in this book is less comprehensive
and explicitly excludes from its central core, international transactions
in convertible currencies and liquid instruments. This exclusion can be
rationalised on four grounds. First, movements of short-terms funds,
to the extent that they do not accompany imbalances in the balance
on basic transactions,[8] require a remedy other than the adjustment
of the underlying economies. Second, the major concern of policymakers is with real variables such as employment rates, real income
and growth rates rather than with movements of short-term international funds in and of themselves. Third, international movements
of short-term funds do not in the absence of any trend or shift in
the relative desirability of foreign and domestic liquid assets, affect
either the net worth or the net reserve position of a nation. Finally,
the argument can be made that balance in the 'real variables' is
necessary but not sufficient for orderly conditions to hold in foreign
exchange markets and that a separate analysis of the set of transactions governed by real variables is warranted.[9] It is possible to contend that so restricted a frame of reference hardly warrants the use
of the word 'payments' in its description, but unfortunately there is
no convenient alternative that is not equally, if not more, misleading.

The remainder of Part I sets the stage for the generation of the
model in Part II. Chapter 2 investigates more deeply the reasons for
rejecting the general-equilibrium framework for policy-making in
payments adjustment and introduces a conceptual framework for a
short-run model that combines period analysis, the target–instruments approach and the trichotomy of basic adjustments, quasi-
adjustments and financing as alternative cures for payments imbalance.[10] Chapter 3 examines the influence of Keynes' constructs
on the model to be evolved and utilises an early model of Keynes of
aggregate international payments adjustment as a basis for the
definition of a key set of relationships in the aggregate theory.
Finally, Chapter 4 is devoted to the somewhat tedious topics of
assumptions, definitions and limitations of the model.

---

[7] Krueger, *Journal of Economic Literature* (March 1969) p. 5.
[8] The concept of the basic balance is discussed in detail in Chapter 4 below.
[9] 'Monetary variables' are considered in Chapter 11 below.
[10] See Fritz Machlup, 'Adjustment, Compensatory Correction and Financing
Imbalances in International Payments', in *Trade, Growth and the Balance of
Payments*, R. E. Baldwin *et al.* (Chicago: Rand McNally, 1965) pp. 185–213.

2 Characteristics of the Short-Run Model

The contention that the general equilibrium approach is unsuited to policy prescriptions for payments adjustments in the modern era must be analysed before a short-run theory can be substituted for it as the core of payments theory. The requirements imposed upon the world by general equilibrium theory for it to be operational are considered first and are followed by a brief examination of the support for general equilibrium that can be derived from the twenty-five-years life span of the Bretton Woods era.

The alternative analytical approaches of period analysis and the targets-instruments framework are outlined briefly and combined with Machlup's trichotomy of solutions for imbalance of basic adjustments, quasi-adjustments and financing. The short-run frame of reference is summarised succinctly in the concluding section.

EQUILIBRIUM ANALYSIS

Given the post-war commitments to high levels of employment in the developed countries and the consequent refusal of national authorities to permit to take place an adjustment process – automatic or induced – that involved unpalatable levels of unemployment, reliance upon equilibrium analysis would be operational only if the world met the following conditions:

1. The equilibrium which will evolve must be a state of high employment and the system must react to any disturbance so that the original or some equally satisfactory equilibrium state is quickly reattained.
2. The social cost of the automatic adjustment to the new equilibrium must be minimal, i.e. not subject to reduction by an alternative, interventionist economic policy.
3. Equilibrium, once attained, must be maintainable, i.e. the policy decisions that stem from equilibrium analysis must

generate a system of responses that will minimise lapses from
full or high employment for balance-of-payments reasons.

In a closed economy, these conditions would summarise the criteria
by which the efficiency of macroeconomic policy would be assessed.
The crucial question then is: does the world of international economic transactions provide the stability of relationships that corre-
sponds with the operational application of equilibrium analysis? If
the adjustment mechanisms are or can be made sensitive and if the
disturbances are few, equilibrium analysis that includes all the
relevant variables will be a reasonable basis for international payments policy. Under such a system the actual number of policy
adjustments that would have to be instituted would be small. If,
however, disturbances are frequent occurrences so that adjustments
must be made frequently and, if the disturbances had considerable
magnitude, with the result that the reaction to one disturbance
would not be completed before the arrival of another, equilibrium
analysis would not be a suitable framework for policy.[1] The institution of a system of freely flexible rates of exchange that would clear
foreign exchange markets automatically, does not eliminate the
shortcomings of a general equilibrium approach. What matters is the
frequency of the need for adjustment and not the speed with which
actual adjustment follows upon perceived need. Of course, those who
recommend freely flexible rates as a solution to payments adjustment
work implicitly in a frame of reference that concerns itself with
short-run equilibria in which the combination of market forces and
institutions are always pressuring the system towards some set of
equilibrium values in the face of frequent and unforeseen disturbances.[2]

There are four main areas which can be expected to give rise to
disturbances with a frequency that is sufficient to substantiate the
need for reliance on short-run analysis for international payments
policy. The four areas are: (1) the behaviour of absolute price levels
in the two nations; (2) the impact of exogenous changes on the path
of adjustment; (3) the time dimension in equilibrium analysis, and
(4) the role of long-term international investment.

[1] The rejection of general equilibrium analysis as a basis for payments adjustment theory does not deny its value for analyses of resource allocation, long-run
problems and of markets in which equilibrium conditions are very rapidly
attained.

[2] The question of the optimality of a system of flexible rates is developed in
Parts II and III below.

(1) In a world of fixed and infrequently adjustable exchange rates, perverse changes in price levels in individual trading nations can constitute disturbances. There has been a tendency to neglect the role of changes in absolute price levels in countries, perhaps because economists with sufficient faith in David Hume's price–specie–flow mechanism could rely upon the monetary authority in the deficit nation being forced, ultimately, to lower the price level.[3]

The classical medicine of adjustment to a disturbance involved two component parts – one was the macroeconomic adjustment of the absolute price level and the second was the microeconomic adjustment of relative prices and resource reallocation. Modern macro-policy can offset the macroeconomic adjustment process and can attenuate the microeconomic adjustment by maintaining aggregate demand in the face of a change in the net contribution of the international sector. While the automatic adjustment process is not completely negated by domestic macrostabilisation policies, its effectiveness is markedly reduced, and the length of time needed for adjustment to a given disturbance much increased.[4] To the extent that the automatic forces of adjustment are countered, self-reinforcing disturbances with cumulative effects must ultimately induce a crisis set of conditions with correspondingly severe social costs.

In a system of flexible rates of exchange, perverse movements of national price levels would be offset by correspondingly greater changes in exchange rates than would otherwise have taken place. Provided that the system of flexible rates is able to withstand the greater strains imposed by perverse behaviour of domestic price levels, lack of national discipline over price levels will not affect the efficiency of adaptation to disturbances that have their origin in real variables.

(2) Any changes in the balance of payments resulting from economic policy actions taken with their impact upon payments

[3] Had the writings of Isaac Gervaise become the keystone of the received doctrine of adjustment, the ability of absolute price levels to run counter to adjustment needs would have received greater prominence. See John M. Letiche, *Balance of Payments and Economic Growth* (New York: Harper Bros., 1959) pp. 26–32. Classicists were aware of the unreliability of the price–specie–flow mechanism in practice in both deficit and surplus countries: See Robert V. Eagly, 'Adam Smith and the Specie Flow Doctrine', *Scottish Journal of Political Economy* (February 1970) pp. 61–8.

[4] For a perceptive analysis of this phenomenon, see Nicholas Kaldor, 'Conflicts in National Economic Objectives', *The Economic Journal*, LXXXI (March 1971) pp. 1–16.

ot

balance clearly understood, can be considered as endogenous. The effect of any such measures will either have been intentional, and therefore can be presumed to be equilibrating, or will have been deliberately offset by another policy measure. It is the impact of other kinds of economic change – exogenous changes – that can induce imbalance of payments and that the adjustment mechanism must be capable of absorbing. The most important and obvious kind of exogenous change is economic growth and related dynamic changes in economic forces over time. If there is one thing that two-country growth models can be said to have substantiated beyond reasonable doubt, it is that the trading conditions necessary for the maintaining of payments balance are likely to change over time. When the possibility of changing and disparate growth rates for many nations of varying importance as trading partners is allowed for, the necessity of adjustment appears inevitable. However, provided that the equilibrium model itself is dynamic and the trend of adjustment is a steady one, the equilibrium framework might still prove adequate to the task. The probability of this happy state of affairs materialising must seem small, if economic growth is recognised as a complex composite of many sources of change. If once added to the complexity of the growth process itself, the further complications that stem from intermittent changes in tastes and design-advantages in differentiated goods then the probability of real world growth paths obeying models based on dynamic equilibrium must be negligible.[5]

Another sort of disturbance that will affect the trading conditions on which payments balance will obtain are the phenomena that arrive in this world at discrete and haphazard intervals and which have no direct relationship with macroeconomic policy or variables. Examples of these are changes in political alignments and commitments that involve a balance-of-payments cost. Changes in membership in trade blocs or the formation of trade blocs can exert profound influences on the pattern of international payments as can changes in

[5] While it is artificial and abstract in the extreme, Johnson's analysis of the range of the different effects on the balance of trade of economic growth must be seen as almost substantive proof of the never-ceasing occurrence of disturbances in the real sector. See Harry G. Johnson, 'Economic Development and International Trade' in *Readings in International Economics*, ed. R. E. Caves and H. G. Johnson (Homewood, Ill.: Richard D. Irwin, Inc., for the American Economic Association, 1968) pp. 281–99. Note particularly the summary table on p. 296.

the known stock of global natural resources and their distribution among nations.[6] Finally, the international system is not immune to the thousand and one changes in tax rates and regulations that are generated by growing bureaucracies without any intent of impinging on payments balance.

It is possible that all of these disparate sources of economic change will have a cumulative impact and that a nation may, for a relatively long period, suffer an adverse secular trend in the trading conditions under which it can achieve payments balance. The possibility of the existence of a secular trend in trading conditions compatible with balance has not yet fully incorporated itself into payments analysis.[7] It is therefore not surprising that the policy-makers of the Bretton Woods era were able to countenance the creation of so great a force as the European Economic Community without anticipating any protracted problem of adjustment.

(3) 'More often that not, time is left out in the construction and operation of equilibrium models.'[8] Such models must clearly refer to stationary states and are of little pragmatic value in a world concerned with adapting to ongoing change.

Dynamic equilibrium analyses – however useful they may be as basic research – have little more to offer as bases for pragmatic policy prescriptions than do their static counterparts. The interest in dynamic models is to examine the way in which economies will interact and, as a consequence, these models also run the risk of having a timeless quality. The sheer intricacy of the analysis limits the number of variables that can be included. Pain and imbalance are eliminated by the assumptions of instantaneous adjustment, permanent full employment and flexible exchange rates. The economies are usually characterised by specific attributes and growth patterns and rates so that the resultant interaction generates a stable growth path for the two nations without any finite time limit.

[6] The discovery and harnessing of energy resources in the North Sea is a case in point.

[7] One diagnosis of the United States deficit avoided explicit consideration of an adverse trend despite dealing with an indication of its existence: 'A second explanation is that a series of random events was somehow biased towards increasing the deficit and negating these measures [to close the payments gap]. This view is unacceptable since it contradicts the meaning of randomness.' See Robert Z. Alibur, *Choices for the Dollar* (Washington: National Planning Association, 1969) p. 20.

[8] Machlup, *Economic Journal* (March 1958) p. 7.

Even if it were assumed that a dynamic equilibrium analysis of a nation's international growth were able to forecast with reasonable accuracy the *trend* rate of change of the exchange rate through time, the relevance of such a model for policy decisions does not follow automatically. If the variation around the trend comprises 'deficit cycles' and 'surplus cycles' that offset each other in the long run, riding out the cycle with the trend exchange rate may be a mistaken policy and, in addition, the trend itself may be affected by the decision to (or not to) ride out the cycle. It is quite possible that the total loss of reserves during a deficit cycle will exceed the international financing capacity that the country has available and it is also possible that the concomitant reduction in its (international) net worth is not the optimum policy for the nation.

(4) In the modern world, long-term capital flows and unilateral transfers constitute jointly an integral and quantitatively important part of international economic transactions. These flows, deriving as they do from stock-adjustment considerations (investments and investment income) and from political considerations (foreign aid and government loans), may fluctuate over time to the point that models based exclusively on well-defined flows are unlikely accurately to represent the real world. Capital account transactions do not occur in isolation but reflect back upon the current account even when the concomitant monetary effects are offset by the respective economic authorities. The net impact of a capital transaction upon international balance depends upon the degree to which the capital movement generates offsetting (or reinforcing) current account flows and upon the time-shape of these flows. The sheer complexity of the joint category suggests that current-account repercussions are unlikely to be a constant proportion of the net capital outflow through time. Long-term capital itself involves three types of investment, each of which is likely to have a different repercussion upon the current account. The reaction of the current account will vary with both the type of direct investment and the characteristics of the host nation. Direct investment can take on three separate forms, and each has its own pattern of current-account impact: a new establishment; an extension to an ongoing foreign subsidiary and a take-over of an existing foreign-owned enterprise. The degree to which an investment will generate a demand for the home country's exports will depend largely upon the availability of capital goods in the host nation so that, as a first approximation, the initial current-account

impact of a foreign investment will be larger when the host nation is a less-developed nation.[9]

Over time, international investment will provide a change in the underlying production–consumption complex of all the nations involved, and these changes will react back upon the trading conditions necessary for payments balance. This is the effect of capital movements that is concerned with the resource allocation pattern of different nations.

It is the result of both the capital movements, with their related current account repercussions, and the effects of the redistribution of a global stock of capital that will disturb the ongoing payments balance. Any model that emphasises the production–consumption complex of two nations may be capable of making approximate allowance for the impact of international capital flows by suitable adjustments of the rate of domestic capital formation. It is less likely that a flow model will be able successfully to incorporate the capital movements themselves and their direct repercussions on the international accounts.

It is also possible that the combinations of international investments and unilateral transfers will be subject to time trends and to shifts over time. Trends if correctly foreseen, present no insuperable problems for equilibrium analyses, but severe and irregular shifts in variables over time are difficult to include satisfactorily in a dynamic framework. It is quite possible that the future volume of international investment will decline as a proportion of global output. It may well be that the decade of the sixties saw a flood of capital movements following a period of forty-five years (1913–58) when conditions in the world were not conducive to international investment (i.e. a large stock disequilibrium existed in 1958), and because of the formation and the success of the E.E.C. Investments in developing countries may also be reduced because of xenophobic tendencies and increasing political unrest in Africa, Asia and Latin America. On the other hand the capacity to absorb capital in these nations might increase dramatically as a result of increases in educational levels and the ability to work with modern technology.

The four areas summarised in the preceding paragraphs support the proposition that equilibrium analysis is unlikely to be able adequately to represent and incorporate the large number of

[9] This is the question of the rate of concurrent induced international saving and is examined in detail in Chapter 7 below.

disturbances that can affect a nation's international accounts. Indeed, it is arguable that the frequency and magnitude of disturbances has increased since the late fifties when the recoveries of individual nations from the effects of the Second World War were virtually complete. Foremost among the causes of the increase in disturbances are the growth of economic interdependence and the accompanying surge of international investment and licensing agreements that followed from the progressive lowering of international barriers to economic activity that characterised the fifties and the sixties.[10]

THE BRETTON WOODS ERA

The international monetary regime developed at Bretton Woods in 1944 provided the world with a monetary system that worked smoothly for almost a quarter of a century. Given the faith in the attainability and the inherent desirability of equilibrium that was a cornerstone of the Bretton Woods monetary system, the longevity of that system could be seen as evidence in support of reliance upon a general equilibrium context as a solution to international monetary strains.

When the Bretton Woods system was formulated, the problems of post-war adjustments dominated the minds of the conferees, and the problems associated with the operation of a global international monetary system in times of normalcy received only passing attention. As the operation of the system evolved there was a general resistance on the part of the International Monetary Fund and the main trading nations to changes in the par values of currencies. This resistance suggests a faith in the existence of an equilibrium set of exchange rates that lasted well beyond the post-war recovery period.[11] In practice, a part of the overall success of the Bretton Woods system was due to the natural development of events during the twenty-five years. A brief survey of the main developments will indicate three vital attributes of the Bretton Woods era that contributed to the longevity of the system, and it will also show why the situation in August 1971, at the end of the Bretton Woods era, was a less than ideal basis for the creation of a new system to be built on the same premises.

[10] See Cooper, *The Economics of Interdependence*, Chs. 1 and 10.
[11] See William R. Allen's incisive critique of the Fund's *Weltanschauung* in 'The International Monetary Fund and Balance of Payments Adjustment', *Oxford Economic Papers* (June 1961) pp. 149–65 and see also the I.M.F. *Annual Report 1964*, p. 28.

European nations slowly rebuilt their economies after the war, and the recovery of their productive potential slowly reduced the disparity between the official, supported rate of exchange of their individual currencies and the rate that would have existed in the absence of trading and capital controls *vis-à-vis* strong currencies. In practice this meant that the degree of severity of controls on current transactions and on the freedom to transfer capital funds abroad were gradually relaxed until some state of normalcy was attained. Thus the rates of exchange of the currencies of the war-torn nations slowly shed the trappings of suppressed disequilibria. Even so, the change from a chronic dollar shortage to a world in which the United States was the main key currency nation and was afflicted with a chronic deficit was remarkably rapid. The existence of dollar deficits meant that European and other surplus nations were able to build up their international reserve positions and, since the reserves were kept in the form of dollar balances, no liquidity or financing strain was imposed upon the United States. The infusion of reserves was greatly needed since the volume and value of international trade were both growing apace and trading nations naturally desired to keep larger liquid balances on hand. Simultaneously the surge in direct and portfolio investment from the United States took place and made its own contribution to the rapidity of the turnabout from dollar shortage to dollar deficit.

At this point it became apparent, at least to one farsighted man, that the elimination of the United States deficit which had ultimately to occur, would bring to a halt the major source of increase in international liquid assets. This elimination of the dollar deficit betokened a shortage of international liquidity as a constant volume of liquid assets became insufficient for an evergrowing volume of international trade. This thesis, associated with its main proponent, Robert Triffin, led the world of international finance to emphasise the need for the creation of international liquidity in preference to concern with the improvement of the process of adjustment. The institution and the creation of Special Drawing Rights in 1970 were the culmination of Triffin's work. The correct rate of increase in the supply of world liquid assets has still not been decided but the original mechanism has been described as 'excessively political.'[12] There is no question that Triffin performed a valuable service.

[12] Lawrence B. Krause, *Sequal to Bretton Woods* (Washington: The Brookings Institution, 1971) p. 16.

However, the emphasis on the need for liquidity creation had inevitably to detract from the attention paid to the process of adjustment – despite the fact that the need for the created liquidity hinged upon a cessation of the United States deficit and therefore, presumably, upon some adjustment process. To some degree the creation of liquidity is a substitute for the improvement of the adjustment processes, so that proponents of greater liquidity tended to discourage schemes put forward for greater flexibility of exchange rates. Triffin himself labelled flexible exchange rates a 'false solution' to the liquidity problem. His reasons appear to be based on the expectation or fear that destabilising speculation would prevent the market for foreign exchange from determining the 'correct' underlying prices.[13] On the other hand proponents of exchange-rate flexibility grew in number during the sixties, and many different schemes were devised to allow the foreign exchange market to follow a trend without giving encouragement to exchange-rate speculation. Others argued for the retention of the adjustable peg but with the recommendation that the pegs be adjusted with much greater regularity and by smaller amounts than in the past. Probably no one would argue that some adjustment mechanism was not necessary and desirable and probably no proponent of exchange-rate flexibility would argue against the desirability of man-made liquidity supplementing gold.

The longevity of the Bretton Woods system owes something to the financing role of the International Monetary Fund and something to the exchange-rate adjustments that actually took place. But the three main sources of the system's strength were the slow release of suppressed disequilibria, the key currency status of the main deficit nation and, very important, the willingness of the United States to see its international liquidity position worsen through gold sales and through increases in its net short-term liabilities to foreigners. After the widespread 1949 devaluation, the European nations (and others) had currencies whose overvaluation was suppressed by controls at the same time that the trend of economic forces over time was to strengthen their currencies in relation to the U.S. dollar. Thus, until 1958 approximately, the system worked smoothly because the natural tendency was equilibrating. After 1958 when concern over the intractability of the United States deficit began to be registered the imbalance was still not large in terms of the resources of the key

[13] Robert Triffin, *Gold and the Dollar Crisis* (New Haven: Yale University Press, 1961) pp. 82–6.

currency nation and most surplus nations were willing to hold their newly-acquired reserves in dollars. Thus the United States deficit on current and long-term capital account was 'easily' financed. Finally, the system worked well because the United States was willing to act as a 'financial residual' by letting its liquidity position deteriorate more or less as the overall payments system needed. The reasons for this behaviour were the conformity of the action with its *credo* and because the nation continued to enjoy a surplus on current account and annual increases in its net international asset position. But the system was vulnerable and failed quickly once the United States was no longer able passively to tolerate the overall deficits coupled with the apparent deterioration of its international asset position as a consequence of deficits on current account in 1968 and 1969.[14]

The net result of the twenty-five years rule of the Bretton Woods system is that the new system must take shape in a world that is, in some respects, the mirror image of that which prevailed in 1950. Then, the United States had an excessive share of the world's total supply of liquid assets – in 1971 the United States has a sizeable negative net short-term position. The new system has a more difficult world to manage. It starts from a position of very unequal distribution of liquid assets in a world which will not tolerate suppression of disequilibria and a world in which capital movements – both short-term and long-term – have attained unprecedented magnitudes. Like Bretton Woods, the new system will have to create a mechanism that permits some approximate balance to be achieved and then a mechanism for maintaining that balance.

Those forces which conspired to provide a twenty-five-years life-span for an institution which placed minimal emphasis on adjustment through external measures, cannot be relied upon in the future. The new system must encompass a mechanism whereby the terms on which transactions with foreigners take place can be deliberately changed relative to those prevailing in domestic transactions. The new system will also need to take into account the positive role played under the Bretton Woods system by long-term capital movements in that they made possible the continued deterioration of the liquid balance of the key-currency nation. The experience

[14] $386 and $899 million respectively: see Department of Commerce, *Survey of Current Business*, 51 (June 1971) p. 30. Since profits retained by foreign subsidiaries are not entered in the U.S. international accounts and since they exceeded the deficits on current account, the net international asset position did not decrease.

of the fifties and sixties showed that the balance on autonomous transactions – the change in the liquid asset position – is not the only or even necessarily the major international target variable of a developed nation in the modern world. The balance on current account can be very important since it indicates, subject to some corrections, the change in the value of the nation's net international asset position. Provided that a nation's current account is in surplus there is a feeling of accumulation of net worth that can rationalise a continuing deterioration of its liquidity position. Finally, the emphasis upon external methods of adjustment is imposed upon the system by the importance of high-level employment as a domestic goal.

PERIOD ANALYSIS

Abstract analysis must simplify the complexities of the real world and must, in so doing, do violence to reality. The rejection of equilibrium analysis in favour of period analysis as a basis for balance-of-payments adjustment policy does not imply that period analysis presents no problems of compromise between analytic clarity and the real world conditions. The choice among alternative approaches must be based on the relative applicability to the problem at hand. Period analysis has been defined as the 'splitting of time into periods such that, apart from exogenous changes, the events of any period can be explained with reference to the events of previous periods.'[15] The larger the number of exogenous variables that must be taken into account, the more relevant is period analysis. However, the number of exogenous variables should be considered as the sum of two distinct types of variable: those that are truly exogenous and those for which exogenously-determined values have to be provided because the variable responds to too many separate forces for its behaviour to be expressed as a function of lagged endogenous variables. In balance-of-payments analysis that explicitly involves flows of long-term capital and unilateral transfers, both kinds of exogenous variables are sufficiently numerous that period analysis becomes preferable.

The hallmark of period analysis is its discontinuity. Because period analysis inherently involves the expectation of some changes in

[15] William J. Baumol (with a Contribution by Ralph Turvey), *Economic Dynamics: An Introduction*, 2nd ed. (New York: The Macmillan Company, 1959) p. 128. This section relies heavily on Ch. VIII.

underlying conditions occurring at frequent intervals, it imposes upon the policymakers a mental cast that is keyed to ongoing dynamic disturbance.[16] It is this characteristic of discontinuity that makes the approach so suitable as a basis for short-run forecasting with econometric models even though the feature of discontinuity does create problems that relate to the internal consistency of empirical models. These problems can be summarised under three headings: length of period, intra-period adjustment and aggregation.

Period analysis relies upon the creation of an artificial discreteness in economic flows. In contradistinction to the sequence of equilibrium analysis – equilibrium, disturbance, adjustment, equilibrium – there is in the pure concept of period analysis a sequence of period, simultaneous shifts in some or all of the exogenous variables, period, and a never-ending sequence of shifts and periods thereafter. Since it is impossible that all exogenous variables change simultaneously, the *length of the basic period* is a primary concern. Intricately involved with the concept of period analysis are the concepts of *ex ante* and *ex post*.[17] *Ex ante* values are planned flows determined in the light of values and expectations that exist at the beginning of a period. *Ex post* flows are those realised during the period after the interactions of the plans of all spending and production units have resolved themselves. To use a familiar example, *ex ante* investment is the sum of all investment plans. These plans will only be realised if the requisite amount of resources is available and no unplanned investment or disinvestment takes place. If spending plans are not compatible with production plans or with production capability, aggregate *ex post* investment will differ from aggregate *ex ante* investment. The difference between *ex post* achievements and *ex ante* plans leads spenders, together with the effect of exogenous changes in the

[16] This whole question of the need for the basis for economic policymaking to 'break out of the cocoon of equilibrium' is brilliantly analysed in Joan Robinson, 'The Second Crisis of Economic Theory', *American Economic Review*, LXII (May 1972) pp. 1–10.

[17] Cooper, *The Economics of Interdependence*, p. 13, has used these expressions in a slightly different way in a balance-of-payments context. In this use he enjoys the approbation of C. P. Kindleberger, see 'Measuring Equilibrium in the Balance of Payments', *Journal of Political Economy*, 77 (November–December 1969) pp. 873–91. Cooper uses the expression '*ex ante* balance' to describe a forecast flow in much the same way as the expression is used in period analysis. However, an '*ex post* balance' refers to a deficit or surplus that obtains after the enactment of some balance-of-payments policy and therefore involves not only the working out of any incompatibilities in the initial values but also the effect of the policy action itself. Cooper's method can mislead and is not used here.

underlying conditions, to revise their plans for the ensuing period. Thus, the length of time between possible revisions of plans on the part of the economic units involved, is an important factor in determining the length of the period. However, for aggregate, empirical work, this specification may be too demanding. Not all of the economic units in a country have the same plan revision time: consumers may reconsider their plans on a week-to-week basis; manufacturing concerns may revise schedules on a monthly basis and agricultural producers may do so annually. In its purest form the period in a model incorporating such a mixture of economic units would have to be the shortest of the decision-revision periods and would have to be one week. But, if data are not available on a weekly basis, weekly empirical analyses are impossible. The form in which data are available will influence the pragmatic choice of the length of the period. At the other extreme, the longest period permissible would be that at which events at the end of the period are about to be influenced by happenings at the beginning of the same period.

In practice the availability of the necessary data is frequently the decisive factor. Models based on quarterly and annual data are quite common even though they may violate some of the strict behavioural assumptions on which period analysis is based.

In period analysis the *ex ante* behaviour of the involved parties may not be mutually compatible so that the *ex post* solution of at least one unit has to be different from its planned behaviour. There are two ways of resolving this problem of intra-period adjustment whereby incompatible plans are accommodated: of these one is particularly suitable for analysis of balance-of-payments models.[18] Any disparity between rates of output and sales (international debits and credits) can be met out of producer's inventory by leaving the price unchanged for the period. This method is called 'the disequilibrium method' and implies an *ex ante* indifference to changes in inventory and a perfectly elastic supply schedule of shipments from inventory at the going price. This solution is easily adaptable to an international payments model when the inventory is specified as short-term international reserves the unit value of which is constant during the period (a constant rate of exchange coupled with constant price levels). Adjustments to inventories will affect behaviour for the following period. In international-payments terms a deficit (an unplanned reduction in the liquid reserve position) will tend to

[18] See Baumol, *Economic Dynamics*, pp. 130–4.

increase the target balance for the ensuing period as well as tending to decrease the forecast balance. In this way, the probability of some deficit-reducing policy measure being enacted is enhanced.

The problems of *aggregation* are mainly those incurred in striking a balance between the impracticable requirements of treating each economic unit separately and the vitiation of the construct by forcing economic units into a Procrustean bed of identical decision periods. However, aggregation does involve the assumption that, if *ex ante* demand and supply for, say, consumption goods were equal, *ex ante* demand and supply for each consumption good are also equal. In aggregative models, inventories again serve as the simplest way of reconciling incompatibility of plans within a period, but unplanned changes in income can occur. These affect the inventory of cash balances of consumers or the inventory of unemployed labour. They affect expenditures plans only for the subsequent period.

THE TARGETS–INSTRUMENTS FRAME OF POLICY REFERENCE

Period analysis as a model of international payments can be expressed in terms of the targets–instruments framework and, since the framework is short-run, there is no need for the target balance of payments to be zero. Targets are determined by the authorities in the light of the 'general interest' function of the focus nation.[19] The variables that are included in the general interest function need not be those included in the period analysis. The international payments target will depend upon domestic goals and their relation to international goals, the expected flow of capital abroad and the expected balance on merchandise as well as on any difference between the actual and the desired position in net international reserve position.[20] The target may also be influenced by considerations of feasibility based on recent international performance and the maximum change that the authorities believe can be imposed upon the system in any single

[19] The targets–instruments approach derives from the work of James E. Meade and Jan Tinbergen. The terminology used here is taken from Tinbergen's *On the Theory of Economic Policy*.
[20] Inclusion of the difference between the actual and desired net reserve positions in the general interest function allows consideration of flows of short-term and monetary international assets to be incorporated into the aggregate theory. In this way, any disturbances in the short-term asset market (excluded from the frame of reference) can be integrated with the adjustment mechanisms required of basic transactions. For example, a reduction in gross reserves might induce a nation to seek an increase in its net reserve position. See Chapter 1 above.

period. The general interest function itself may specify more than one
payments target as different sub-balances of the international
accounts have different implications for domestic or national goals.
The balance on goods and services provides an indication of the
contribution of the foreign sector to domestic employment – the
value of this target may be less important than the absence of change
since it is difficult quickly to reallocate resources from depressed and
relatively specialised export industries.[21] The balance on current
account denotes the change in the nation's net international position.
The basic balance on current and long-term capital account provides
a good indicator of the nation's international payments position
abstracting from transitory elements.[22] Finally, the balance on
autonomous transactions denotes the overall change in the gross
liquidity position. While the individual balances will move in the
same direction more often than not, they are capable of diverging,
particularly when there are sudden and sizeable changes in the
composition and the magnitude of capital flows. The incorporation
of national targets into payments analysis introduces an element of
greater realism since it stresses that role of nationalism in economic
policymaking. The level of employment and the international asset
position are matters of national concern. It is unrealistic for policymakers in a developed nation to look for other developed nations to
assist them in achieving full employment. Equally a nation's international policy is based on self-interest, and self-sacrifice in order to
assist other nations to achieve their goals is the exception rather than
the rule.[23]

The Tinbergen framework for analysis of quantitative policy distinguishes four basic types of economic variables: target variables
which are to be achieved; instrument variables by which the targets
will be achieved; data which are the values of variables that are given
and which do not change during the period under consideration and
irrelevant variables that do not affect the targets though they may, of
course, be important in their own right. Targets are the numerical
values or ranges of values determined for the target variables by
policymakers. Instrument variables designed to effect payments

[21] The definitions of the different sub-balances are given in Chapter 4 below.
[22] See Walter S. Salant and Associates, *The United States Balance of Payments
in 1968* (Washington: The Brookings Institution, 1963) pp. 5–9.
[23] Joan Robinson, *The New Mercantilism* (Cambridge: Cambridge University
Press, 1966) develops this theme with respect to international investment and
commercial policy.

targets are 'balance-of-payments policies' and can be defined as 'a government action whose primary purpose is not related to a domestic economic need and that would not be undertaken except for a perception of a disequilibrium in the balance of payments'.[24] Balance-of-payments policies therefore include a certain subset of the totality of instruments available to a national government. The subset includes all those instruments that affect the terms on which transactions between residents and foreigners take place, as well as the instruments that affect the desired total volume of transactions in so far as a change in the desired total will affect the volume and composition of transactions desired with foreigners. Foremost among the instruments are exchange-rate changes, changes in the domestic price level, tariffs, quotas on imports, subsidies on exports and impediments to capital movements.

There is, however, a crucial difference between the characteristics of instruments designed for international payments adjustments and those affecting domestic targets. International instruments either involve changes in ratios (relative price levels or exchange rates) or they involve impositions of absolute magnitudes whose effects can be neutralised by counteracting policies on the part of trading partners. Because instruments aimed at domestic targets may have repercussions either upon other sectors or upon the effectiveness of other domestic instruments, interdependencies can affect the choice among the set of available instruments for any given situation. The international instruments suffer from a different kind of interdependency. The effectiveness of an international instrument relies to a large degree upon a passive reaction by the authorities in trading-partner nations as far as their own target variables are concerned. An offsetting action on the part of trading nations will negate the original action. The clearest example of interdependence of international instruments is the phenomenon of offsetting devaluations of national currencies restoring the *status quo ante* and nullifying the design of the original devaluation to change the rate of exchange between two currencies. Domestic interdependence of instruments does not necessarily involve an incompatibility of targets. International interdependence does derive from an incompatibility of short-run targets.

[24] Lawrence B. Krause, 'A Passive Balance-of-Payments Strategy for the United States', *Brookings Papers on Economic Activity* (3: 1970) pp. 339–60. The definition needs broadening to allow for the possibility of a change in the payments target.

Foreign retaliation to a change in balance-of-payments policies by one nation can involve either a reduction in the size of the change actually induced in an instrument variable or a change in the data. A 10 per cent devaluation matched by a 5 per cent counter-devaluation by all trading partners would reduce the change in the instrument variable (the rate of exchange) to 5 per cent. A 10 per cent surcharge imposed upon all imports is an absolute change in (a vector of) instruments: a retaliatory 10 per cent surcharge on imports imposed by trading partners would have to enter any formal exposition of the model set up in a targets–instruments framework, as a change in the data. Clearly any instruments which can be expected to bring about an offsetting change in the data is of little worth.

The targets–instruments framework has, when considered as the basis for a methematical–econometric basis for policy actions, many potential pitfalls.[25] Principally the process relies upon the definition of targets by policymakers according to their own interpretation of the social welfare function. However, in the practical world of quantitative goals, this attribution of numerical targets is not difficult nor is there great room for subjective interpretation. It is only when qualitative analysis and subtle trade-offs between inherently desirable ends become involved that the definition of targets becomes impracticable. If, as has already been suggested, realisation of quantitative targets is prerequisite to the achievement of any secondary or qualitative goals, then the targets–instruments is a valid, workaday approach to economic policy. Difficulties will arise when the coefficients of instruments change over time, when targets cannot be precisely formulated and when the interrelationships between flows are subject to wide year-to-year variability. The difficulties do not, of course, argue that attempts should not be made to apply theory to policy – particularly since every policy decision must be based upon some presumption of a quantitative relationship that, in the absence of objective forecast, derives from a combination of received wisdom, instinct and desire. The final difficulty in policy selection lies in the choice of alternative packages of instruments because, on a pragmatic level, there can be no guarantee that a unique solution exists – particularly in the international sphere where every action must be accorded some probability of retaliatory offsets.

[25] These are summarised in Marina v. N. Whitman, *Policies for Internal and External Balance* (Special Papers in International Economics No. 9, International Finance Section) Princeton, 1970, Ch. IV.

The introduction of a time dimension into formal analysis of quantitative policy complicates the solution of the model. A time dimension in which target values can change over time and in which various exogenous forces can arise to cause changes in the data or even, *in extremis* and paradoxically, to make the irrelevant variables relevant, can complicate the analysis to a point at which formal solutions must lose reliability as a basis for real-world policy. Clearly the more short-run the analysis, the easier will it be to forecast exogenous changes and to incorporate them into the model as given and the easier will it be to attribute reasonable values to the target variables. It may be possible to define intermediate targets which will serve for short-run analysis and which will also represent steps along an approach to a specific long-run target. A long-run goal might be a balance on autonomous transactions coupled with a surplus on current account. However, such a goal might not be attainable in a short-run planning period from the existing situation, and intervening targets would comprise growing current account surpluses and declining overall deficits until the full target was achieved some *n* years later.

In practice nations would attempt to forecast the size of any deficit or surplus on the most important (dominant) balance in the international accounts. This forecast would be based upon the continuation of existing policies and such exogenous changes in the data as could be foreseen. The forecast deficit would then be compared with the target. If they were not tolerably close, a policy action would be instituted so that the revised forecast balance would be expected to be tolerably close to the target. The issue then becomes one of a choice among alternative instruments given the domestic targets.

MACHLUP'S TRICHOTOMY EXPANDED

Disparity between the target and the forecast balance allows policymakers two courses of action. The disparity can be tolerated (by changing the target) or it can be corrected by the institution of some policy measures. The correction of the disparity allows two alternatives – lasting or basic measures or temporary, suppressive measures. Toleration of the disparity means that it will be financed, and correction by a basic measure involves the reallocation of resources within nations and changes in real incomes. The set of options was completed by Machlup who gave definition to the third (suppressive) category of policies.[26] Machlup's definitions complement an analysis by Harrod.[27] These approaches demonstrate the need for an additional, fourth category of forces that can affect a nation's payments position, and the four categories combine to form a general analytic framework that fits well with the dynamic qualities of period analysis.

The suppressive category of 'compensatory corrections' includes those policy actions that involve something more positive than the mere financing of a deficit and yet are designed to gain time or save reserves rather than to eliminate or erode the root cause of the deficit. Compensatory corrections are defined as resulting in a reduction of the need for adjustment. In contrast to real adjustments, which operate only on the current account by changing relative incomes, prices and resources allocations, compensatory corrections are described as resulting either from 'independent spontaneous developments' or from balance-of-payments policies in deficit and/or surplus countries.[28] A variation on Machlup's theme was made by John H. Williamson who defined 'basic adjustments' as those capable of inducing a change in relative international prices that would eliminate or reduce a deficit. The elimination of the deficit in this way would not impede the focus nation in the realisation of its long-run targets because of balance-of-payments measures that lingered on and whose release would cause the deficit to reoccur. In contrast Williamson uses the term 'quasi-adjustments' to describe those measures that will eliminate an imbalance of trade at the cost of a departure from a desired resource allocation, from a given (internal) income distribution or from some achievable level of output.[29] There is one significant difference between the two sets of definitions that makes the terms basic adjustment and quasi-adjustment preferable to Machlup's: the income effects of a deliberately induced recession are a quasi-adjustment according to Williamson's nomenclature and a real adjustment for Machlup.

The deliberate deflation of a domestic economy because of a deficit in the balance of payments will involve two separate effects. The reduction in demand will lessen the demand for imported goods and

[26] Machlup, 'Adjustment, Compensatory Correction and Financing.'

[27] Sir Roy Harrod, 'Assessing the Trade Returns', *The Economic Journal*, LXVIII (September 1967) pp. 499–511.

[28] Machlup, 'Adjustment, Compensatory Correction and Financing', p. 209.

[29] 'The Crawling Peg', *Essays in International Finance*, No. 50 (Princeton, New Jersey), p. 10.

services and will release capacity in the export sector. To the extent that unemployment results, the process is a quasi-adjustment: hardship is inflicted on the economy, domestic goals are sacrificed and the improvement will be lost when the suppression of demand below potential output is released. However, if the rate of change of the absolute price level is negatively related to the unemployment rate, the reduction in demand will also change relative international prices over time and will constitute a basic adjustment. The second-best connotations of a quasi-adjustment, other than deliberately-induced recessions, can be illustrated by the use of the term 'qualitative' in Tinbergen's sense. A quasi-adjustment has an adverse qualitative effect upon the economy although this cost may be tempered slightly when import duties or equivalent measures generate some small improvement in the net barter terms of trade. This improvement is likely to be short lived, for it is doubtful that trading partners would long tolerate such impediments to trade without retaliation of some kind. For a surplus nation a quasi-adjustment would take the form of a general lowering of import duties which might improve global resource allocation. Such an action is unlikely since it would tend to reduce the 'normal' tariff level of the surplus nation and would in that way sacrifice some of the gains from trade currently enjoyed. Thus, unless some expendable quasi-adjustments are in force in the surplus nation, it is to be expected that the surplus nation will be in favour of a basic adjustment though it may not take the initiative. It is important to recognise quasi-adjustments for the second-best options that they are and not to excuse them on the grounds that it is not possible to say *a priori* in a world of many imperfections whether or not a given quasi-adjustment will improve resource allocation. Quasi-adjustments are measures taken to reduce deficits. They are avowedly temporary and are undertaken because, for some reason, a basic adjustment is either not economically or politically desirable at the time.

Harrod's contribution was to conceive of the full-growth balance-of-payments surplus or deficit such that 'an improvement in the balance of payments due to repression of domestic growth below its potential would not be reckoned an improvement at all.'[30] To estimate whether the payments position has improved by the full-growth criterion it is necessary for imports to be subdivided into three categories:

[30] Harrod, *The Economic Journal* (September 1967), p. 500.

(1) Imports that are required to contribute to the industrial process, the rate of growth of which is a function of the rate of industrial production.

(2) Imports that are needed, but whose path of growth is not to an important extent a function of the growth of industrial production.

(3) Imports that may either grow or decline, by an amount which is a function of our competitiveness.

The first two categories are termed 'required imports'. Imports of the third category are subtracted from total exports, necessarily influenced by the degree of overall competitiveness, to obtain a value for 'net exports'. Assuming trade to be balanced originally, net exports must grow at the same rate as required imports if payments balance is to be maintained. The full growth rate of increase in net exports is, therefore, a target figure which abstracts from such temporary phenomena as extraordinary rates of stock-building or stock-reduction of imported goods or from the saving in imports achieved by unsatisfactory levels of domestic employment. Presumably the effects of any other quasi-adjustments would also be deleted from any reduction of the deficit during the period analysed. A continuous full-growth balance would testify to the absence of need for any basic adjustment.

The application of the concept of full-growth balance to the actual data of the United Kingdom's balance of payments between 1964 and 1966 showed that the basic adjustments had either been negligible or had had a negligible effect within the two-year period. Virtually

TABLE 2-1

Balance of Trade in 1966 Compared with 1964
(£ million)

Actual improvement	Improvement due to deviation of actual balance from the 'full-growth balance'	
	Decline in stock building	112
	Shortfall in industrial production	94
	Improvement in terms of trade	178
+ 400		384
Improvement in 'full-growth balance': 16 million		

Source: Harrod, *Economic Journal* (September 1967) p. 509.

all of the recorded improvement in the balance of trade is traced to such transitory phenomena as the reductions in stocks of imported commodities, to the process of domestic deflation or growth retardation and to a change in the terms of trade. The role of the Wilson Government in the improvement of the British balance of trade is therefore seen as negligible. Harrod's data are given in Table 2-1.

Both analyses rest on a firm basis of achieving international balance without reliance on temporary interferences with the freedom of movement of goods, services and capital and of accomplishing any adjustment that may be needed by means of a basic adjustment. Harrod would have the international payments position conceived in terms of the need for or the absence of need for basic adjustments, and Machlup and Williamson both recognise the costs incurred by the impositions of quasi-adjustments in terms of economic goals and hold quasi-adjustments as inferior policy measures. The distinction between the two types of policy measures is recognised by Meade when he draws the distinction between an 'actual' balance-of-payments deficit and a 'potential' balance-of-payments deficit – the difference between the two deficits being the flow of accommodating finance saved by government measures specially devised to restrict the demand for foreign currencies.[31] Both categories of policy are expenditure-switching policies in Johnson's sense of switching world expenditure from foreign output to domestic output.[32]

The distinction between basic and quasi-adjustments is made quite clear by Figure 2-1. The Figure measures the balance of trade vertically and the competitiveness of the focus nation horizontally so that the sensitivity of the trade balance to changes in competitiveness can be drawn as a positively-sloped schedule. The competitive position is conceived of as the ratio of foreign price levels to domestic price levels interrelated by the rate of exchange between the two currencies.[33] The ratio is defined in such a way that an increase in its value will amount to a depreciation of the domestic currency in

---

[31] J. E. Meade, *The Balance of Payments* (London: Oxford University Press, 1952) p. 15.

[32] Harry G. Johnson, 'Towards a General Theory of the Balance of Payments', in *International Trade and Economic Growth* (London: Geo. Allen and Unwin, 1958) pp. 153–68, and reprinted in Caves and Johnson, *Readings in International Economics*, pp. 374–88, hereinafter referred to as 'Towards a General Theory'.

[33] The concept of the competitive ratio is analysed in detail in Appendix 4-A below.

terms of foreign currencies and will be assumed to cause an increase in (reduction of) any balance-of-trade surplus (deficit).

$$C = \frac{P_f}{P_d} \cdot \frac{1}{r}$$

where P_f and P_d are, respectively, indices of prices of tradable goods and r is an index of the rate of exchange defined so that an increase in r represents an appreciation of the currency of the focus nation. In Figure 2-1, tastes and 'normal' levels of tariff protection are

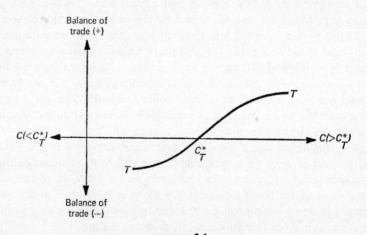

FIGURE 2-1

Competitiveness and the Trade Balance

assumed to be given for the period in the absence of some balance-of-payments policy. Acceptable levels of employment are also assumed to be given. There is, then, some value of the competitive ratio, C, which, if it were to be instituted at the beginning of the period by means of a basic adjustment, would generate balanced trade for the period as a whole. Call that value C_T^*. This is the value of the competitive ratio that accords with the payments target and it may or may not be the actual value of the competitive ratio that prevails in the international market place (C_P). If the prevailing ratio is less than the trade target ratio, the focus nation will experience a deficit and vice versa. The TT schedule shows the responsiveness of the trade balance to changes in C_P. There is no implication that a basic adjustment made at the beginning of period t_1 will achieve its full effect in that period. The diminishing marginal effectiveness of basic adjustments within a single period – beyond some certain size of adjustment – is shown by the S-shape of the schedule.

Basic adjustments are defined as causing changes in relative international price levels and are shown by movements along the *TT* schedule. In contrast quasi-adjustments involve changes in the underlying conditions which are subsumed by the Figure and must therefore involve a shift in the *TT* schedule. Assuming no forecasting errors the value of the *TT* schedule corresponding to the prevailing competitive ratio is the *ex ante* balance. To remove any deficit or surplus, it is necessary to make a basic adjustment of the magnitude of $(C_T^* - C_P)$. The *ex post* balance will then be equal to the target balance (zero). The alternatives to a basic adjustment are to finance the deficit by conceptually setting the target change in net reserves equal to the vertical distance between the *CC* axis and the *TT* schedule at the prevailing ratio, or to sacrifice some domestic goal by shifting *TT* by a quasi-adjustment until the *TT* schedule intersects the *CC* axis at the prevailing competitive ratio.

Harrod's system is essentially dynamic since it incorporates the effects of growth. Growth entails an increase in required imports which, in turn, necessitates a larger surplus on net exports. The increase in required imports in effect will tend to shift the *TT* schedule downward in each period. This shift must be offset either by an increase in the competitive position or by some counterforce that exerts an upward pressure on the whole *TT* schedule. This counterforce can be generated independently of policy actions (for example, by growth in foreign nations) and, in that case, must be an 'independent spontaneous development' of the kind that constituted one of Machlup's categories of compensatory corrections. However, this inclusion of spontaneous events in 'corrections' is undesirable on two counts: semantically, a correction implies a positive action resulting either from the working of natural forces which tend automatically to restore equilibrium from some disequilibrium situation, or from conscious rational action to set something right: analytically, the inclusion of independent spontaneous developments in 'corrections' ignores the possibility that spontaneous phenomena can be aggravating as well as corrective. For these reasons autonomous or independent spontaneous developments will be classified separately. This problem of distinguishing between external influences and induced effects is also apparent in Harrod's analysis since he does not make a categorical distinction between the favourable effects of the British balance of trade that result from domestic deflation and those that result from favourable shifts in the terms of trade. In terms of Figure 2-1, the difficulty arises from the failure explicitly to distinguish between shifts in the TT schedule that are policy-induced and other shifts which happen independently of balance-of-payments policy actions. In what follows the term quasi-adjustment will be used to denote only deliberate balance-of-payments policy actions.

It will be useful to distinguish between the values of variables that represent the full achievement of domestic targets and those that are affected by the existence of quasi-adjustments. An asterisk is used to denote fully-achieved targets and the indicators that correspond to those targets. Thus, C_T^* indicates the value of the competitive ratio needed to achieve balanced trade in the absence of any policy measure by the government of the focus country and when trading partner nations are also achieving their goals. The compatible real income is shown by Y^*. Clearly, the equality of C_P and C_T^* will not generate balanced trade when trading partners are suffering from a cyclical decline, but it does represent the value of the competitive ratio that the focus nation should maintain if the temporary decline in aggregate demand abroad is not to be accentuated. For any given set of standard policies in foreign countries and a given trading matrix in the world, C_T^* is unique. A value of the competitive ratio, C_T, would imply the existence of a balance-of-payments policy in the form of a quasi-adjustment instituted by the authorities in the focus country *or* in its trading partners. Because there exist many different types of quasi-adjustments that can be applied with varying degrees of severity, C_T can only be unique when defined in a particular context which specifies the set of quasi-adjustments actually in force.

The third category of forces working on a nation's balance of trade will be called 'change of data effects' or, more simply, 'data-effects'.[34] Data-effects comprise all factors that bring about shifts in the TT schedule either independently of any policy actions or without the induced shift in the schedule being an intended consequence of or an important variable in the decision. This category is necessarily very broad. Data-effects can include the balance-of-payments repercussions of different rates of economic growth at home and

[34] 'Data' is used here in Tinbergen's sense of variables of given magnitudes that are external to the complex under analysis.

abroad as well as of changes in tastes following income redistribution. Purely exogenous economic phenomena and political decisions can also give rise to data effects. These might include the discovery of a natural resource and its integration into the productive system, a change in the level of military commitments abroad or the relinquishing of ties with a trading partner and, possibly, of preferential tariff agreements with a former colony.

Both quasi-adjustments and data-effects can be either beneficial or adverse to the balance of trade. Ordinarily adverse quasi-adjustments would represent the downward shifts in the TT schedule resulting from the relinquishing of earlier policy measures designed to protect international reserves (presumably because the need for them had been outgrown or because they had lost their effect). In the absence of concomitant basic adjustments, quasi-adjustments that have only a short period of effectiveness would seem to be of doubtful value since for every beneficial shift of the TT schedule, there is the prospect of an equal adverse shift.[35] The effects on the balance of trade of the focus nation of quasi-adjustments instituted by foreign governments must be considered as data-effects. It may be possible to distinguish four categories of data-effects. The first category would impart some trend to C_T – presumably a monotonic one. The second category would be random phenomena that might be expected to cancel themselves out over a (long) period of time. A third category would be one that imparted to C_T a cyclical pattern around its trend and finally there are data-effects which generate a once-and-for-all shift in the TT schedule. Quasi-adjustments by foreign governments will comprise mainly reversible data-effects since they cannot be kept on indefinitely without engendering retaliation or losing their effectiveness.

Data-effects can occur, within the set of assumptions that governs period analysis, only in the intervals between the periods. Thus for each nation the totality of data-effects can be expected to introduce a shift in the TT schedule in each period except in the happy, but improbable, case in which data-effects cancel each other out. For each succeeding period the value of C_T needed to achieve payments balance can be expected to change. Depending upon the magnitude

[35] It may be argued that since the eventual removal of a quasi-adjustment is socially desirable, the quasi-adjustments should consist of measures which provoke public antipathy since these will be the more quickly revoked when the trade balance permits. For developed nations, this argument suggests that taxes on foreign travel may be valuable quasi-adjustments if the measures can effect sufficiently large improvements in the current account.

and the mix of the data-effects, the time-path of C_T can be expected to show both trend and cyclical component elements. If the change in C_T exceeds any change in C_P brought about by 'the classical medicine', each period will require consideration of a change in the package of balance-of-payments policies including changes in the par value of the currency and the maintenance or relinquishing of quasi-adjustments already in force. If the future time-path of C_T can be forecast or anticipated, it would be possible to choose among policy options on a basis of expected efficiency.

The cause of an imbalance in trade and the different implications of the alternative policy options can be described in another way. The value of C_T is a numerical indicator of the terms of trade or the trading conditions which must exist among nations if trade is to balance. The value of C_P is an indicator of the terms of trade as they actually exist in the market place as a result of the decisions of the monetary authorities. Imbalance results from the failure of the existing monetary conditions to correspond to what may be described as the 'real' forces. When a basic adjustment is made, the monetary conditions are adapted toward the real conditions. When a quasi-adjustment is made the real conditions are changed to bring them into equality with the prevailing monetary conditions – provided always that the quasi-adjustment is not offset by retaliatory action Financing the deficit merely leaves the disparity between the two sets of conditions in force for the period.

THE SHORT-RUN MODEL

The major dimensions of national economic policy can be defined quantitatively as desired numerical values for the target variables of employment rate and international payments. Such is the ponderousness of those adjustment mechanisms that do exist, that there can be no reliance that either of the two interrelated targets will be achieved with any degree of automaticity.[36] The similar aggregative quality of the domestic and international target variables is itself an argument for treating both in the same analytic framework and, given the short-run actual or potential variability of the component variables, it is axiomatic that the short-run analysis that underlies macro-stabilisation policy should also provide the foundation for the formulation of international payments adjustment policy.

[36] See Whitman, *Policies for Internal and External Balance*, pp. 1 and 2.

The use of a short-run framework for analysis of international payments adjustment has the added pragmatic virtue that it is able explicitly to recognise that national economic policy may seek the furtherance of national ends in its international transactions. These goals may reflect a desire to change the net international asset position of the nation through private international investment, or a desire to use international transactions to facilitate the achievement of internal balance. Internal and external targets are seen to be interrelated by their joint inclusion in the nation's general interest function. There is therefore a degree of substitutability between domestic and international ends. It is the question of the relative emphasis placed upon the domestic goal at the expense of the international goal that is at the core of any discussion as to whether the balance of payments constitutes a goal or a constraint.[37] In fact the true constraint on international policy is the degree to which other nations will offset unilateral policy actions in order to safeguard their own ends. When, as during the Bretton Woods era, the institutional setting was quite rigidly defined, any attempt to achieve external balance other than by internal policy, was likely to involve contravention of the existing system and would be more likely to arouse offsetting action on the part of other nations which would feel themselves to be simultaneously relieved from the institutional constraint.

The recognition that international economic policy, and balance-of-payments policy in particular, is merely a part of an overall international posture, necessarily involves the possibility of non-zero target payments balances. This possibility is at the core of mercantilist theory but was lost when payments adjustment analysis was fitted into a general-equilibrium framework. In practice, the national payments target can be defined in any of several sub-balances of which one will be dominant at any particular time. Except for a possible surplus (deficit) on current account deliberately offset by a corresponding deficit (surplus) on capital account, payments analysis has tended to concern itself almost myopically with the balance on goods and services or with the balance of trade. The multiplicity of

[37] The distinction between a goal and a constraint is, at bottom, only an indication of the relative importance attached to the variable under scrutiny – always provided that the policy option does not encounter the true international constraint of intransigeance on the part of foreign nations. This problem is clearly treated in Salant, *The U.S. Balance of Payments in 1968*, pp. 243–5 and in J. J. Polak, 'International Co-ordination of Economic Policy', I.M.F. *Staff Papers*, 9 (July 1962) p. 151.

dimensions in which the dominant goal can be defined will serve to measure changes in the net contribution to domestic employment, changes in the net international asset position, and changes in the net and in the gross liquid reserve positions.

The short-run model explicitly excludes international transactions by the private sector in short-term assets and other internationally-liquid assets from its scope. This exclusion derives primarily from the belief that, while net reserve positions are acknowledged to be important, gross reserve positions and the distribution of the stock of international short-term assets among nations have little effect upon international economic policy. The exclusion also reflects the fact that monetary imbalance will require a separate set of policy variables from those usually associated with payments adjustment. This is particularly true if there exists some critical disturbance in international monetary markets that is not tied in with a serious problem of imbalance in the balance on basic transactions. The exclusion of monetary assets from the core of the analysis should not be interpreted as a 'money does not matter' posture. The role of domestic money in acknowledging the magnitude of real variables and price levels within a nation is acknowledged. What is judged to be of secondary importance is the distribution of matching liquid assets and liabilities among nations – just as sectoral distribution of gross liquid assets and liabilities is not considered a primary consideration in a closed economy.

The short-run model relies fundamentally upon period analysis so that exogenous changes and changes in national targets or values can be introduced into the analysis at discrete intervals. Policymakers must be presumed to generate a set of international targets for each period. These targets are not necessarily optima and may be interim targets subject to further emphasis in the ensuing perod. At the same time, the policymakers will hold some expectation – formed intuitively or by econometric estimation – of what will actually evolve in the period under consideration given a continuation of existing policies by the focus nation and given estimates of policy actions and economic activity on the part of foreign nations. The desired and expected outcomes are then compared and, if they are approximately equal, no question of instituting a change in international payments policy arises. If the two are not equal, then the policymakers must determine whether or not the best policy is to finance the disparity between desired and actual. Such a policy effectively involves changing the target to fit reality and could involve a recognition of the inability of the focus nation to make any effective change in the balance at that time because of the balance-of-payments constraint imposed by foreign behaviour. The alternative to changing the target is to institute a positive policy. That policy could involve a basic adjustment or a quasi-adjustment or a combination of measures. The package that would be used would depend, *inter alia*, on the type of disturbance and its expected duration.

The increased importance of data-effects as potential disruptors of the ongoing state of affairs is reinforced by the possibility that changes in national values or in the data can induce nations to change the dominant dimension in their own payments target. A change in the dominant target – from, say, the balance on current account with its emphasis on the change in the net international asset position to the basic balance with its emphasis on the change in the net reserve position – can bring about a change in policy without there being any change in any of the forecast balances.

3 The Debt to John Maynard Keynes

Any work that avowedly accords high levels of employment primacy of place among short-run economic goals, must rely to a very large degree upon the work of Keynes. For Keynes, between the wars, the important task was not so much to use the international sector to help to achieve full employment as it was to gain some release for the domestic economy from a world in deep economic despair. In 1930 he advocated the imposition of capital controls to prevent (short-term) international capital movements from hamstringing expansionary domestic monetary policy,[1] and fourteen years later, then Lord Keynes, he pleaded again for a monetary system that would permit the national economy a sufficient degree of independence to allow it to pursue its own macrostabilization policies:[2]

> We are determined that, in future, the external value of sterling shall conform to its internal value as set by our own domestic policies, and not the other way round. Secondly, we intend to retain control of our own domestic rate of interest, so that we can keep it as low as suits our own purposes, without interference from the ebb and flow of international capital movements or flights of hot money. Thirdly, whilst we intend to prevent inflation at home, we shall not accept deflation at the dictate of influences from

[1] John Maynard Keynes, *A Treatise on Money, II* (London: Macmillan and Company, 1930) pp. 306–19. Note particularly the conceptualisation of the Interest Equalisation Tax on page 315. Hereinafter this work will be referred to simply as *The Treatise* and page references will refer to the original (1930) edition rather than to the recent edition in the Collected Writings.

These concerns with national autonomy found their ultimate expression in Article VI of *The Articles of Agreement of the International Monetary Fund* which condoned control of capital transfers provided that the controls did not interfere with payments for current transactions. Article VI can be traced in turn to Section VII of the *Proposals for an International Clearing Union*, (H.M.S.O. 1943).

[2] Address before the House of Lords on the International Monetary Fund, May 23, 1944, *The Parliamentary Debates* (Hansard) (London: H.M.S.O., 1944) fifth series, vol. 131, p. 843.

outside. In other words, we abjure the instruments of bank rate and credit contradiction operating through the increase of un-employment as a means of forcing our domestic economy into line with external factors.

In the second half of the twentieth century the problems are quite different, but a description of the importance of Keynes' thinking and writing in the geneology of the aggregate theory of international payments adjustment transcends mere doctrinal interest. The present theory has as one of its bases, concepts that closely resemble concepts first put forward by Keynes in *The Treatise*. The short-run model clearly derives many of its characteristics from *The General Theory of Employment, Interest and Money* and from the writings of those who built upon the methodological platform that *The General Theory* has provided.[3] The net result of these similarities is to make the theory of payments adjustment more easily understood by everyone who has a working familiarity with 'the comparatively simple fundamental ideas which underlie' Keynes' theory[4] and who has not had time to delve into the arcane world of international economic adjustments.

But the similarities must not be exaggerated: they exist in general, not in the particular. Keynes' vision[5] of the workings of the British economy in the thirties does not lend itself to direct extension to the international economy – either between the wars or in the post-Bretton Woods era. Keynes' own proposals for international pay-ments in 1933 were designed to finance very large amounts of external debt so that national governments could generate domestic expansions without any balance-of-payments – *financing* constraint.[6] The similarities between the two theories derive from similarities in goals and in the underlying approach to policymaking. The differ-ences are to be found in the behavioural assumptions about national macroeconomic performance suitable for a world of normalcy and in the operative *milieu* of the policy variables. *The General Theory*

[3] (London: Macmillan and Company, 1936), hereinafter referred to as *The General Theory*.

[4] The description derives from Keynes himself, see 'The General Theory of Employment', *Quarterly Journal of Economics* 51 (February 1937) pp. 209–23: reprinted in *The New Economics*, ed. Seymour E. Harris (New York: Alfred E. Knopf, 1947) pp. 181–93.

[5] The word is used in Schumpeter's sense: see Joseph A. Schumpeter, *History of Economic Analysis* (New York: Oxford University Press, 1954) p. 41.

[6] See *The Means to Prosperity* (London: Macmillan and Company, 1933) pp. 25–37.

has an interventionist philosophy in the two extreme situations for which Keynes drew policy conclusions from his theory – deep depression and a severe inadequacy of aggregate demand in the thirties and severely excessive aggregate demand in *How to Pay for the War*.[7] The belief is that the performance of the economic system can be improved to a significant degree and even made to function acceptably well, by deliberately influencing a few key aggregates. His theory of international payments presented in *The Treatise* provides a framework for analysing which key international economic aggregates should be influenced and in what way. Neither of the two models precludes the development of and use of systems of economic institutions that will reduce the need for conscious decision-making – e.g. sensitive automatic stabilisers and flexible exchange-rate systems. The main difference in *milieu* is crucial. In a world in which separate nation states exist to act in their own self-interest, income distribution and the distribution of any burden of adjustment among nations are questions of paramount importance. In a closed system, changes in income distribution can be imposed upon the system in the name of the general economic good. There is no equivalent authority internationally. In an international system, subsections of the world economy possess a degree of autonomy and they have preference functions that weight the welfare of residents and citizens much more heavily than the welfare of foreigners.

There are analytic similarities that must be interpreted with caution and not exaggerated but which, subject to the *caveat*, do provide expositional insight into the way in which the analysis of *The General Theory* is applicable to the world of international payments adjustment. The two alternative quantitative policy measures available in the closed economy – fiscal policy and monetary policy – have their international equivalents – financing and external adjustment respectively.[8] In a depressed closed economy, fiscal policy requires that the central government be indifferent to its own pecuniary welfare (narrowly conceived) and use its own unlimited financing powers to *finance* expenditure-generating projects. In this process it would be likely to alter the 'terms of trade' between surplus and deficit units. Monetary policy aims directly to influence the return to savers and the cost of financing capital expenditures and therefore

[7] (London: Macmillan and Company, 1940).
[8] Fiscal policy here abstracts from any changes in tax rates upon different sectors and is used solely in the sense of changes of the deficit-surplus type.

allows the system to *adjust* in favour of spenders and borrowers. Just as Keynes's solution for internal balance during the depression called for fiscal policy and therefore for financing, his international programme in the thirties and in the post-war era also called for an entity with tremendous financing powers. But financing was not likely to provide an enduring answer to the problem of international payments because of the difference in the *milieu* between closed and international economies. This can be illustrated by analogy with domestic fiscal policy conducted on a voluntary basis. No national or federal government could hope to indulge in expansionary fiscal policy if its constituent parts had the power to opt out of the process of incurring debt jointly and no supranational agency could hope to redistribute without limit reserves from surplus to deficit nation unless it possessed powers of coercion.[9] Monetary policy (and changes in tax rates and subsidies on different undertakings and transactions) alters the conditions on which different types of expenditures are made and dragoons the system into adjusting in much the same way as a change in exchange rates will tend to restore international payments balance.[10]

The failure of modern payments theory to incorporate capital movements means that the profession neglected the model presented by Keynes in *The Treatise*.[11] The next task is to summarise that model. That Keynes developed a model that included capital movements as a specific entity should occasion no surprise given the fact that, under the gold standard, movements of interest-sensitive capital could negate attempts to pursue expansionary monetary policy. As a means of escape from this state in which the nation's liquid reserves were hostage to interest-rate differentials, he recommended controls over capital movements, and he also recognised that, for London at least, a lowering of the bank rate would bring about not only an exodus of short-term funds but also an increase in foreign demand for medium-term and long-term loans. Thus, the basic macroeconomic model in *The Treatise* was internationalised. There were three international flows that were incorporated into the model: gold exports and imports, 'Foreign Lending' and the 'Foreign

---

[9] This is essentially the point made by M. June Flanders in 'International Liquidity is Always Inadequate', *Kyklos*, XXII (Facs. 3, 1969) pp. 519–28.

[10] Milton Friedman, 'Discussion', in *The International Adjustment Mechanism* (Boston: The Federal Reserve Bank of Boston, 1970) p. 109, notes that monetarists are almost invariably in favour of exchange-rate flexibility.

[11] *The Treatise*, I 131–2, 161–6, 213–16 and 326–42.

Balance'. Foreign lending was defined as the negative balance on capital account and constituted the (net) increment of home-owned capital located abroad exclusive of gold. The foreign balance was the balance on current account (including investment income) and constituted the excess of the value of home-owned output of goods and services placed at the disposal of foreigners over foreign-owned output acquired. The foreign balance was always equal to the sum of foreign lending and gold imports. Total investment was the sum of home investment (the increment of total capital situated at home exclusive of gold), of foreign lending and of imports of gold. Since the foreign balance was equal to the sum of gold imports and foreign lending, the foreign balance represented the contribution of the international sector to total investment and was therefore named 'Foreign Investment' – a term which is in current use as a component of national income accounts.

External equilibrium or balance existed when no shipments of gold were taking place, therefore, when foreign lending equalled the foreign balance. Total equilibrium existed when home saving (total saving less foreign lending less gold imports) was equal to home investment in addition to external balance and, by definition, total investment was equal to total saving.

International capital movements were deemed to depend upon *relative* interest rates at home and abroad – though equality of rates was not a precondition for no foreign lending – and the foreign balance was dependent, in any given situation, on the relative prices of goods and services that entered into international trade. There was no direct connection between the functional determinants of the two flows, so that a disturbance in the foreign sector could only be corrected through the domestic sector. Attempts by the monetary authorities to maintain external balance by changing the bank rate would inevitably react back on the rate of home investment. The costs of adjustment were seen to depend upon the relative sensitivities of the functional relationships and the possibility of effecting an increase in the foreign balance by a lowering of the domestic price level was seen as a painful process. The cost of adjustment was seen to vary substantially not only with the 'sign' of the disturbance but also with the source of the disturbance – the current or the capital account. A fall in foreign prices would diminish the foreign balance but would not, in the new equilibrium, after a fall of the domestic price level of equal proportions and assuming no distributional effects, change the real incomes of either nation or relative prices – only money prices would have changed. When, however, the disturbances was an increase in foreign interest rates (due presumably to improved investment opportunities abroad), foreign lending (capital exports) would increase, gold would flow out of the country and the bank rate would have to be raised to the detriment of domestic investment. This would, in turn, reduce the domestic price level and increase the foreign balance. The new equilibrium would have higher rates of foreign lending and of the foreign balance and a lower rate of domestic investment as well as a lower level of income at home because of the deterioration in the net barter terms of trade. The distinction between the two disturbances adumbrates Hicks' emphasis on the difference between real and monetary adjustments.[12] But the degree to which the economy will suffer as a result of an increase in foreign lending will depend upon the sensitivity of the foreign balance to changes in relative prices and to the impact of increased foreign lending upon the demand for the exports of the lending country. If foreign lending also gave rise to an increase in the demand for the country's exports of capital goods, the necessary price-level adjustment would be smaller, and, *pro tanto*, more easily effected. The longer-run effects on the welfare of the lending or investing country could not be obtained from *a priori* reasoning.

The model was an important step forward in balance-of-payments theory but it was destined to be shunted aside in the revolution in thinking that followed on the publication of *The General Theory*. In the thirties and the forties, the assumptions of *The Treatise* were not relevant to the real world, but the main features of the international model regained a degree of relevance in the fifties when nations started borrowing and investing internationally again on a significant scale, and when they maintained high levels of employment domestically by subordinating external balance to the needs of internal balance where necessary. However, several aspects of the model need modification if it is to be developed into a useful analytic base for current operations. The primary shortcoming is, of course, the static, long-run equilibrium and full-employment characteristics of the model. Even though it did allow for capital flows, it was not able to incorporate the inevitable increase in the foreign balance as foreign ownership of assets and investment income increase over time. The

[12] J. R. Hicks, 'An Inaugural Lecture', *Oxford Economic Papers*, 2 (June 1953) pp. 117–35.

model contains the seeds of its own destruction as long as foreign lending is positive. The presumption must have been that these changes in flows were so small relative to other flows as to be negligible. The same device is used in *The General Theory* in which net capital formation is not considered to have any effect on the ultimate value of output and employment. A virtue of the model is that the process of adjustment is made to and is allowed to take place in a manner consistent with the then prevailing world conditions – the shortcomings of the adjustment process for modern analysis is that the adjustment process described is achieved through internal adjustment by the sacrifice of a high-priority domestic goal.

The aggregation of capital movements into one category of interest-sensitive capital does not adequately reflect the composition of capital movements in the modern world. It is currently useful to distinguish three types of private capital movements: short-term, portfolio investments and direct investments. While short-term investments are quite sensitive to interest-rate differentials, both the generating and the recipient nation attempt to offset their impact upon the domestic economy by neutralising the inflow or outflow. Thus, except for any investment income generated by the flows, their effects are exerted mainly upon a nation's international liquidity position and not upon its quantitative achievements.[13] Portfolio and direct investments are both likely to represent long-term commitments on the part of the investor and therefore have impacts upon the real incomes and rates of capital formation in the two countries concerned. While portfolio investment can be thought of as interest-sensitive, direct investments cannot. Direct investments take place because the investor expects to realise a higher rate of return from a real asset owned abroad than he could expect to earn in a domestic outlet. There is no reason to suppose that interest-rate differentials constitute an important determinant of flows of direct foreign investment because expected rates of return on these investments are likely to be quite intramarginal and, as such, not sensitive to interest rates. However, direct investments are not financed exclusively with equity capital. Any supplementary loan capital that is not supplied out of the liquid reserves of the parent corporation, could be obtained either from host-country or from investing-country financial intermediaries.

[13] These flows are not a part of the formal model developed in Parts II and III but they are reintroduced into the analysis to a limited degree in Chapter 11 below. Their exclusion does not indicate a lack of importance.

One determinant of the source of such funds would be relative costs of borrowing (interest rates) but the differential would not be the crucial determinant since foreign borrowing would not involve an exchange risk. The overall flow of long-term, capital, foreign investment, will be sensitive to the interest rates that prevail in the two countries to some degree, but the coefficient of sensitivity will depend upon the composition of the aggregate and, if the composition fluctuates significantly, will have little reliability.

The remaining shortcoming of the model in *The Treatise* is the identification of foreign investment with the foreign balance instead of with foreign lending. The identification is not wrong in any logical sense of the word but it does inhibit the analytic flexibility of the model by disguising the close relationship between domestic saving and the foreign balance. There are two possible explanations for Keynes' choice of the foreign balance as the equivalent of investment rather than saving. First, Keynes could have examined only the equilibrium properties of the model when foreign lending was equal to the foreign balance and when there was no superficial reason to prefer one pairing to the other. Secondly, Keynes might have been influenced by his distinction between available and non-available goods – consumption goods and investment goods. Since the United Kingdom had a comparative advantage in capital goods (non-available goods), the foreign balance would be naturally identified with non-available goods and therefore, in *The Treatise*, would constitute investment.[14]

The basic framework is improved if Keynes' definitions are modified and his model recast in terms of international investment (I_I) and international saving (S_I). The concept of the foreign balance is logically a concept of saving since it measures a flow of goods and services produced by domestic factors of production and used to acquire an asset that will permit future consumption, rather than for purposes of current consumption. Walter S. Salant has noted this discrepancy between the nomenclature accorded to the balance on current account in the national income accounts and the accepted definitions of investment and saving.[15]

'Investment' is accepted as meaning the purchase of goods and services for capital purposes. 'Saving' is accepted as meaning the

[14] See *The Treatise*, I 127–8.
[15] Walter S. Salant, 'International Transactions in National Income Accounts', *The Review of Economics and Statistics*, XXXIII (November 1951) pp. 304–5.

difference between income and current expenditure. Any net acquisition of financial claims on others (including accumulation of cash) is therefore an excess of saving over investment. This is generally recognized for units within an economy, e.g., households and firms, or for groups of them. Why should it not be recognized for an open national economy? What is now called 'foreign investment' is exactly such an excess of national saving over national investment: the net acquisition of financial claims on other countries (including gold).

Salant's argument should be amended to state that 'foreign investment' is an excess of national saving over domestic investment since nations can invest internationally by acquiring real assets and equity claims, so that his definition should be broadened beyond the acquisition merely of financial claims. International investment differs significantly from domestic investment in one dimension. In a closed economy the acquisition by an individual of an outstanding bond does not represent investment on the part of the economy. However, the acquisition of a bond from a foreigner increases the nation's total stock of wealth (its net worth) and therefore does represent investment by the community. The foreign bond will yield a flow of investment income and contribute to national income as long as the asset is held, in exactly the same way that an addition to the nation's stock of capital goods would yield a flow of income for the life of the capital good.

The distinction between international saving and international investment can be made quite clear by conceiving of a nation's international net worth. International net worth is defined as the sum of all international assets minus the value of all international liabilities. International assets comprise portfolio (including short-term) assets which represent claims on foreigners, real assets which represent tangible assets owned abroad by citizens and monetary assets such as gold and foreign convertible currencies. International liabilities comprise real assets owned at home by foreigners, portfolio assets issued by residents and owned by foreigners and monetary liabilities owed to foreigners. International saving involves an increase in international net worth – the foreign balance. International investment takes place when citizens of a nation acquire (illiquid) foreign assets through portfolio investment or direct investment in order to acquire a flow of income in the future. If all of the surplus on current account were to be taken in gold, the non-consumption would have been devoted to hoards and no international investment would have taken place.

Using the definitions of international saving and investment given above, a simple flow model of *ex post* relationships can be created. Using Y to represent income or output, C to represent consumption, S and I to denote saving and investment respectively and the subscripts I and D to distinguish international and domestic flows, the modified model of *The Treatise* can be written quite simply as:

$$Y = C + I_D + I_I \tag{3-1}$$

$$Y = C + S_D + S_I \tag{3-2}$$

$$S_I = X - M = I_I \tag{3-3}$$

Government expenditures are subsumed under consumption and investment. Unilateral transfer payments are assumed to be zero so that the balance on current account is equal to the export surplus over imports $(X - M)$. I_I represents autonomous foreign investments. Equation (3-3) shows the condition necessary for a sustainable equilibrium without any international movements of monetary assets.

Equation (3-1) denotes the intent of the nation in increasing its total net worth. The intent has two dimensions: the rate of total addition to net worth and the division of that total between increments to the stock of domestic capital and its international assets. A surplus of exports over imports is a consequence of the intent to increase the international net worth although, in times of deep depression, positive international saving could be an end in itself. On the other hand, equation (3-2) subdivides total non-consumption into that accomplished domestically and that accomplished by consuming less foreign goods than are generated by sales to foreigners.

Thus, in the context of this simple model of *ex post* relationships, payments balance requires that the flows of international saving and investment be kept equal. If international investment is not sensitively controlled by any available macropolicy instrument, then international saving must be made equal to international investment. This involves a process of adjustment of the domestic economy. Nations with spare liquid assets available to them, including lines of credit, can temporarily finance any excess of international investment over international saving. If international saving rates are not adjustable – because of a fixed exchange-rate system and prices that are sticky – then international investment must be curtailed by some means. If international saving exceeds international investment, the excess flow of foreign currency can be hoarded as gold or as liquid balances.

In a world in which ongoing changes are continuously taking place, an equilibrium, *ex post* system of analysis is not a suitable vehicle from which to devise policies to maintain prescribed values of target variables in the short run. This lack of appropriateness derives both from the disregard of disturbances once an equilibrium has been reached and from the lack of concern with the sacrifice of domestic goals during the period of adjustment from one situation – acceptable or otherwise – to a situation of equilibrium. Despite the fact that equilibrium represented, by definition, the achievement of a satis-factory performance as far as quantitative goals were concerned, the failure to consider the effects of changes in the level of income was the hallmark of *The Treatise*.[16] The apparent disequilibrium frame of reference that is inherent in *The Treatise* derives from the identifica-tion of causes of changes in the level of prices.[17] Changes in the price level would, domestically and internationally, bring about a new equilibrium albeit very slowly and always assuming there was no continuous series of disturbances that were all self-reinforcing. It was, however, *The General Theory* that developed the disequilibrium system of analysis necessary for the conduct of short-run economic policy. The fundamentally disequilibrium system of *The General Theory* exists in the fact that any equality between planned saving and planned investment (except at full employment rates and in a disturbance-free world) is a short-period equilibrium that contains the seeds of its own destruction through an inevitable tendency for one or other of the constituent parameters to shift over time in response to some underlying, temporal pressure. The most famous example of this characteristic of a constituent variable in the model being a function of time as well as of economic variables is Patinkin's analysis of the short-run and the long-run supply schedule of labour.[18] The concept of 'underemployment equilibrium' is chimerical in any long-run sense.

Keynes never married the simple international flow model of *The*

[16] Cf. *The General Theory*, pp. vi–vii.
[17] See Sir Roy Harrod, 'Reassessment of Keynes' Views on Money', *The Journal of Political Economy*, 78 (July/August 1970) pp. 617–25.
[18] Don Patinkin, *Money, Interest and Prices* (Evanston, Ill.: Row, Peterson and Company, 1956) pp. 233–40.

Treatise with the analytic concepts that he developed in *The General Theory*. Indeed while the core details of the proposed International Clearing Union are supplied in *The Treatise* and are reiterated in *Means to Prosperity* his thinking about international economics and international adjustment was never able to relate to any sense of normalcy.[19] His international concerns were always dominated either by freeing domestic economic policy from balance-of-payments constraints or by the need for post-war financing.[20] Thus he was never able to integrate the concepts of foreign lending and the foreign balance into the short-run analysis of *The General Theory* and was unable to consider ongoing variability in foreign lending (as opposed to a once-and-for-all shift in a schedule) as a continuing source of potential domestic instability or as a balance-of-payments adjustment problem.

The combination of the international flow model of *The Treatise* and the distinction between planned and actual flows (from *The General Theory*) would have enhanced analysis of international adjustment in the thirties. This can be shown by using the combination to clarify an aspect of the Reparations Problem – namely to distinguish quite clearly between the two component elements of the problem, the Budgetary problem and the Transfer problem. According to the Dawes Committee the Budgetary problem involved the extraction of the necessary money out of the pockets of the German people and the Transfer problem involved the conversion of the funds so obtained, into foreign exchange. A reparations payment is equivalent to a mandatory portfolio investment made by the paying country. Failure to make the reparations payment when due results in the debit being carried forward to the future to the detriment of the international net worth of the paying country. International net worth also suffers if the reparations payment is made by borrowing in a foreign capital market. The existence of a schedule of reparations payments implies the automatic deterioration of international worth in each period by the amount of the payment unless the payment is made with the proceeds of a positive foreign balance (international saving).

Equations (3-1), (3-2) and (3-3) posit *ex post* equality between S_D

[19] But see the discussion below on the need for variability in exchange rates, pp. 104–8.
[20] See, for example, Keynes' two-part letter to *The Times*, 17 and 18 April 1939, entitled 'Crisis Finance'.

and I_D, between S_I and I_I and therefore between total saving, S, and total investment or change in net worth, I. The distinction between the two sources of saving and between the two uses to which the non-consumption can be put allows for explicit analysis of inequalities in planned saving and planned investment domestically and internationally as well as in total. The reparations problem is solved when actual international saving equals planned international investment.[21] Using R to represent the reparations payment and asterisks to denote planned flows and assuming that domestic saving cannot be negative, the conditions for a successful reparations payment can be expressed as:

$$(S - I_D)^* = (S - I_D) = R = I_I^* \qquad (3\text{-}4)$$

$$S_I^* = S_I = R \qquad (3\text{-}5)$$

Equation (3-4) shows the conditions that satisfy the Budgetary problem – that the actual excess of total saving over domestic capital formation equal the scheduled reparations payment (the planned international investment). Total non-consumption is then adequate to the change in total net worth that is envisaged. The transfer problem is solved when equation (3-5) is satisfied – when actual international saving is equal to planned international investment. Given the fulfilment of the Budgetary problem, the successful resolution of the Transfer problem requires that actual international saving equal the excess of total saving over domestic capital formation. Multiplier repercussions are avoided if both problems are solved since international saving provides the impetus to income that high saving takes away. If the transfer problem is not solved but the budgetary problem is solved, the paying country will experience a contraction. For the equilibrium to continue it is not only necessary that the paying country continues to save internationally but it is also necessary for the recipient country to dissave internationally by an equal amount.[22]

It is apparent from the model of *The Treatise* that, if payments balance is defined as *requiring* no international movements of liquid

[21] The reparations payment is assumed to be the only international capital movement and therefore is equal to planned international investment. The modifications made to the model in *The Treatise* by expressing it in equations (3-1), (3-2) and (3-3) do not affect the analysis.

[22] Compare this condition with the discussion of the need for compatible international targets considered in Chapter 10 below, pp. 178–86.

assets and that this is to be achieved each year, then international saving and international investment must move in unison. In a world in which the flows of international investment are not constrained by capital controls, stamp taxes or similar impediments, planned international investment can be subject to sizeable year-to-year fluctuations. The target rate of international saving would also be required (under the assumption of complete balancing each year) to fluctuate from year-to-year by an equal amount. If the instrument variable predominantly associated with international saving is the rate of exchange, there is some value of the rate of exchange that is appropriate for each year – that is for each position of the international investment schedule. Thus, if lags in the effectiveness of instruments are ignored, effective policymaking then becomes an exercise in fixing the values of instrument variables that will 'hit a moving target'. If the target moves each year around some trend value, it becomes sufficient to 'aim the instrument at the trend'.

The concept of a moving target is touched upon in *The General Theory* when, in the relevant closed economy model, Keynes conceived of 'the neutral rate of interest'.[23] This rate of interest was a derivative from Keynes's version in *The Treatise* of Wicksell's natural rate and was the rate of interest that would generate full employment given the other parameters of the system. Thus, if an economy that used the rate of interest as the sole instrument for controlling aggregate demand, the neutral rate would be the value of the single instrument variable appropriate for the year. Keynes did not develop the theme but there is, clearly, a neutral rate for every possible position of the investment schedule in a two-sector model. If the investment schedule shifts annually, then the appropriate value of the instrument – the neutral rate – also changes each year. At first blush there would appear to be a distinction between the means of control of the instruments in the international and closed models. It appears that, in the international model, the rate of (international) saving is being made to conform to the flow of planned international investment, while in the closed model the rate of investment is being curtailed to equal a given volume of saving available at full employment. However, the apparent difference is exaggerated. It is true that in the closed-economy model, saving dominates investment at full employment and the rate of interest separates intramarginal from extramarginal investment projects. In the international model,

[23] *The General Theory*, pp. 242–4.

abstracting from any impact the rate of exchange may have upon
consumption and the rate of interest may have on international
investment, the rate of exchange does not affect the total amount of
saving but rather affects the distribution of a given volume of saving
between domestic and international saving. If planned international
investment is not sensitive to the domestic rate of interest it is, by
definition, intramarginal. Thus, the rate of exchange serves only to
allocate saving between two end uses, total saving still dominates
total investment and the rate of interest serves to separate intra- from
extramarginal projects. If some international investments were sensitive to the rate of interest, then an increase in the rate of interest
reduces the change required in the rate of exchange.

In a three-sector model including a government sector, the neutral
rate will vary with the size of the government budget deficit or surplus
as well as with the position of the domestic investment schedule. For
any given rate of interest, there is also a 'neutral budget deficit' that
will generate full employment, given the other parameters of the
system.

While Keynes never committed himself explicitly to the concept of
estimating and instituting values for policy tools that would achieve
full employment, it is clear that he stopped short of so doing by only
a very little.[24] It is possible that the severity of the disequilibrium
made him unconcerned with the niceties of small adjustments in the
neighbourhood of full employment. But *The General Theory* and the
post-war success of employment policies built on reasoning that
derived from it undoubtedly laid the foundation for the targets–
instruments framework of analysis developed by Meade and
Tinbergen.[25] While the mathematical formulation of the problem –
particularly as a set of linear equations – was beyond Keynes'
concepts, the system is built upon an inversion of the traditional
analysis and can therefore be legitimately traced to Keynes' work.

The single most important contribution to the practice of economic
policy to be derived from Keynes' writings and thinking is the idea of
the use of the huge economic entity that is government as a deliberate
offset to vagaries in the economic behaviour of the private sector.
The idea of monetary policy serving as an adjustment mechanism to
influence the size and direction of private sector financial flows was

[24] See Axel Leijonhufvud, *On Keynesian Economics and the Economics of
Keynes* (New York: Oxford University Press, 1968) pp. 343–7.
[25] See Whitman, *Policies for Internal and External Balance*, Ch. 1.

not new with Keynes. What was new with Keynes was the idea that monetary policy could be used aggressively in pursuit of internal balance and without regard to the pecuniary interests of the central bank, and the corollary that changes in the international net worth and liquidity position should be financed by the use of the government's credit in international markets. In other words, when monetary policy was to be used for internal balance, external imbalance was to be financed by the massive borrowing power of the government and, if possible, by the creation of an institution that would facilitate massive international borrowing by governments. Since the domestic expansion would induce an international payments deficit largely as a result of private sector transactions, the government could be seen as offsetting private excesses or shortcomings. When government expenditure policy was to be used, the government was to act as a residual supplier (or agent for absorption) of effective demand that was able to act in this way because of its unlimited debt capacity in its own national currency. Central banking theory had recognised the need for a lender of last resort as a means of preventing financial panics. Keynes' analysis demonstrated the need for a spender of last resort and, as a consequence, for the best substitute he could envisage for an international lender of last resort.

Given the reliance on the process of financing (as opposed to adjustment) of both government expenditure policy and of a passive attitude towards the balance of payments, it is not surprising that a comparison should be made between the budget of the central government and the international accounts.[26] Any such comparisons should be treated with great circumspection because internal deficits are capable of being financed by credit-creation powers under the control of the borrower, while external deficits cannot be financed without limit. Both sets of accounts embody data on policy instruments and both represent cash-flow contraints which must be satisfied. There is, however, one similarity between the two sets of accounts that is enlightening and that is the degree to which it is legitimate to finance a deficit in autonomous cash flows in order to offset an increase in the asset position. Just as the international accounts separate transactions on current and on capital account, so too a budget document can separate disbursements made for current expenditures and those made for the acquisition of an asset. Quite recently the concept of a capital budget was considered and rejected

[26] Polak, I.M.F. *Staff Papers* (July 1962) p. 156.

in the United States by a presidential commission. The rejection was supported by one analyst who argued that, in the political climate of the United States, such a concept would lead to an unfortunate bias in expenditure patterns, would confuse the analysis of fiscal policy and would add still more confusion to the question of the economic effects of changes in the volume of public debt outstanding.[27] The case in favour of a capital budget is the greater conceptual accuracy of accounting which would allay some of the opposition to an overall cash-flow deficit on the part of the central government – provided that the deficit was less than the capital surplus. The introduction of a capital budget would show the change in the net worth of the central government. The questions of the change in net worth and the separation of the capital and current accounts have their exact counterparts in the international accounts. Ultimately the constraint of liquidity will become effective but, in the interim, a combination of a deficit on cash flow coupled with a surplus on current expenditures is a sign of economic health. Failure to have considered the capital account separately from current transactions and monetary movements would have presented a very misleading picture of the United States international transactions for the generation ending in 1970.

It may appear from the preceding pages that Keynes paid scant heed to adjustment as a means of eliminating imbalances on international account. This conclusion would be only partly correct and, in any assessment of Keynes' grappling with the processes of international adjustment, it is important to distinguish between situations in which there existed what might be called a 'fundamental equilibrium' and those in which the imbalance was transitory.

The main goal of Keynes' thinking was always domestic prosperity, so that where he espoused the concept of exchange rate fluctuation, it was as defensive barrier to protect domestic prosperity.[28] Thus his concern was with a managed currency. This concern showed itself in his attempt to prevent the British return to the full gold standard in 1925 at the pre-war parity of £ = $4·86 and in his recognition of the deflationary impact that such a policy would bring about.[29] Keynes'

[27] See Samuel B. Chase, Jr., 'Federal Budget Concepts: A Critique of the Report of the President's Commission', in *The Federal Budget in a Dynamic Economy* (New York: The American Bankers Association, 1968) pp. 34–5.
[28] As in *The General Theory*, p. 270.
[29] See Donald Winch, *Economics and Policy: A Historical Study* (London: Hodder & Stoughton, 1969) Ch. 5, for an insightful history of the problem. It is

own solution was a managed currency with, undoubtedly, some devaluation of sterling, although the precise amount of devaluation necessary varied according to movements in the British and American price levels as well as according to the degree of freedom accorded to capital movements.[30] The essential reason for devaluation was that it was a more efficient way of achieving a cut in real wages – a point he was to make later with respect to the choice between monetary expansion and domestic deflation.[31] Here Keynes clearly recognised the need for adjustment. Another example of his recognition of the need for adjustment is to be found in his analysis of the German transfer problem, where he argued for a substantial depreciation of the German mark in terms of foreign currency.[32] The third instance in which the possibility of adjustment was considered was in the posthumous article where he mentioned exchange variation as 'a quicker and less painful aid' to the ongoing classical medicine.[33]

In the absence of any destabilising capital movements and assuming a reasonably realistic rate of exchange to have been achieved, Keynes seems not to have seen any great need for exchange-rate adjustment. While he incorporated the classical adjustment mechanism into his discussion of his international model in *The Treatise* and countenanced there the possibility of changes requiring adjustment occurring in both the capital and the current account, real changes in trading and investment conditions do not seem to have concerned him in his later work. Certainly the proposals for some supranational monetary organisation seemed to regard changes in exchange rates as infrequent occurrences, and in a note, published in 1943, he seemed to regard differential rates of inflation as the prime cause for any necessary realignment of exchange rates – if the initial

---

perhaps symptomatic of the era that in discussion of the relative price levels that permitted a return to the gold standard at the $4.86 rate, no mention was made of the interdependence between the viability of the move and the level of unemployment – the concept of a full-employment rate is not visible.

[30] After the original devaluation, variation in the gold-rate was not an integral part of the plan in the absence of inflation or deflation in the United States. See *A Tract on Monetary Reform* (London: Macmillan, 1924) Ch. v.

[31] *The General Theory*, p. 268.

[32] 'The German Transfer Problem', *Economic Journal*, xxxix (March 1929) pp. 1–7, reprinted in *Readings in the Theory of International Trade*, ed. H. S. Ellis and L. A. Metzler (Philadelphia, 1950) pp. 161–9. Note that here Keynes is still not conceptually including income-adjustments in his thinking process.

[33] 'The Balance of Payments of the United States', *Economic Journal*, LVI (June 1946) pp. 172–87.

exchange rates were fixed correctly, the only important disequilibrium for which a change in the exchange rates is the appropriate remedy would be if efficiency wage-rates were to move at materially different rates.[34] The use of the word 'materially' coupled with the gist of the last pages of the posthumous article in which he allows for the classical medicine 'to do its work',[35] suggests that Keynes foresaw any need for adjustment being accomplished largely by the classical mechanism and consequently did not expect that discretionary changes in exchange rates would become an important adjunct to policymakers' tools. This faith in the ability of the classical mechanism to iron-out any changes in national competitiveness that might occur is compatible with the expectation of a higher average rate of unemployment than has, in fact, been experienced.[36]

There was some lack of cognizance on Keynes' part of the possible need for ongoing and fairly frequent discretionary adjustments of exchange rates in a world of normalcy. Whether this was due to his preoccupation with violently abnormal periods, with a concept of normalcy that was insufficiently optimistic, or whether it was because he foresaw capital controls being maintained by all countries and tightened at the first sign of a serious deficit is not known. Certainly the very large post Second World War volume of capital movements – both portfolio and direct – and the generally high rates of employment are both in conflict with his analytic frame of reference.

The theory to be developed in this book was not intended at the outset to be a marriage of Keynes' macroeconomic thinking to balance-of-payments theory. The fact that there will be a large element of Keynes' constructs evident in the final framework is a tribute to the wide applicability of Keynes' analysis. Donald Winch has remarked that 'one of the incidental tragedies of the failure of

[34] 'The Objective of International Price Stability', *The Economic Journal*, LIII (June-September 1943) pp. 185–7. Lord Robbins, *The Economist in the Twentieth Century* (London: Macmillan and Company, 1954) p. 53 seems to have been unaware of Keynes' thinking on this subject. The belief has been echoed by Milton Friedman as recently as 1969, see *The International Monetary Mechanism*, p. 116.

[35] *Economic Journal* (June 1946).

[36] Keynes, in a letter to Lord Beveridge in 1944, thought a target rate of unemployment of 3 per cent to be overoptimistic – cited by R. F. Kahn, 'Lord Keynes and Inflation', *The Listener*, May 3 1956, p. 543. The social insurance scheme in the *White Paper on Employment Policy* (Cmd. 6527, H.M.S.O., 1944) 'balanced' at 8 per cent unemployment. As a working assumption in discussions of post-war national income, Keynes used 5 per cent of the insured population.

post-war planning in the international field was the fact that it was here that Keynes sacrificed most of the last years of his life'.[37] Not that the proposal for a clearing union, the ultimate International Monetary Fund and the American Loan were not worthwhile achievements, but because of his involvement in public affairs, Keynes never found the time to marry his vision of the macro-economic world developed in *The General Theory* to economic relations among nations. The idea for a supranational monetary organisation belonged to *The Treatise* and the similarity between domestic saving and investment and international saving and invest-ment developed in *The Treatise* was never updated.

In a closed economy, savings and investment could not be relied upon to achieve equality at the correct, full-employment rate within a socially-acceptable period of time, even though there did exist a powerful mechanism for equating the two. In the international world, the flows of international investment and saving have determinants that are just as disparate as those governing full-employment, saving and investment. The difference is that, in the international world, there exists no powerful mechanism to equate the two within a socially-acceptable period of time.

[37] *Economics and Policy: A Historical Study*, p. 279.

4 The Accounting, Formal Definitions and the Assumptions

The main proposition underlying the formal payments-adjustments model is that planned international investment and planned international saving respond to two separate sets of determining variables. While the two flows do interact, there is no dominating force that can be relied upon to establish equality between the two flows with any degree of automaticity, and it is quite possible that a nation will find it either impossible or undesirable to finance any excess of planned investment over planned saving. Thus frequent or continuing policy adjustments may be necessary if a satisfactory international performance is to be achieved. The failure of international investment and international saving to become equal to each other may be due to institutional rigidities, to the ponderousness and inefficiency of such equilibrating mechanisms as do exist or to perverse variability in any exogenous forces. Alternatively the international system may fail to adjust automatically because the authorities in either the deficit or the surplus nation are unwilling to incur the costs of adjustment – measured by the consequent failure to achieve domestic goals – so that any equilibrating mechanism is deliberately counter-acted.

Before the theory can be stated with any precision, it is necessary that the accounting concepts be clearly specified, that the variables in the model be defined and that the assumptions and limitations of the analysis be set out.

As noted in Chapter 2, the theory makes no pretence of solving with a single frame of reference the twin sets of analytic problems posed by the international accounts of a reserve-currency nation. It is crucial that the problems of the movement of volatile, liquid funds be separated from those problems that result from changes in the conditions underlying transactions in goods and services and international movements of long-term commitments of capital. What is of concern to policymakers aiming at quantitative goals is the need or lack of need for adjustment of the focus economy. Adjustments can cause the economy temporarily to lapse from high employment levels as resources are shifted among sectors and, possibly, as changes in real income levels are experienced.[1] Thus what is needed is an indicator of the degree of 'international health' of the economy. For any nation but particularly for nations whose currencies serve as reserve currencies, it is possible for monetary disturbances to take place which affect a nation's international liquid asset position but which do not indicate the need for any adjustment of the economy.

Balance-of-payments accounts, defined to comprise all autonomous international transactions, are designed to measure any change in a nation's (net) liquid asset position. The accounts are based upon a concept of cash flow. When transactions among nations were limited to transactions of current goods and services and a means of settlement, a change in the liquid asset position was an important indicator of the 'health' of an economy. Equally, under a full gold standard, a change in the liquid asset position was recognised as an integral part of the adjustment process that enabled the classical medicine to do its work. A change in the liquid asset position can still, in the modern world, indicate the need for adjustment of the domestic economy even if the deficit is located primarily in the short-term capital account (in which case it must be assumed that private capital movements correctly foresee or obey some disturbance which has not yet made its impact felt upon current transactions). However, it is also possible that a change in the liquid asset position can take place without indicating any need for readjustment of the domestic economy. This possibility holds for all nations that do not have strict controls over the export of short-term capital (resident-owned or foreign-owned) but will be most apparent for reserve-currency nations.

Any cash-flow measure will indicate a combination of any change in net worth as well as any change in gross liquid assets. Changes in liquid asset positions caused by, for example, an outflow of short-term capital owned by residents or by foreigners, do not indicate any failure to achieve social goals or any change in the real wealth of the nation. Any such movements of short-term capital represent

---

[1] This echoes the distinction made in *The Treatise*, I 326–9, between disturbances that affect the new equilibrium level of income in the focus country and those that do not.

offsetting changes in both assets and liabilities. As a consequence it may be desirable or necessary to repair the liquidity position, but these measures do not directly require an adjustment of the domestic economy, and particularly not to the point that the loss in gross reserves be fully offset by an increase in international saving. However, if a deficit on cash-flow indicates a decrease in net worth, this could impinge directly upon the national set of goals and could require an adjustment of the focus economy. Because movements of liquid assets among currencies do not necessarily have any direct impact upon the viability and performance of either economy in any 'real' or long-term sense, the effects of international flows of short-term capital will normally be neutralised as much as possible in both countries. One reason for ignoring short-term capital movements of this kind is that they may reverse themselves quite quickly and there is no need to inflict upon an economy the pain of two offsetting adjustment processes in short succession. A second reason for not adjusting the economy is that short-term disturbances may indicate a structural defect in the international monetary system whereby the global desires for international liquid assets are not met by the creation of a sufficient quantity of international liquidity and this shortage is reflected in drains on the gross reserves of key-currency nations.[2] Operational problems of data accuracy and correct categorisation of transactions aside, it is this possibility of conflict within a single indicator that makes a single figure for an international deficit or surplus inadequate for analysis of international economic policy needs.[3] The two problems of liquidity needs and adjustment needs can be independent of each other. The liquidity position will affect the range of acceptable values of the international target and will *require* adjustment only through its impact upon the general interest. It is necessary to derive an indicator of international performance *apart from* the flows of short-term assets. Such an indicator would reduce the probability of adjustment policies being instituted when there was no need, as well as reducing the probability of the need for the institution of adjustment policies being covered up by short-term phenomena.

[2] This phenomenon is analysed in Walter S. Salant, 'International Reserves and Payments Adjustment', Banco Nazionale del Lavoro *Quarterly Review* (September 1969) pp. 283–308.
[3] C. P. Kindleberger, *Journal of Political Economy* (November–December 1969) recommends two measures as constituting the minimum satisfactory number of indicators: changes in net worth and in gross reserves.

The international target (what is desired) will be the product of interaction between domestic goals, international net worth considerations and by the liquidity position of the nation (as well as by the data). In contrast, the actual international performance of the economy (what is) will be primarily indicated by a figure that excludes autonomous transactions in short-term capital.

THE ACCOUNTING

Allusion was made in Chapter 2 to the possible existence of multiple international goals or targets. If multiple goals exist, then each goal will require its own performance indicator. The most straightforward way of identifying the distinct goals is to develop a system of international accounts *ab initio* and to identify each possible goal with a different sub-balance. Departures from orthodoxy in the system of accounts set out below are, at most, slight.

The most important single category of transactions among nations is the sale of commodities and services by residents of one country to residents of another country. The purchaser's currency is exchanged for the foreign-made good so that an import represents a debit in the international accounts. These transactions form the basis for the received body of payments-adjustment theory. Each export uses factors of production as inputs and therefore detracts from the maximum amount of goods and services available for domestic use or absorption.[4] Each import increases the amount of goods and services available for domestic absorption by adding to the available bundle of goods without using up factors of production. This sub-balance can be referred to as the Balance on Goods and Services or the Balance of Trade (B_T). Since B_T is based on transactions in goods and services that require inputs of factors of production for their export, it follows that B_T is the main indicator of the direct effect of the international sector on the demand for labour in the focus country. Thus, B_T assumes importance when policy is aimed at achieving high employment levels through the international sector. The labour content may vary among different categories of exports

---

[4] Absorption is defined as covering all categories of expenditure on goods and services within a nation that use factors of production in their creation. In the simplest case it is equal to the sum of consumption, investment and government expenditures on goods and services including imports. When $B_T = 0$, absorption is equal to output. See S. S. Alexander, 'Effects of Devaluation on a Trade Balance', I.M.F. *Staff Papers*, II (April 1952) pp. 263–78.

so that the absolute value of B_T may not be a good indicator of the number of jobs 'exported' or 'imported'. However, in the absence of severe compositional shifts, a change in B_T will indicate a change in the impetus given to domestic employment levels by international transactions.

The balance of trade does *not* include investment income. This exclusion represents a small departure from orthodoxy. Included with investment income are related flows which do not involve the use of domestic factors of production in the period in which the credit is earned. Dividend and income receipts, together with royalties, fees, etc., are the product of capital formation transferred in earlier periods and produced in earlier periods. Fairly clearly, the net flow of investment income will be determined by forces that are different from those that influence the components of B_T.

Investment income is included in the second important category of transaction – unilateral transfers. Unilateral transfers are current payments in the international accounts that do not generate any *quid pro quo* in the current period. Unilateral transfers comprise gifts, foreign aid, pensions paid to non-residents, private remittances, charitable donations as well as investment income. Receipt of a unilateral transfer is distinguishable from a credit earned by a commodity or service export because of the difference in current factor inputs required.

Together the sub-balances on trade and on unilateral transfers constitute the Balance on Current Account (B_C). The balance on current account represents the amount by which claims on foreigners net of foreign claims on the focus nation have increased during the period under review. It is therefore the measure of *ex post* international saving.

The third sub-account is the long-term capital account and comprises the net acquisitions of long-term illiquid claims on foreigners by both the private and government sectors. Normally, private long-term investments are divided into (long-term) portfolio[5] and direct investments. Portfolio investment implies a lack of control over the operation of the debtor or issuer of the equity: direct investment implies control over the asset acquired or, in the case of a business subsidiary, operating control. There is an apparent problem

[5] Some definitions include private holdings of short-term assets (other than money) in portfolio capital. Liquid or short-term assets are explicitly excluded from the definition of portfolio investment used here.

of classification since it is extremely difficult to separate portfolio assets into those that are and are not illiquid. The crucial aspect from an international payments point of view is the intent of the holder and, using this criterion, new issues of long-term securities should be considered to be long-term but other instruments including equities could be considered long-term because of their (lack of) maturity date or short-term because of the relatively efficient markets in which they can be traded. Tangible assets and equity in business that are under the control of the equity owners can normally be considered to be long-term commitments of funds from the creditor to the debtor nation. A third category of long-term debt is inter-governmental debt. Extensions of loans net of repayment and any debt incurred constitutes changes in a government's net international position on long-term. There is one qualification that must be applied to this type of debt. Governments have been known to incur long-term debt for balance-of-payments purposes.[6] Financing an international payments deficit on long-term does not constitute an autonomous transaction and therefore should be excluded from the long-term government account.

These three categories of transaction comprise the Balance on Capital (B_K) and provide an *ex post* measure of international investment. ($I_I = -B_K$).

The sum of B_C and B_K is defined as the Basic Balance (B_B). The basic balance was originally conceived as an indicator that eliminated most transitory effects and served to illustrate basic or underlying economic trends. Presumably, it is these underlying trends that exert their influence upon real income, employment levels and upon policy goals so that B_B is perhaps the best indicator of what has been referred to as a nation's 'international health'. A basic balance of zero would show that the increase in the international net worth of a country was just equal to the long-term assets which it had acquired.

For completeness, it is necessary to introduced a fourth sub-account comprising autonomous movements of liquid assets – called the monetary balance (B_M). Finally, there remain accommodating flows that combine with the four sub-accounts to produce the necessary accountant's identity. The relationship between the accounts can be summarised in tabular form:

[6] For example, the United States acquired the so-called 'Roosa Bonds' during the sixties.

(a)	Balance on trade
(b)	Balance on unilateral transactions
$(a+b) = c$	Balance on current account
(d)	Balance on long-term capital account
$(c+d) = e$	Basic balance
(f)	Monetary balance
$(e+f) = g$	Balance of payments on autonomous transactions
(h)	Balance on accommodating flows
$(g+h)$	Accountant's identity

FORMAL DEFINITIONS

This section is quite short. Its purpose is to define the state of balance in international payments as it will apply in the model. The section will also define component concepts which are used in the definition of balance and will introduce the concept of an indicator of the relative competitiveness of a national economy in its international transactions.

A nation's international payments position is defined as being satisfactory or in balance when its international transactions are unconstrained by balance-of-payments considerations and are compatible with the highest available level of achievement in the national set of target variables (the general interest). Thus a satisfactory payments position exists when neither special measures nor accommodating monetary flows are needed to align its international targets and its international performance. The absence of accommodating (or capital) flows is the standard definition for payments balance but, in the definition given here, the exclusion of short-term capital movements from consideration delimits the need for balance to those underlying flows that determine living standards and rates of capital formation. These flows can be identified, quite simply, as consumption, and international and domestic investment.

The process of adjustment can be defined as the process of removing imbalance 'through changes in relative incomes, prices and resource allocations'. This is the definition evolved by Machlup and it limits the effect of adjustment to the current account balance or to the flow of international saving.[7] Thus, it would be possible to define imbalance as the existence of the need for adjustment when no special measures were in effect and to emphasise the interrelation between the international performance of an economy and its absorption of current material benefits – imbalance testifying to the need for some reallocation of the internal production mix and/or some change in the rate of absorption.

A formal definition of full balance is: international payments balance exists when, for a specified short period of time and in the absence of any special measures designed to improve the balance on current account, the desires of the nation to acquire illiquid foreign assets coupled with any desired change in the international liquid reserve position of the economic authorities is equal to the flow of international saving. Symbolically:

$$I_I + \Delta R^* = S_I \qquad (4\text{-}1)$$

where R^* is the liquid reserve position of the authorities and Δ denotes a change, so that ΔR^* denotes the desired change in liquid reserves to be achieved during the period. In terms of the accounting balances, balance is defined as:

$$-B_K + \Delta R^* = B_C \qquad (4\text{-}2)$$

For practical purposes, the expression 'a specified short period of time' can be taken to mean a calendar year. The expression, 'in the absence of any special measures designed to improve the balance on current account', is the equivalent of Nurkse's classic requirements for his definition of international monetary equilibrium,[8] and refers both to the failure to attain domestic target levels of employment for balance-of-payments reasons as well as to the imposition of impediments to current account transactions (quasi-adjustments). 'The desires of the nation to acquire illiquid foreign assets' does not necessarily imply complete neutrality on the part of the authorities between domestic and foreign investment but does imply the absence of any interference with international investment standards for balance-of-payments reasons. Finally, the desired change in the international liquid reserve position of the economic authorities

[7] Machlup, 'Adjustment, Compensatory Correction, and Financing of Imbalances in International Payments', p. 208.

[8] See Ragnar Nurkse, 'Conditions of International Monetary Equilibrium', in *A.E.A. Readings in the Theory of International Trade*, ed. H. S. Ellis and L. A. Metzler (Philadelphia: Blakiston, 1950) pp. 9–11.

needs to be specified separately from the flow of international invest-ment. Although it represents an autonomous acquisition of assets that is seen as long-run in nature, the assets themselves are quite likely to be liquid and the determinants of ΔR^* will differ from those of I_I.

The change in the desired liquid reserve position and in the flow of international saving have both been implicitly specified as exact values. It is quite possible that either item has a range of values compatible with the achievement of domestic targets. If some range of values is allowed for in the definition, it could read '. . . coupled with any tolerable change in the international liquid reserve position of the economic authorities is equal to any flow of international saving compatible with the achievement of domestic goals'. The concept of a range of acceptable values for the component flows complicates the exposition without making any significant contribu-tion to the analysis. Therefore unless explicitly specified, it will be assumed that national targets set exact rates of international invest-ment, international saving and changes in the liquid reserve position. If the desired or target change in the liquid reserve position is zero, a nation achieves full international balance when its planned international investment – free of restrictions applied for balance-of-payments reasons – is equal to its international saving – achieved without the use of 'artificial aids'. Under the background conditions specified, balance is achieved when the basic balance is zero.

The attainment of an equality between international investment and saving when special balance-of-payments measures have been instituted can be referred to as a quasi-balance. Even more than a position of full balance, perhaps, a quasi-balance is subject to disturbance because of the probability that other nations will lose patience with the qualitative aspects of the quasi-adjustments by which the quasi-balance is obtained and may offset their impact.

Given that the desired change in the international liquid reserve position and the flow of international saving are exact values, the definition of balance is an equation. It might be reasonable, though a shade mercantilistic, to expect a surplus to be included in the definition of a satisfactory performance – that is, to express the definition of satisfactoriness as an inequality. Assuming there is a zero desired change in the liquid reserve position of the authorities, the definition, specified as an inequality, would amount to $B_B \geqslant 0$ – assuming there are no special measures in force to improve the current account for balance-of-payments reasons. A surplus on basic balance would *not* represent a satisfactory international achievement because the surplus itself necessarily involves a reduction in the levels of the domestic target variables that could be reached. However, the argument against specifying the definition in terms of an inequality does not depend upon the untenability of a surplus for two reasons: a surplus is tenable for quite lengthy periods if other nations are, in practice, willing to lose liquid reserves as a group for a number of years, and the specification and achievement of targets must be limited to short-run situations.

The definition of a satisfactory international performance in the form of an equation is compatible with the possibility that a nation will seek to acquire a degree of insurance against an error in forecasting by achieving an overall payments surplus. The reason for a policy of this kind is to be found in the asymmetry of the costs of falling short of and exceeding payments balance by equal amounts – a surplus involving, in the short run at least, a far smaller sacrifice in terms of domestic goals and involving far more palatable adjustments. The insurance will take the form of setting a higher ΔR^* than would be set if the costs of a deficit and surplus were equal. Since the desired increase in the reserve position is itself an element in the equation, a neo-mercantilist policy is quite compatible with the definition of balance.[9]

It has been contended that the international target of a nation will be determined by interaction between its domestic goals, international net worth considerations and by its liquidity position. International saving is only equal to the increase in international net worth under quite specific circumstances. International saving is defined as the (flow) value of the excess of current receipts over current payments – the balance on current account. International net worth is the (stock) balance of all international assets and liabilities. The flow of current international saving is only exactly equal to the increase in international net worth when the value of a nation's outstanding assets and liabilities – measured in some international numeraire – does not change on balance. It is extremely improbable in practice that there will, in any year, be no change in the values of outstanding assets and liabilities although, under normal circumstances, the net change can be expected to be fairly small relative to the total values of assets and

[9] But see Joan Robinson, *The New Mercantilism*, pp. 10 and 13–20, for an analysis of why nations will strive to attain and/or keep a surplus.

liabilities. A period of widespread expropriation of foreign assets or of default on securities could cause sizeable changes in international net worth apart from the flow of international saving. The major source of change in the value of international assets and liabilities is likely to be profits retained in the country of operation by subsidiaries of foreign parent corporations. Provided that the accounting procedures of the International Monetary Fund are followed, this source of error will not be important since the I.M F procedure requires that retained earnings of subsidiary corporations be included in repatriated profits and entered in the current account and be offset by a debit entry in direct investment in the capital account.[10] In what follows, it will be assumed that no change in the values of existing assets and liabilities takes place and that therefore, international saving is equal to the increase in international net worth.

The process of basic adjustment can have its effect only on international saving (B_C) and must work through the current account by affecting relative money incomes and prices and, through these, resource allocations in the two trading countries.[11] If variation in the level of employment and output is temporarily assumed to be zero, the variation in money incomes must derive from the income effects of the change in relative prices.

THE ASSUMPTIONS

The theory is constructed for a two-country world consisting of a focus or domestic nation and the rest of the world (the foreign nation). It is assumed that the focus country possesses the main attributes of an optimum currency area – that factors of production are mobile within the nation and that the flow of international saving is sufficiently sensitive to changes in C for the adjustment process to be considered efficient in some absolute sense of that word.[12] The limitations that are inevitable in a two-country framework are reduced if the 'rest of the world' is not considered as a static, monolithic entity but is recognised as being capable of internal evolutions that will affect the terms on which transactions will be made over time

[10] International Monetary Fund, *Balance of Payments Manual* (Washington, D.C.: 1961) pp. 68 and 183.

[11] Machlup, 'Adjustment, Compensatory Correction and Finance', p. 208.

[12] See Robert A. Mundell, 'A Theory of Optimum Currency Areas', *American Economic Review*, 51 (September 1961) pp. 657–65.

with the focus nation. Thus, the flow of international saving will vary over time for any given value of C for the focus nation.

The focus nation is assumed to have a defined 'general interest' function that provides its authorities with a set of criteria by which the authorities can attempt to maximise the national welfare. The set of values for the target variables will be fixed for a given set of parameters and will be changed in the light of new information. Thus international policy will be defined but will be subject to change if the international behaviour of trading partners changes. If domestic parameters change or if international forecasts are not borne out, the authorities may consider a change in international policy to be necessary – in other words, the failure to achieve the international economic target will lead the economic authorities to consider adjustment or some substitute policy. If a new policy is considered worthwhile, attempts will be made to institute that policy. It is not necessary in order to have an understanding of payments adjustment to conceive of the rest of the world as having its own collective set of international criteria on which it will base its composite reaction to any change in posture by the focus nation or in response to internal changes. However, the focus nation is likely to formulate its own expectations, and therefore its international targets, as though there were a single composite entity *en face*. The characteristics of this composite will be drawn from the economic characteristics of the focus nation's trading partners and will be weighted by the importance of the individual nations as trading partners. Thus, since the greater part of a developed nation's international transactions is with other developed nations and since some basic features of developed nations are quite similar, the concept of a single rough-hewn policy for the rest of the world does not seem an unjustifiable simplification. Both sets of general-interest functions must presuppose that the size of the liquid reserve positions – both absolutely and relative to some optimum – are given as is the set of international monetary institutions so that the ease and cost of financing a deficit are data. Equally the two functions prerequire a given domestic economic structure.

The main features of the practical alternatives that face the authorities in the focus country can be sketched in. The contention has already been made that, in developed nations particularly, a high employment level is a paramount target. Almost equally important is the issue of price stability. In nearly all countries these two goals are in direct conflict with each other. It is possible to specify a nation's domestic tolerances with what might be termed an Adams Box.[13] In Figure 4-1, the axes denote rates of inflation and unemployment and the box defines the ranges of unemployment that the electorate considers tolerable – the lower limits of the box being the pragmatic minima. Provided that the structure of the economy is

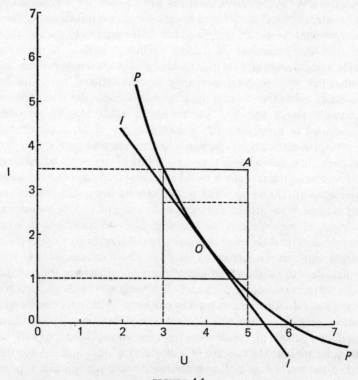

FIGURE 4-1
The Range of Domestic Policy Tolerances

such that its inflation-unemployment trade-off – represented in the Figure by a Phillips Curve with its standard shape showing asymmetric wage and price rigidities[14] – merely touches the box at

[13] From John Adams, 'The Phillips Curve, a "Consensual" Trap, and National Income', *Western Economic Journal*, VI (March 1968) pp. 145–9. See also E. Ray Canterbery, *Economics on a New Frontier* (Belmont, Calif.: Wadsworth Publishing Company, 1968) pp. 30–9.

[14] There is no contention here about causation and it is recognised that Phillips Curves are, at best, only a partial explanation of the inflation since they can and do shift.

point A, the domestic policy mix is defined. If the curve cuts the box (as does PP in the Figure), there exists a feasible range of policy mixes among which one will be chosen. If, for simplicity, community indifference curves are assumed to be parallel to the negatively-sloped diagonal of the box, an optimum policy mix is conceptually defined. If for some reason the Phillips Curve lies to the north-east of A, an incomes policy is in order together with other crisis measures.[15] There is no reason to suppose that the positions of the Phillips Curves at any one time or the limits of tolerance are the same in both nations. It is quite possible that the two best domestic policies are not compatible with ongoing international payments balance in a world of fixed rates of exchange because of unequal rates of inflation in the two nations. This incompatibility, which will exist except in very rare cases, will tend to reduce the size of the box. If the best domestic policy leads to ongoing balance of payments strains because of a steady deterioration in C over time, the rate of inflation must be reduced. Thus, the upper limit of the box will shift downward (the dotted line in the Figure) and the maximum rate of inflation will be reduced to $2\frac{3}{4}$ per cent and the minimum level of unemployment raised from, roughly, 3 to $3\frac{1}{2}$ per cent for the Phillips Curve actually drawn. This process may be one of the meanings of the expression, 'the discipline of the balance of payments'.

It is possible to relate the size and the position of the Adams Box to balance of payments. The box will be constant in size and position for all surpluses on the basic balance (adjusted for ΔR^*) but will shift outwards and contract as the deficit on international payments increases.[16] Since the Phillips Cuve will be largely independent of the basic balance or even of the balance of trade, it will cut the box at different positions as the deficit increases. Thus, as the deficit grows larger, the range of policy options in the domestic sphere will decrease and ultimately 'crisis conditions' will ensue. The size of the deficit at which the box loses contact with the Phillips Curve represents the maximum rate of international dissaving that the nation will accept (the flow of investment being given).

The assumptions about the behaviour of the two nations can now be summarised. Both nations will attempt to achieve levels of

[15] This does not controvert the desirability of a policy of maintaining continuous downward pressure upon the Phillips Curve at all times by means of a guidelines policy.

[16] See Figure 5-2 below, pp. 90–2.

domestic performance that fall within their respective range of tolerances. There is no guarantee that the two sets of behaviour will be compatible in a world of fixed exchange rates and, in that case, the behaviour of one of the nations will be constrained by international considerations. The subservience of domestic policy to international payments problems does not ensure the removal of any deficit – either through adjustment or through the imposition of some impediment to trade or other second-best policy. It follows directly from the assumption of behaviour characteristics on the part of the focus nation of the kind specified above, that the model is unlikely to have any applicability to a developing nation – particularly not to one that has only limited capacity for monetary discipline.[17]

The following assumptions are made about the relationships of international economic flows to changes in policy in one of the trading nations and to other exogenous variables. All the relationships posited assume the absence of simultaneous other changes in the system and, in this sense, are *ceteris paribus* relationships. They need not hold in a situation of multiple simultaneous disturbances of different magnitudes.

(1) An increase in the level of capacity utilisation (employment) in one country will cause its balance of trade to deteriorate both when no foreign reaction is assumed (through a multiplier) and when an induced foreign reaction or expansion is assumed. Since an increase in capacity utilisation does not in itself allow for any increase in the national stock of capital, this assumption does not necessarily imply that economic growth by one country with the rest of the world stagnant will necessarily cause the balance of trade to deteriorate.

(2) A deficit on the balance of trade can be removed by an effective increase in the nation's competitive position or ratio (C). In terms of the orthodox literature with its emphasis on trade flows, this assumption implies that the foreign exchange market for a country's currency is stable, or – even more traditionally – that the sum of the elasticities of the two import demand schedules exceeds unity.[18] No assumption is made about the size of the change in the net barter terms of trade relative to the ratio of the prices of tradable to nontraded goods. It is assumed that the net barter and the single factoral

---

[17] Milton Gilbert contends that such countries defy economic analysis because the problem is one of the failure of political authority: see *The International Adjustment Mechanism*, p. 21.
[18] With all the manifold assumptions.

terms of trade move against a nation that has to increase its competitive ratio to achieve a surplus or eliminate a deficit on current account. It follows from this assumption that for a nation to achieve a surplus on the balance of trade (and, by extension, on current account) it will have to suffer some loss in its absorption potential in addition to the surplus on trade account.

(3) Finally, it is assumed that any transfer will be undereffected in the classical frame of reference of a stationary state with both economies fully employed. If the transfer is undereffected it will have a positive effect upon the balance of trade of less than the debit occasioned by the transfer and will therefore have a negative effect on international saving. An increase in C will therefore be necessary to maintain a given rate of international saving in the event of an increase in the deficit on unilateral transfers. Given the behavioural assumptions made above, it is probable that some or all of any deflationary effects of a transfer will be offset by the transferring country. Offsets are also likely to be instituted in the receiving country if the receipt of the transfer is likely to induce inflation. Offsetting policy actions of this kind would substantially reduce the likelihood that a transfer would be effected in the real world.

(4) The creation of an analytic framework that will incorporate capital movements that can be considered long-term commitments and other transfers in balance-of-payments analysis need devote no more than passing reference to mundane operational problems. The impossible task of diagnosing in fact what capital movements are and are not long-term commitments need not be dwelt upon here. It suffices to identify all long-term private capital movements as autonomous as well as all increases in liquid reserves of the authorities even though the latter be short-term. Other capital movements are considered to be outside of the framework of the analysis and can, for convenience, be characterised as being accommodating. In this frame of reference the fundamental truth of balance-of-payments analysis is retained: a nation must 'pay its way'. This cash-flow concept was the original fact that dominated the international accounts when transactions were almost exclusively current transactions. The introduction of long-term commitments of capital to foreign countries merely re-emphasises the fact that a nation can only increase its international net worth by saving internationally and that the cash surplus on current account must equal the cash deficit on capital account.

CONCLUSION

Part I has laid the groundwork for the theory to be presented in Part II. A brief summary is warranted at this point.

Analysis of international payments adjustment is not adequate to the task of policy prescription in the modern world unless it contains capital movements, unilateral transfers and related flows as integral elements of the theoretical framework. Further the framework must take account of (1) the present, inescapable policy emphasis in developed nations on high levels of domestic employment and (2) the fact that the resistance to inflation in surplus countries and the resistance to the unemployment that accompanies absolute reduction in price levels in deficit countries effectively precludes reliance upon the classical mechanism of adjustment. Finally, the increased interdependence of the developed world, the variability of certain international flows, particularly of capital and transfer flows and of their repercussions on the current account, and the greater frequency of shifts in world trade structure have required that the system of analysis be a short-run rather than an equilibrium framework.

The analytic framework to be developed will have the disequilibrium approach that characterises *The General Theory* in which Keynes sought to rid the world of the notion that, in a closed economy, internal balance could be reached with any degree of automaticity. The short-run disequilibrium approach of period analysis is appropriate for the problem at hand and is compatible with the targets–instruments concepts developed by Tinbergen as a basis of a theory of economic policy.

The combination of the introduction of capital flows and the non-equilibrium frame of reference makes a non-zero balance on current account or basic account, a legitimate short-term policy goal. A deficit of this kind can be financed either by a reduction in the gross and net reserve positions or by the attraction of interest-sensitive funds so that the gross reserve position remains unchanged. If the deficit is to be financed by maintaining the gross reserve position unchanged, the concept is approached part way and, in turn, partially justifies the analysis developed originally by Mundell, of achieving internal–external balance under a system of fixed exchange rates by joint manipulation of interest-rate and expenditure policies.[19]

[19] R. A. Mundell, 'The Appropriate Use of Monetary and Fiscal Policy for Internal and External Stability', I.M.F. *Staff Papers* (March 1962) pp. 70–9.

Any policy of financing a deficit by maintaining constant the gross reserves of the deficit nation is viable only in the short-run and is rational only if the limitations of financing a deficit are explicitly included in the calculus of the authorities of the focus nation. The Mundell analysis is the essence of period analysis, ignoring as it does the waning of the flow of short-term funds that must occur with the passage of time and a constant international interest-rate differential.[20] Financing a deficit is a legitimate policy only if the focus nation is unconcerned with the deterioration in its international net worth, foresees a reversal of the cause of the deficit in the future or is acquiring long-term assets net at a rate exceeding the deficit.

APPENDIX 4-A

THE COMPETITIVE RATIO

The need for a measure of the 'international health' of an economy or for an indicator of its competitiveness, has already been mentioned. The device to be used, the competitive position or ratio, has been touched upon in Chapter 2 (see pp. 29–31). This appendix considers the analytic problems inherent in the concept of the competitive ratio and of measuring changes in that index number. The qualifications and the assumptions are spelled out with reference to the values of the ratio that exist (C_P) and that will balance the trade account (C_T). These considerations will also apply to the values that will balance the current account (C_C) and the basic balance (C_B) when these measures are introduced in Part II.

The ratio has been defined as:

$$C = \frac{P_f}{P_d} \cdot \frac{1}{r}$$

such that an increase in the value of C_P will, *ceteris paribus*, increase the trade balance. The term, P_f and P_d, are index numbers of the absolute price levels of tradable goods in the local currencies of the foreign and focus (domestic) nation respectivly. The symbol, r, stands for an index of the rate of exchange measured as the number of units of foreign currency needed to buy one unit of domestic

[20] See Thomas D. Willett and Francesco Forte, 'Interest-Rate Policy and External Balance', *Quarterly Journal of Economics* (May 1969) pp. 242–62.

currency so that a depreciation of the domestic currency reduces r and increases the value of C. The measure, C, must be specified in terms of a base year. It is probably desirable to specify the rate-of-exchange index in terms of the base year for the competitive ratio. Since the foreign country necessarily comprises the 'rest of the world', it is necessary to specify exactly the assumptions that govern the compilation of P_f and the definition of r as well as to specify the assumptions that apply to the computation of the index of the domestic price level for internationally tradable goods. Further the implications of a change in one of the component elements for the change in the value of C must be precisely understood.

The concept of the competitive ratio can trace its genealogy back to the 'cost ratio' used in an early analysis of the internal–external balance problem. 'The "Cost Ratio" . . . is some sort of index measuring the competitive position of Australian industries – e.g. the ratio of an index of international prices (prices of imports and exports) to an index of local wages, with weights reflecting the sensitivity of supply and demand for different commodities to changes in relative costs.'[1] The competitive ratio is defined in prices rather than in costs since it is money prices that determine international trade flows in the short run[2] but it is a reasonable presumption that prices and costs will tend to move together.

The concept of a competitive ratio which, if attained, would yield balanced trade bears no relation to that ephemeral entity, the equilibrium rate of exchange.[3] A value of C_T involves only balance not equilibrium. The balance need only hold for a single period and is as liable to be disrupted by forces which are already in the process of working themselves out as the impact of a change in an instrument variable waxes or wanes with time as by new external disturbances. However, the computation of a value for C does require the assumption of quite precise values for all the other variables that affect

[1] T. W. Swan, 'Longer-Run Problems of the Balance of Payments', in *Readings in International Economics*, ed. R. E. Caves and H. G. Johnson (Homewood, Ill.: Richard D. Irwin, Inc., 1968) pp. 455–64.

[2] Cf. Bertil Ohlin, *Interregional and International Trade* (rev. ed.) (Cambridge, Mass.: Harvard University Press, 1967) p. 7 – 'The Immediate cause of trade is always that goods can be bought cheaper from outside in terms of money than they can be produced at home and vice versa.'

[3] See Joan Robinson, 'The Foreign Exchanges', in *Essays in the Theory of Employment*, (Oxford: Blackwell, 1947). Reprinted in *Readings in the Theory of International Trade*, ed. H. S. Ellis and L. A. Metzler (Philadelphia: Blakiston, 1949) pp. 83–158.

demand-and-supply patterns in international markets. The level of income in both countries must be accurately specified – this in contrast to the range of values for income that was defined as potentially satisfactory according to the set of national goals. Given the tendency toward increasing rates of import demand as higher income levels strain manufacturing capacity – irrespective of price competitiveness – the values of C_T can be expected to be quite sensitive to small variations in income levels within the range acceptable to the authorities.[4] The second assumption that needs to be made about national income levels can most easily be made in reference to Figure 2-1. In that figure the positively sloped TT schedule's position is based on given levels of income in both countries. Yet any change in the value of the trade deficit or surplus that accompanies a basic adjustment will tend to alter the level of income unless offset by simultaneous expenditure-reducing (increasing) policies in the deficit (surplus) nation. Allowing for a basic adjustment to have been initiated by the deficit nation, it is assumed that an expenditure reduction of the same magnitude and of a known type is introduced at the same time so that income in the deficit country is constant for all ranges of the competitive ratio. The specification of the type of expenditure-reducing policy is necessary since alternative macropolicies will have different effects upon the trade balance. At the same time as the basic adjustment is made, those countries in the rest of the world destined to suffer income reductions through the erosion of their trade surpluses will offset this by known expansionary policies. These behavioural assumptions fit into the framework of period analysis.

The formula for C, as defined above, makes no allusion to the existence of tariffs or of their effect upon the values of the indexes of absolute prices of tradable goods in the two countries. Properly, both P_f and P_d should be qualified by the domestic and the foreign level of tariffs. These tariffs are the 'normal' level of tariffs that derive from commercial policy and their level is subject to change in either direction as commercial policies change and as bilateral or multi-lateral tariff reductions are negotiated. A change in the mix of imports can alter the effectiveness of the tariffs for the trade balance without any individual tariff being changed.

The two prices indexes are weighted averages of the prices of

[4] See John J. Arena, 'U.S. Imports and the Manufacturing Utilization Rate', *New England Business Review* (August 1967) pp. 3–7.

tradable goods and the weights are determined by the importance of the individual commodities in the trade pattern. As C changes, the relative importance of individual goods in the pattern will change and the weights will change. Similarly as relative prices for individual commodities change – even with C remaining constant in the aggregate – the weights will change. The indexes are therefore assumed to adapt to a changing mix of goods in much the same way as Swan's cost ratio. Clearly a change in the distribution of import duties will affect the relative demand for goods and, therefore, the weights. The weights that apply to the value of C_T or C_T^* should also be used in the compilation of the price indexes for C_P which is to be compared with them.

The aggregation of the rest of the world into a single country raises problems of definition of the exchange rate to be used in the formula. One foreign currency must serve as a numeraire exchange rate for the rest of the world. Once the numeraire currency has been selected, the effective rate of exchange governing the international transactions of the focus nation can vary without the official rate of exchange altering. This divergence between the numeraire and effective rates of exchange will occur when third-country currencies appreciate or depreciate and affect trade flows.[5] Any such changes in the par values of third-country currencies will affect the prices of individual commodities and the weights attached to them. Thus, third-country depreciations will make their effect felt in the value of C through a change in P_f rather than a change in r. The aggregation of the rest of the world into one country also tends to gloss over the indirect effects on the focus nation that result from changes in the balance-of-trade targets of one of the foreign nations or from date-effects leading to readjustments within the rest of the world.

The disequilibrium version of period analysis assumes all prices to be held constant within a period. The relationship between the value of the trade balance and the competitive ratio must be uniquely defined for any value of C instituted at the beginning of the period and, therefore, for any basic adjustment. However, there exist data-effects that will make themselves seen as internal variations within the competitive ratio and that, in this way, could give the illusion of an imprecise relationship. Changes in the *relative* prices of tradable goods in either or both price indexes are capable of changing the

[5] See Fred Hirsch and Ilse Higgins, 'An Indicator of Effective Exchange Rates', I.M.F. *Staff Papers* (November 1970) pp. 453–87.

resultant balance of trade without affecting the value of the competitive ratio. Equally changes in government revenue and expenditure patterns could alter the balance of trade for any given value of the competitive ratio. Finally, there is one set of prices which can affect the balance of trade and which is not included in the competitive ratio at all – the prices of domestic goods in the two countries. Any change in the relative price of domestic goods *vis-à-vis* tradable goods will have a direct effect upon the demand for imports and the supply of exports, and therefore upon the trade balance. Thus if the absolute price level of domestic goods varies in either country without affecting the price level of tradable goods, the value of the trade balance for any given value of the competitive ratio will change. All three of these phenomena are the result of data-effects and, if changes in relative prices occur without a change in the tastes of the two populations, they are likely to be the result of an earlier basic adjustment that had not reached its full effect at the beginning of the period.

Interdependence among the elements comprising the competitive ratio can mean that a proportionate change in one of the elements will bring about a less than equal proportionate change in the competitive ratio. There are three different examples of interdependence that merit explicit consideration.

(1) The sensitivity of C to a change in the rate of exchange or in one of the price indexes can be reduced by international trade in intermediate goods or primary products that are incorporated ultimately in tradable goods. If the domestic currency depreciates, the domestic price index is likely to increase as the higher cost of foreign inputs is reflected in the prices of finished manufactures. Similarly a decrease in the domestic price level will have its effect eroded when domestic exports are inputs into foreign tradable goods that compete either with the finished exports or with the import-substitutes of the focus country. The relationship between the domestic cost-of-living index and the par value of the domestic currency can deter a nation suffering simultaneously from inflation and a trade deficit, from a depreciation of its currency.

(2) It is possible that depreciation of the domestic currency may, for political as well as for economic reasons, be accompanied by the elimination of some previously imposed quasi-adjustments. This conjoint policy will reduce the improvement in the trade balance that may be expected from a depreciation since C_T and C_P will both move

in the same direction. C_T^* will not be affected by the negative quasi-adjustment and the true deficit will be reduced.

(3) A depreciation of the currency will bring about a decrease in real absorption, and with it a decrease in real income for pressure groups. If the resistance to decreases in real income leads to an upward shift in the Phillips Curve in the same period, the increase in C from the depreciation is likely to be partly eroded by an increase in P_d. It is probable that there will be some delay between the depreciation and any upward shift in the Phillips Curve. An erosion of C through an increase in P_d can also take place if the tradable goods industries experience increased costs or if they have less than infinitely elastic supply schedules. This is the reverse of the classical medicine operating to diminish the effectiveness of depreciation.

In equilibrium analyses of the trade balance, such interdependencies qualify the use of the elasticities approach which must, if it is to be used, define elasticities as a measure of response of quantity to price after all the repercussions of a general equilibrium adjustment have been worked out.[6] The analytic value of the concept of a competitive ratio is that it makes explicit the effects of the inter-dependence among its component elements as well as emphasising the potentially unbalancing role of changes in absolute price levels.

[6] R. F. Kahn, 'Tariffs and the Terms of Trade', *Review of Economic Studies*, xv (No. 11, 1947) pp. 14–19.

Part Two
The Aggregate Theory

5 The Theory Developed for the Balance of Trade

The task of Part II is to assemble the concepts and the methodological tools introduced in the preceding pages into an aggregate, short-run theory of international payments adjustment. This first chapter develops the model in the more familiar analytic realm of a two-country world in which the only international transactions involve current (or factor-using or factor-saving) trade in goods and services as well as a means of payment.[1] The theory will necessarily emphasise the determinants of what is expected to occur rather than the international payments target. In a world limited to current transactions the only potential difference between the target and a zero balance is the desire of the focus country to increase its stock of internationally liquid reserves. For simplicity it is assumed that ΔR^* is zero. The next three chapters introduce unilateral transfers, transactions on capital account and the latter's progeny, investment income, and consider the implications of these flows for the theory developed in Chapter 5. The final chapter in Part II presents the model as a single set of interrelations among international targets and instruments that determine the existence or lack of a satisfactory payments position.

The goal of the national economic authorities will be to minimise the social costs of any disparity between the international target and the forecast value of the target variable. This chapter has five sections. The first categorises the types of disturbances that may create a disparity between target and forecast and the second considers how these disturbances can be instigated, aggravated or offset by domestic policies and policy errors. The social costs of adjustment are analysed in the third section. The non-optimality of freely flexible exchange rates, as opposed to authoritative intervention, is considered in section four and the model is summarised in the concluding section.

[1] Investment income is excluded in accordance with the accounting procedures developed in Chapter 4.

TYPES OF DISTURBANCE

The most important distinction among types of disturbances lies
between real disturbances and monetary disturbances. Friedman
distinguishes between the two at the beginning of his classic essay,[2]
describing disturbances in real conditions as stemming from weather,
technical conditions of production, consumer tastes and the like, and
in monetary conditions as arising from divergent degrees of inflation
in various countries. Unfortunately the distinction is not developed
as an integral part of the argument. In contrast, Johnson gives
the appearance of categorising all continuing deficits as monetary
phenomena. His argument depends upon the necessary role of credit
creation by the monetary authorities in frustrating an automatic cure
for any deficit – self-exhaustion for a stock disturbance and the
inexorability of the classical medicine for a flow disturbance. Since
the monetary authorities can create only domestic and not international money, deficits are decreed to be monetary phenomena. An
alternative monetary cause of a deficit is the lack of a sufficient stock
of international reserves to allow the cure to be effected by the
'natural self-correcting process'.[3] Johnson seems to limit the definition of a deficit to situations which the authorities do not wish to or
are unable to finance since, somehow, the drawing down of international reserves in the dishoarding disturbance does not constitute a
deficit.[4] Johnson avoids categorising all deficits as monetary in origin
by a hair's breadth and limits himself to the statements that distinguishing between real and monetary disequilibria is 'not logically
valid' and that the concepts of real and monetary may be helpful in
'isolating the initiating causes of disequilibrium or the most appropriate type of remedial policy to follow'.[5] The emphasis is on the cure
for a disequilibrium situation rather than on diagnosis of the cause of
the payments imbalance.

From some given position that has the appearance of a stationary
disequilibrium, the process of reattaining equilibrium probably
depends only on the conditions that prevail and not upon the
character of the original disturbance. Labelling such a disequilibrium

---

[2] Milton Friedman, 'The Case for Flexible Exchange Rates' in *Readings in
International Economics* pp. 413–37.

[3] H. G. Johnson, 'Towards a General Theory', pp. 157–8. The distinction
between 'stock' and 'flow' disturbances is discussed below in this section.

[4] *Ibid*. The analysis is not clear at this point.

[5] *Ibid*.

as a monetary phenomenon is merely to argue that both of the means by which basic adjustments can be made – the gold standard or price–specie–flow mechanism and a change in the par value of the currency of the deficit nation in terms of the numeraire currency – are monetary mechanisms. If an imbalance is to be analysed before it reaches some sort of stationary disequilibrium situation, the source and category of the disturbance are of some importance since they can affect the costs of reattaining balance, the choice of instruments to achieve balance again and the speed with which remedial measures should be undertaken.

The competitive ratio, period-analysis framework allows the difference between real and monetary disturbances to be easily identified. A monetary disturbance is one which brings about a change in the value of C_P as a result of something other than a policy measure. This will usually imply that C_P will change away from C_T^*. A monetary disturbance will take effect predominantly in the P_f/P_d ratio and will usually consist of a change in absolute price levels in one or both countries. A real disturbance changes the value of C_T^* as a result of some data-effect. A real disturbance can be either balancing or aggravating but, for purposes of analysis, it is simplest to start from an original position of balance so that a comparison can be made between imbalance-creating monetary and real disturbances.

The difference in the effect of a monetary and a real disturbance is most clearly seen in a comparison of the patterns of resource allocation needed for balanced trade in the deficit (focus) country before and after the disturbance. Any such comparison must abstract from other contemporaneous disturbances and must also be quite explicit about the time lapse since the disturbance took place. Assume the absence of any other disturbance and a government policy of adjustment that sets the money level of absorption equal to that required for the ultimate reattainment of balance. International claims are met by drawing down international reserves. Consider, as a real disturbance, a change in foreign tastes away from the commodities exported by the focus country and, as a monetary disturbance, a 5 per cent increase in all money prices in the focus country.

If the analysis is set in an equilibrium mould so that the time lapse between the original and post-disturbance equilibria is ignored, there will have been a change in relative real incomes and in relative prices after the real disturbance. No change in real variables will have been necessary after the monetary disturbance in a static world and the system will have reverted back to its original position. Once the time sequence is explicitly introduced, the difference becomes more substantial. The authorities would, after a real disturbance, allow the classic medicine so to work on relative prices that the resource allocation would slowly veer in the direction of the new resource allocation required for balance. The export sector would decline and resources would shift into the import-substitute and domestic-goods sectors. After the monetary disturbance, the official policy would lead to a depressed situation in the export and import-substitute sectors of the economy. Prices and employment in both of these sectors would decline and the depression would be transmitted to the domestic-goods sector. The brunt of the adjustment would fall upon the tradable-goods sectors. But no reallocation of resources is required and the costly interplay among sectors will have served no useful purpose for domestic resource allocation. When the possibility of rates of investment in different sectors being influenced during the adjustment process is admitted into the analysis, the social costs of a monetary disturbance can increase substantially. The depressed tradable goods sectors will receive less than their appropriate share of investment – at least in the first few periods – and the stock of capital could become mal-distributed in comparison with the original allocation of resources. This process, to the extent that it occurs, will tend to enhance the social costs of adjustment and to lengthen the time needed for the re-establishment of balance.

The dangers of maldistribution of investment are even greater when the deficit tends to be ignored and aggregate demand is maintained by the stimulation of domestic consumption.[6] Given that the tradable-goods sectors tend to be low-profit sectors in a period of deficit and that investment is demand-induced, investment in these sectors will be discouraged. However, even under these circumstances there is a distinction between the effects of monetary and real disturbances. If the real disturbance is a decrease in foreign demand for exports, no new export capacity is required, so that a reduction of investment in that sector is itself a part of the classical medicine. If the disturbance is monetary, the relative lack of investment in the export sector works against the resource allocation ultimately necessary for balance. To the extent that the reduced rate of invest-

[6] Nicholas Kaldor, *The Economic Journal* (March 1971).

ment in the export sector also retards the introduction of new technology, the social costs of adjustment can be enhanced. When a real disturbance is the underlying cause, special depreciation allowances or tax credits on investment in the export sector involving equipment that embodies new technology might be warranted. Such measures would not be necessary for a monetary disturbance if the disturbance were quickly offset.[7]

The real disturbance involves an increase in C_T^* and any mal-distribution of investment inherent in the adjustment process can further increase C_T^* and move the terms of trade further against the focus country. The monetary disturbance does not involve any ultimate shift in the terms of trade as a result of the original disturbance but can involve such a shift if the classical medicine is relied upon to effect its cumbersome cure.

Finally, a monetary disturbance can have political repercussions that will work against the institution of an adjustment. The tradable goods industries of a country in surplus because of a monetary disturbance will experience increased (and spurious) prosperity that can be expected to evaporate completely with adjustment. If these industries are important, they will be able to and will exert political pressure that will accentuate the difficulty of achieving adjustment by political negotiation with the government of the surplus nation. The longer the surplus has lasted, the greater the degree of 'unwarranted' investment that will have been generated within these industries and the less willing will the industries be to renounce their 'edge'. The behaviour of basic industries in West Germany in the last years of the Bretton Woods era is a case in point.

If the distinction between real and monetary disturbances is vital to balance-of-payments theory, the distinction among different categories of real disturbances is almost equally important. Harry G. Johnson's essay that distinguishes between stock deficits and flow deficits, must be considered a major contribution.[8] According to Johnson, 'refined theoretical analysis has generally been concerned with flow deficits, without making the distinction explicit'. A stock deficit results from a once-and-for-all change in the composition of

---

[7] A different real disturbance would generate a different set of effects. The point made is that there is practical value in distinguishing between the two categories of disturbance and among real disturbances. A taxonomic analysis of all possible real disturbances is not necessary here.

[8] 'Towards a General Theory' – even by Johnson's standards and not only in this narrow area – see particularly pp. 158–61.

the focus nation's assets and must necessarily be a temporary affair whereas a flow deficit is not of inherently limited duration and must, therefore, require a deliberate change in economic policy if the deficit is to be terminated by means other than the classical medicine.

While the distinction between stock and flow disturbances is fundamental for a purely theoretical approach, a pragmatic approach can better utilise a distinction between three types of real disturbances: trend, permanent or shift, and reversing. These are illustrated

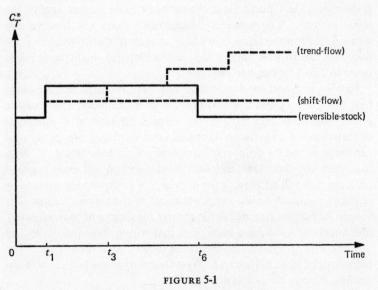

FIGURE 5-1

Alternative Types of Disturbance

Note: The discrete changes emphasise the limitations of the period analysis frame of reference.

An increase in C_T^* denotes a disturbance that induces a deterioration in the trade balance in the absence of an adjustment.

in Figure 5-1. A trend disturbance will cause C_T^* to increase monotonically over time. Such a disturbance could find its roots in either a gradual reduction in a technological lead or in the disparate effects upon the trade balance of economic growth. A permanent or shift (flow) disturbance would come from a once-and-for-all change in the circumstances underlying international trade: an example of this type of phenomenon might be the discovery and integration into the productive system of an import-competing natural resource, a change in political commitments or a sizeable change in the membership in a trade bloc. Finally, the reversing disturbance can be either a stock disturbance which exhausts itself after a finite number of periods or a temporary flow phenomenon such as a crop failure. It is quite possible that the sum of effects of a series of shift disturbances will over time engender what appears to be either a reversing or a trend disturbance. However, there is also the possibility that some disturbances will occur which are big enough to overwhelm simultaneous data-effects and to constitute shift disturbances. It is equally possible that what appears to be a trend disturbance is, in fact, a long-drawn-out adjustment to a fundamental shift in the structure of international economic relationships.[9] It is probable that simultaneous data-effects will, in the real world, combine to provide occasional substantive shifts in the value of C_T^* but that there will tend to be an irregular movement around some trend.

Monetary disturbances can result in trend disturbances as one nation tends to inflate faster than its trading partners or in a shift disturbance as a burst of inflation causes a once-and-for-all shift in the prevailing competitive position. Note again that monetary disturbances manifest themselves as shifts in C_P. In a world in which real and monetary disturbances are taking place simultaneously, changes in the balance of trade come about because of a change in $(C_P - C_T^*)$. *Both* components of the difference can behave independently of each other in a world in which the self-correcting mechanisms that accompany data effects are negated by macrostabilisation policies.

The future time shape of C_T^* cannot be forecast with complete accuracy, but some idea of its trend, of its reversibility and of the position relative to trend at any time should be ascertainable. The three types of real disturbances will, optimally, require different counteracting policies: a trend disturbance will require a series of basic adjustments; a shift disturbance will require a single basic adjustment; and a reversing disturbance may be financed or suppressed and a basic adjustment may be suboptimal. Each type of disturbance can engender different considerations about the timing of policy actions and, as a consequence, about the mix of policy measures to be applied. The inclusion in the disequilibrium framework of deviations about some trend in C_T^* (possibly a zero trend)

9 See footnote 5 in Chapter 2 and also p. 15.

allows quasi-adjustments – even given their clear second-best connotations – to be legitimate policy measures under some circumstances.

The greater degree of interdependence that exists now among the economies of rich nations and that may be supposed to increase even further, must lead to an increased frequency and a greater amplitude of disturbances to payments balance.[10] *A fortiori*, it may be presumed that the probability of reversing disturbances has also increased. This expectation of more frequent data-effects and more frequent reversing disturbances will be reinforced when capital movements are introduced into the analysis in the subsequent chapters.

DOMESTIC POLICY IMPLICATIONS FOR THE TRADE BALANCE

Even in the absence of data-effects in the international sphere, an ongoing balance can quite easily be disrupted by the failure of macropolicy in the focus country to achieve its targets. Since macropolicy is never likely to become an exact science, occurrences of this type are likely to happen fairly regularly. There are three aspects of domestic macropolicy that can have direct repercussions upon the trade balance: (1) that the target mix of inflation and unemployment is incompatible with a constant competitive position given the targets and policies of trading partner nations; (2) that the increase in the price level will exceed or fall short of the target rate; and (3) that the rate of absorption will exceed potential national income.

(1) The possibility that target rates of inflation in the two countries are incompatible will necessarily give rise to a monetary disturbance over time. Policies that can counteract the discrepancy are to engineer a shift in the Phillips Curve, to accommodate domestic goals to the rate of inflation permitted by foreign targets, and frequent depreciations of the domestic currency in terms of the international numeraire. The solution of frequent changes in the currency's par value is almost equivalent to adopting a system of flexible rates of exchange. The danger lies in the possibility that some real disturbance will occur for which a system of flexible rates is not suitable, and that the continual depreciation of the currency internationally will tend, itself, to shift the Phillips Curve upward as inflationary expectations reinforce themselves. A more probable solution is that the goals of the domestic economy will be changed to

[10] Cooper, *The Economics of Interdependence, passim*, but particularly p. 150.

achieve some viable rate of inflation. The process whereby domestic targets interrelate with payments constraints is illustrated in Figure 5-2.[11] As the trade deficit increases – presumably measured in some

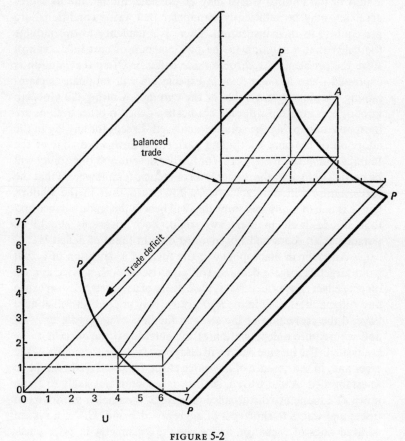

FIGURE 5-2

Domestic Policy Goals and the Trade Balance

average that would be sustained over a number of periods given fixed rates of exchange – the tolerance of the electorate for inflation is reduced and the Adams box collapses and shifts outward. In the process the indifference curves of the authorities also become

[11] This is an elaboration of Figure 4-1: see page 70 above and the relevant text.

flatter. As a result the rate of inflation is reduced at a social cost of an increase in the rate of unemployment. The reduction in national income will reduce the value of C_T^* necessary for balance. Engineering a shift in the Phillips Curve may be possible, though the measures necessary may be sufficiently unpopular that 'crisis conditions' are prerequisite to their institution. There is a tendency to overindulge the belief that a solution to the phenomenon of cost inflation will solve the problem of a chronic trade deficit.[12] Often the solution is expressed more in hope than in expectation and rationalises maintaining the existing par value of the currency. Cutting the Gordian knot of cost inflation will only eradicate a deficit if other nations are incapable of copying the solution achieved. Except for any lag in the adoption of the cure by trading partners, a downward shift of the Phillips Curve will merely prevent further deficits and this ability will be partially offset by the higher level of income (employment) that the focus nation will now achieve. A downward shift in the Phillips Curve is one of many measures that will benefit the trade balance and that are desirable in their own right. Such measures should be pursued at all times and not invoked only in times of deficit.[13]

(2) An error in macropolicy in the form of a deviation of actual from target aggregate demand will give rise to both a price and an income effect. The price effect is the essence of a monetary disturbance and will manifest itself in the P_f/P_d ratio. Any price effect will endure beyond the correction of the error in the flow of aggregate demand and will require a depreciation of the currency if the effect is to be eradicated. The income effect will disappear with the correction of the error and, in the absence of any price effect, balanced trade would be re-established. A short-lived, shallow recession is not likely to cause much of a monetary disturbance because of the smaller sensitivity of prices and wages to shortages of aggregate demand. Under a system of fixed rates of exchange, and given the asymmetry in price sensitivity, a macropolicy error allowing excessive expansion will be more disruptive of payments balance than one that generates a recession. Once an inflationary error has been committed, the fear of inducing a further (secondary) inflation by making a basic adjustment can

[12] For example, see Christopher McMahon, *Sterling in the Sixties* (London: Oxford University Press for R.I.I.A., 1964) *passim*, but particularly p. 2.

[13] Sir Roy Harrod cites a list of such measures in *Reforming the World's Money* (London: Macmillan, 1965) p. 56. If effective these measures would constitute positive data-effects, but to rely upon their success would smack of over-optimism.

retard the adjustment process. This fear will also lead to second-best quasi-adjustments being used without any valid reason for preferring them to basic adjustment other than that they suppress the secondary inflation at least temporarily.

When an inflationary surge is mistakenly injected into an economy, the foreign sector performs two different safety-valve operations. First, it siphons off aggregate demand into imported goods and thereby reduces the amount of impetus that is felt by the domestic economy. Secondly, it holds down the overall index of inflation by continuing to supply imports at the price levels existing before the inflationary surge. The greater is the elasticity of substitution between imports and domestic goods, the greater will the first effect be. The more open the economy, the smaller is the importance of domestic prices in any overall inflation index. The monetary disturbance will have resulted in negative international saving, but the eradication of the deficit will in turn eliminate the second, price-stabilising effect of the foreign sector. Ultimately the focus economy will have to endure the full impact of its inflationary spurt – either in the form of loss of international reserves as excess demand leaks into imports or as the tempering effect of unadjusted foreign prices is eliminated with the removal of the deficit. The use of quasi-adjustments in the hope of escaping secondary inflation is self-deluding in that quasi-adjustments will lose their effectiveness with time.

When escalator clauses in wage contracts (and even for pensions paid to retired people) are a common means of protection against the erosion of real income by price increases, the effectiveness of a depreciation of the currency and of the classical medicine of adjustment can be seriously impaired. Any increase in foreign prices will affect the base on which the escalator clause is computed, so that foreign price increases can quickly lead to domestic cost increases and, in turn, to increases in the price of finished goods. Since differential rates of domestic aad foreign inflation measured in a single currency are at the heart of the adjustment process, the better that wage-earners are able to protect themselves against price increases, the less effective will the international process of payments adjustment be likely to be. The cause of this side-effect of escalator clauses is that they do not distinguish domestically between income preservation in the face of a monetary disturbance and shifts in the intersectoral terms of trade. It might appear, therefore, that there would be a potential increase in the efficiency of the adjustment

mechanism if the base from which escalator clauses were computed
was to be calculated solely on the costs of value added domestically.

The usefulness of a separate domestic base for computing cost-of-
living escalators can be assessed for the two kinds of disturbance. If
a real disturbance takes place so that C_T^* increases for the focus
country, it is necessary either that foreign prices rise or domestic
prices fall. Assume foreign prices are effectively increased by a
depreciation of the domestic currency. The exclusion of foreign prices
from the base for the escalator will restrain an otherwise inflationary
force and will keep domestic costs and prices at a lower level than
they would otherwise have been. The effectiveness of the adjustment
process (the depreciation) will have been increased. The same
mechanism applies if the change in the terms of trade were favourable and if, under a gold standard regime, foreign prices fell: the
exclusion of foreign goods from the base for escalator clauses would
prevent a decline in domestic costs from happening automatically. If
a monetary disturbance in the form of an increase in the foreign price
level occurred, the exclusion of foreign prices from the escalator base
would prevent domestic prices from increasing in sympathy and from
easing the strain of adjustment placed on the foreign nation, but
the domestic price stability of the 'innocent' country would be
improved. Equally a nation would be immunised from a fall in
foreign prices and, in the absence of a simultaneous real disturbance,
would have to depreciate its currency by the *full amount* of the decline
in foreign prices.

The exclusion of foreign prices from the base for computing
escalator clauses would be likely to increase the effectiveness of the
adjustment process for real disturbances, but will fail to ease the
adjustment to a monetary disturbance. For nations such as West
Germany, the device might be useful since it would immunise the
country from inflation in its trading partners. Nations that tend to
experience higher rates of inflation than their trading parters should
continue to include foreign goods in the escalator base. Nations
experiencing long-term trends in C_T^* or frequent shift disturbances
might profitably exclude foreign prices from the escalator base.

(3) No nation can achieve balance unless its rate of absorption
is equal to its rate of output. If balance and domestic goals are to
be achieved simultaneously, macropolicy must generate a rate of
absorption equal to full-employment output. A failure to achieve the
correct rate of absorption can stem from a simple error or it may

derive from a policy of achieving full employment domestically despite the absence of trade balance.[14]

Any error in macropolicy in the focus country will be reduced or eliminated in the ensuing period. Thus, unless the error has generated other disturbances as side-effects – most probably, monetary disturbances – the effect of the error on payments balance will be purely transitory. Assuming balance to have obtained before the error, a one-period recession will cause a temporary surplus. The reattainment of domestic targets in the following period will generate balance again without the institution of any adjustments. When income in the focus nation does deviate from target, the balance of trade should be computed in terms of full balance,[15] as though the employment target were in fact being achieved. These calculations will assist in the identification of any data effects that might otherwise be covered up by the effect of the policy error as well as drawing attention to any monetary disturbances. This concept has recently been partially developed and put to use by the computation of 'cyclically-adjusted balances'.[16]

If the rate of absorption is deliberately set by authorities at a level other than that at which it will equal full-employment output, an imbalance on trade account is, temporarily, a part of the policy package. If absorption exceeds output, the trade deficit must be financed by the exchange equalisation account or its equivalent. The monetary drain that accompanies the deficit will be deliberately offset by credit creation by the domestic monetary authorities or will be offset as a part of a stock disturbance as the private sector reduces cash balances in favour of a higher rate of absorption. Conversely if the level of output or income exceeds the rate of absorption, the authorities must be neutralising the monetary inflow if the price–specie–flow mechanism is to be avoided. Either imbalance can continue as long as the authorities are both willing and able to finance the international deficit or absorb the surplus into hoards or

---

[14] This section assumes that economic policy abroad is optimal. A foreign error inducing a recession will reduce the achievable level of employment in the domestic country but the depression in the export industries and the payments deficit should be financed since the error will be speedily removed and amounts to a very short reversible disturbance. The *quid pro quo* for this policy is the fact that a domestic error is mitigated by foreign leakages. An error in policy is clearly distinguishable from a change in target rates of employment.

[15] See Harrod, *Economic Journal* (September 1967).

[16] See *The Annual Report of the U.S. President's Council of Economic Advisers, 1972* (Washington 1972) pp. 152–3.

until the wealth effects of a protracted surplus or deficit changes the underlying conditions.

A deficit can occur because income has been inflated and the prevailing competitive ratio allowed to deteriorate or because the competitive ratio has been permitted to deteriorate and income increased to sustain tolerable levels of employment. Either of these deficits occurs because the terms of trade prevailing in the international market place (C_P) are more favourable than those needed for trade balance(C_T^*). This inequality between the competitive ratios needed for balance, and actually in existence, causes the inhabitants of the focus nation to act as though their real incomes were greater than they in fact were. Yeager explains the phenomenon as being caused by means of a 'quasi-subsidisation' of consumers of imports (consumers of tradable goods) and of a 'quasi-taxation' of producers.[17] The subsidy effect results from the maintenance of the overvaluation of the currency $(C_P < C_T^*)$ by the authorities cheapening certain goods in money terms and thereby increasing the perceived real income of people who consume tradable goods. The tax effect works through the relative depression in the tradable-goods industries which suffer reduced receipts measured in domestic currency and receive less than their true real income. If the elasticities are not perverse, the quasi-subsidy will outweigh the quasi-tax. The size of the excess of absorption over income to offset a given disparity between the prevailing competitive ratio and the ratio needed for full balance will depend upon the 'general-equilibrium' elasticities of demand and supply of tradable goods as well as upon the elasticity of substitution between domestic and tradable goods. The actual elasticities involved will vary with the time since the establishment of the original imbalance and may not, in fact, be true general-equilibrium elasticities, but they will be combinations of price and income elasticities. The greater the net leakage of the nation's absorption into net imports per unit disparity in the competitive position, the greater will be the need for the domestic authorities to bolster income to maintain high levels of employment.

The relationship between the excess of absorption over income (the trade deficit) and the discrepancy in the two measures of the competitive ratio or terms of trade is shown in Figure 5-3. The schedule, TT, shows the sensitivity of the trade balance to a terms-of-

[17] Leland B. Yeager, 'Absorption and Elasticity: A Full Reconciliation', *Economica* (February 1970) pp. 68–77.

trade discrepancy under conditions of full (high) employment in both nations. Figure 5-3 differs from Figure 2-1 in one important way. Figure 2-1 shows the change in the prevailing competitive ratio needed to eliminate a given deficit *within a single period*. Figure 5-3 shows the amount of excess of absorption over full-employment

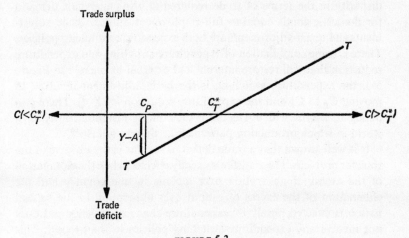

FIGURE 5-3

Excess Absorption and the Terms of Trade

income that is necessary to preserve domestic full-employment for a given discrepancy in the two sets of the terms of trade. Figure 5-3 shows the total impact of a shift in the prevailing competitive ratio in the original *and* in the succeeding periods. It is, therefore, a multi-period relationship. The excess of absorption over income is measured vertically downward from the horizontal axis at the value of the prevailing competitive ratio.

To eliminate the deficit the authorities must reduce absorption so that it is set equal to full-employment output (an expenditure reduction). In the absence of accompanying international policy actions, actual absorption (and employment) will fall short of target by an amount equal to the trade deficit. The expenditure-reducing policy must be matched by an expenditure-switching policy that will increase the total world demand for home-produced goods by making them relatively cheaper than foreign-produced goods. The more sensitive is the distribution of world demand to a change in the prevailing competitive ratio, the greater will be the elasticities of demand and supply and the steeper will be *TT*. Thus, the inter-relationship between absorption theory and the elasticities approach lies in the fact that the elasticities determine, under conditions of high or full employment, the necessary amount of excess absorption required by a given disparity in the terms of trade or determine the disparity in the terms of trade required to bring aggregate demand for domestic goods equal to full-employment output. Basic adjustments and quasi-adjustments are both expenditure-switching policies. There is some combination of expenditure-switching and expenditure reduction that will restore internal and external balance.[18] In Figure 5-3, the expenditure switching is the basic adjustment involved in moving C_P to C_T^* and the expenditure reduction is $(Y\text{-}A)$. These two policy measures will not achieve their effect instantaneously in a world in which production patterns take time to adjust.[19]

It is well known that a trade deficit or surplus is the obverse of the transfer problem. The transfer is exactly effected when the elimination of the excess of absorption over income in one country and the elimination of the excess of output over absorption in the second nation is effected purely by expenditure-changing policies and does not involve any expenditure-switching policies in the process. This concept of effecting a transfer is a general equilibrium concept and would seem to be an extremely improbable occurrence in the short-term.

THE SOCIAL COSTS OF ADJUSTMENT

Kaldor's analysis of the implications of a policy of 'consumption-led' growth indicates one element of what might be called the costs of a failure to adjust *in anticipation* of international disturbances. The cost is incurred because the pattern of investment will be suboptimal during the period in which the domestic currency is overvalued. Except for responses to foreseen disturbances by suitable investment patterns, any reallocation of resources will involve some social cost. No economy can transfer resources among sectors without some frictional unemployment of factors of production and, probably, without some waste of capital (human and/or physical) that is specific to declining industries.

[18] Harry G. Johnson, 'Towards a General Theory', pp. 161–4.
[19] Note that the *TT* schedule in Figure 5-3 is drawn so that the change in C_P is matched with an appropriate expenditure reduction.

When a real disturbance occurs so that C_T^* changes without any indication of a reversal, the focus nation will undergo a process of adjustment. There will be two elements involved in that process: the change in real income consequent upon the change in C_T^* – an increase or reduction in the gain from trade; and the loss of output involved in reallocating resources among sectors until full balance is reattained. These two elements have been called, respectively, the continuing cost and the transitional cost of adjustment.[20] There is a question as to whether the continuing cost is or is not a cost of adjustment. A disturbance can generate a favourable change in C_T^* for the focus country so that any change in the level of absorption is positive. More important is the problem of whether a reduction in the rate of absorption compatible with balance is a 'cost of adjustment' in the full sense of the expression. The so-called continuing cost is an unpleasant result of a favourable shift in the terms of trade elsewhere in the world. Global gains from trade may increase or decrease as a result of a disturbance, but there is a danger in labelling the negative aspect a cost while ignoring the positive aspects of the disturbance.

Transitional cost is, however, a useful concept. Both countries undergo a transitional cost in response to a real disturbance. For the deficit country, transitional cost can be defined as the loss of absorption and international reserves undergone between the onset of the disturbance and the re-establishment of full balance in excess of the loss that would have been experienced had the world economy been capable of instantaneous adjustment. The definition can also be adapted to define the transitional cost of the surplus nation. The amount of transitional cost to be shared between the two nations for any disturbance will depend upon the disturbance itself, upon the flexibility of the two economies, the effectiveness of balance-of-payments policies (including the speed of diagnosis and of action), and the extent to which one nation believes it can impose a larger part of the transitional cost to the other nation. If the transitional cost can be shifted by the adoption by the deficit country of a particular kind of quasi-adjustment – most probably an increase in the level of tariffs or a decrease in import quotas – then it is possible that the surplus country will impose countermeasures to prevent the shifting

---

[20] Benjamin J. Cohen, 'Adjustment Costs and the Distribution of New Reserves', *Princeton Studies in International Finance*, No. 18 (Princeton, N.J., 1966) pp. 5–11.

of the transitory cost. It is therefore possible that the total transitory cost can be expanded beyond the minimum as both nations are tempted to employ mutually-offsetting quasi-adjustments.[21] The important aspect of quasi-adjustments that erect barriers to trade is their ability to cause a shift in the terms of trade in favour of the nation imposing the quasi-adjustments.

Very little attention has been given to the problem of costs of adjustment in response to a disturbance – possibly because of the affinity of analysts for the equilibrium approach.[22] The following attributes of the adjustment process seem intuitively logical and are assumed here for the purposes of analysis of the alternative policy options.

1. A basic adjustment made in response to a real disturbance will involve some social, transitional cost.
2. The amount of social cost will vary with the magnitude of the disturbance, given the structural characteristics of the two countries, and the relationship will probably approximate a one-to-one ratio.
3. The social cost per unit of payments deficit will vary positively with and more than proportionately than the speed of adjustment – that is the amount of additional basic adjustment put into effect in each period.[23]
4. While some adjustment can be accomplished through normal growth processes, there exists some rate of basic adjustment which represents a pragmatic maximum. (In Figure 2-1 this rate is reached when the *TT* schedule becomes parallel to the horizontal axis).

If the four behavioural relationships hold, it becomes possible to deduce certain criteria which can be used to guide the policymakers in the formation of adjustment policies.

From points 3 and 4, there is a maximum basic adjustment that

[21] Cohen attempts to analyse the way in which transitional costs will be divided. See 'Adjustment Costs and the Distribution of New Reserves.'

[22] Two exceptions are Sir Roy Harrod, 'The Speed of Adjustment' and Peter B. Kenen, 'Financing and Adjustment: The Carrot and the Stick'. Both essays are contained in William Fellner, Fritz Machlup, Robert Triffin *et al.*, *Maintaining and Restoring Balance in International Payments* (Princeton, N.J.: Princeton University Press, 1966) pp. 137–43 and 151–5.

[23] This attribute must assume that the rate of adjustment exceeds some minimum at which the gains from disruptions avoided are offset by the effects of perverse patterns of investment.

may be instituted in a single period. If the total adjustment in any period in response to a disturbance exceeds that maximum, it becomes necessary to conceive of a multi-period adjustment strategy. A multi-period strategy raises two separate issues: what is the correct sequence of the sizes of basic adjustments and would a multi-period adjustment programme create any concomitant problems?

Any basic adjustment will achieve its full impact only over a number of periods. In terms of Figure 2-1, the multi-period effect of a basic adjustment should be seen as a movement along the C-axis in the period in which the adjustment was instituted and as a series of shifts of the TT schedule in later periods. Most of the transitional cost incurred (per unit of deficit) will be incurred in the period in which the adjustment is made, because the adjustment will have its biggest proportionate effect in that first period. However, some transitional costs from the first adjustment will carry over into ensuing periods. The fact that some of the adjustment impact of the first adjustment will also carry over into the ensuing periods suggests that the new adjustments made in the following periods should become increasingly smaller in order that the total adjustment per period be kept approximately constant. Any attempt to decrease the total transitional cost per unit of adjustment by spreading out the total basic adjustment over time is likely to reduce the speed with which the deficit is erased. Consequently the slower adjustment process will cause a greater deterioration in the deficit nation's stock of international reserves. There will be some trade-off in the preference function of the authorities between reductions in international net worth (through international dissaving) and increases in the transitional costs of adjustment.

If private speculators foresee the inevitability of further adjustments being made in the future in response to a deficit, it is possible that destabilising flows of hot money will be fostered. These problems could be solved by interest-rate differentials of sufficient size, by official intervention in the forward currency markets, and/or by the imposition of controls or taxes on flows of liquid capital between the two nations. Any of these cures will achieve less than perfect efficiency and the social cost of any measures imposed to counter hot money flows must be set against the reduction in transitional cost that the imposition of countermeasures may achieve. An alternative to a policy of gradual basic adjustments would be a complete basic adjustment – depreciation – by the deficit country coupled with the imposition of prearranged quasi-adjustments by the surplus country. The quasi-adjustments should apply to both the exports and the imports of the surplus country and would be reduced gradually to zero. Such a degree of co-operation between nations exceeds that which seems currently to be available.[24]

If the social cost of adjustment increases with the size of the adjustment necessary (point 2) and if the amount of resource reallocation required can be expected to increase over time because of the existence of a deficit, there is a strong argument for early diagnosis and prompt policy action. The reduction in transitional cost that will be achieved by prompt action is to be found in the decrease in the necessary speed of adjustment and in the saving of international reserves. If payments imbalance also leads to the maldistribution of domestic investment, prompt action also reduces the total reallocation necessary and, therefore, total transitional cost. The argument for prompt action clearly applies to monetary disturbances as well as to real disturbances.

If a reversal of a deficit through the exhaustion of a stock disturbance which gives rise to it, or through the future existence of countervailing disturbances is foreseen, *the transitional costs of adjustment in both directions must be set against the real cost of financing the total deficit*. The damage done to international net worth will involve both the expected duration of the deficit as well as its average severity. Other factors affecting the optimal policy mix when a reversal is anticipated, will be the weights applied by the authorities to any failure to achieve domestic targets, the actual reserve position of the focus nation and the cost and availability of international credit.

When different types of disturbance are considered, quasi-adjustment are no longer necessarily excluded from the optimal policy-mix by virtue of their inherently second-best attributes. Clearly a quasi-adjustment that involves the deliberate deflation of any economy as a means of reducing the demand for imports cannot be justified. Nor, because of the inefficiency of the instrument variables, can domestic deflation be justified as a means of achieving a basic adjustment through changes in relative absolute price levels. Quasi-adjustments that consist of impediments to international trade could be justified as short-term expedients. The crucial aspect

[24] The problems imposed by hot money flows are discussed in Chapter 11 below.

involving the use of quasi-adjustments as components in a balance-of-payments policy package is the degree to which they will be offset by trading partners and thereby increase the total transitional cost of adjustment. If the surplus nation condones the use of quasi-adjustments as legitimate temporary devices, they can be used to reduce the transitional costs of the deficit nation provided always that any social costs of resource misallocation that ensue, do not exceed the saving in transitional cost. Since adjustment is a finite process, a quasi-adjustment cannot, by itself, be a counter to a permanent shift in C_T^* (See Figure 5-1). However, a quasi-adjustment can be a useful adjunct to a basic adjustment or financing if the rate of adjustment would otherwise be too great for minimisation of transitional costs or if the reserve loss incurred with a lower rate of adjustment, would be excessive.

A more important use of quasi-adjustments as complete or partial alternatives to basic adjustment and financing exists when the disturbance is considered to be temporary and reversible. The value of a quasi-adjustment in countering a temporary disturbance is that it may reduce the loss of reserves that would be incurred by financing at a smaller social cost than that which a basic adjustment would involve. When a disturbance is expected to be reversed in the short term, basic adjustment will involve two self-cancelling adjustments, and each of the adjustments will generate transitional costs. Generally quasi-adjustments that cover all imports will involve some cost of misallocation of resources but, given that the existence of a deficit shows some misallocation of resources if the disturbance is a real one, the misallocative cost of a general surcharge on imports could be quite small. If the disturbance is concentrated in a particular sector or trade category and if that sector can be treated in isolation by a specific quasi-adjustment, the smaller is the social cost of a quasi-adjustment likely to be. The greater the certainty with which the ultimate reversal is foreseen, the stronger is the argument for preferring a quasi-adjustment to basic adjustments. The shallower and the more short-lived the disturbance, the stronger the argument for financing the deficit. The deeper is the disturbance, the more likely is a quasi-adjustment to be used – however, the quasi-adjustment must be able to counter the disturbance directly.[25] The problem is

[25] In the case of a crop failure, quasi-adjustments would not be a useful instrument since it would not affect supply and since demand cannot realistically be reduced.

essentially one of cost minimisation and can only be solved if and when some estimates of the magnitudes involved can be formed. The use of a quasi-adjustment by the deficit nation may also be the best policy from the point of view of the surplus nation in that any basic adjustment by the deficit nation will induce resource reallocation in the surplus nation as well. For the surplus nation the costs to be compared are those of reallocating resources through short-lived and reversible basic adjustments, any maldistribution of investment because of financing or reversible basic adjustments, and the failure to gain reserves when the deficit nation institutes a quasi-adjustment.

THE NON-OPTIMALITY OF FREELY-FLEXIBLE EXCHANGE RATES

The non-optimality of a system of freely-flexible rates of exchange as a system for achieving international payments adjustment follows automatically from the analysis of the preceding section. A change in the effective rate of exchange of the currency of the focus country constitutes a basic adjustment.[26] If the change in the exchange rate system merely offsets a monetary disturbance, it prevents resource-misallocation. Any system which automatically invokes basic adjustments for any disturbance will not permit discretionary financing of temporary deficits and is, therefore, sub-optimal. Because of the professional popularity of a system of freely-flexible exchange rates, this weakness requires further elaboration, but it does not preclude that flexible exchange rates might not be the best pragmatic system of international monetary arrangements available in an imperfect world.[27]

Any consideration of a system of flexible rates of exchange must define the role permitted to national monetary authorities. Milton

[26] See Hirsch and Higgins, I.M.F. *Staff Papers* (November 1970) for a description of effective rates of exchange.

[27] My thinking on this topic has been greatly helped by Herbert G. Grubel's paper 'The Optimum Stability of Exchange Rates and a Southeast Asian Payments Union' in H. G. Grubel and T. Morgan (eds), *Exchange Rate Policy in Southeast Asia* (Lexington, Mass.: Heath Lexington, 1973). While the emphasis in the text hinges on the unnecessary real costs incurred by basic adjustments in the fact of reversing disturbances and disruptive shift disturbances, Grubel lists three other disadvantages deriving from unnecessary fluctuations in exchange rates: the greater the instability of exchange rates, the less the usefulness of money in its traditional roles, the greater the costs of foreign transactions and information gathering, and the greater the private risks from asset holding achieved with no social purpose.

Friedman argues the case for flexible exchange rates in terms of complete reliance upon private transactions. Johnson expressed the view that intervention in the foreign exchange market by national monetary authorities is permissible but should be conducted only if the authorities are likely to be more intelligent and efficient speculators than are private speculators.[28] The value of a system of flexible exchange rates can be assessed first in the Friedmanian framework. Then, in the light of the shortcomings of a purely private system, the advantages and disadvantages of government intervention can be considered.

If a system gives rise to a series of instantaneous basic adjustments and is construed as sub-optimal, the weakness must lie either in the areas of the timing and the speed of adjustment, or in the possibility that the basic adjustment is not called for by the underlying real variables. The latter possible weakness of a flexible-rate system is the time-honoured point of opposition by proponents of systems of fixed rates of exchange. The argument relies essentially upon the possibility that speculation in the foreign exchange market by traders will cause changes in exchange rates of significant amplitude and frequency that do not reflect the real needs of the economic system. These fluctuations would inflict social costs to no social purpose. The argument that destabilising speculation would in fact occur is not proven. However, the following argument assumes that speculators do not create unnecessary fluctuations but it does recognise as a weakness of the system of flexible exchange rates that monetary movements made in response to interest rates could cause an appreciation or depreciation of the focus country's currency so that the trade account was forced into deficit or surplus to counteract the effect of the monetary movements in the foreign exchange markets. Thus a system of flexible rates of exchange might engender the 'wrong' rate of exchange, and if monetary flows were not constant through time, some variability in the rate of exchange might result from monetary flows quite apart from any speculative pressures.

In the absence of autonomous monetary flows, a system of flexible rates of exchange will ensure that $C_P = C_T^*$ at all times – assuming that the government of the focus country maintains a satisfactory

[28] Friedman's presentation is given in 'The Case for Flexible Exchange Rates' in *Readings in International Economics*. Harry G. Johnson, 'The Case for Flexible Exchange Rates', 1969, in 'U.K. and Floating Exchanges', *Hobart Papers*, No. 46 (London, 1969) ignores the possibility that private and official speculators may have different goals.

level of domestic employment. The mechanism can best be described in terms of the comparative behaviour of the time-paths of C_T^* and C_P.[29] A flexible-rate system will work perfectly when the time-path of C_T^* is smooth and monotonic and C_P follows C_T^* exactly. The smooth monotonic path of C_T^* ensures that any transitional costs are not aggravated by the speed of resource reallocation required or by reversibility problems. (Note that destabilising speculation would cause the time-path of C_P to fluctuate cyclically around the smooth time-path of C_T^*.) The weakness of a system of flexible rates will occur when the time-path of C_T^* contains cyclical movements of its own and/or sharp shifts. A continuous equality of C_T^* and C_P under these conditions would incur greater transitional costs of adjustment than are necessary because of, respectively, reversals and too-quick adjustments.

The test of a system of freely flexible rates under these circumstances is the ability of the private market place to reduce the variability of C_P so that it approximately follows what would be the trend of C_T^*. In effect, private traders would be arranging financing for the deficit country.

Friedman's treatment of this aspect of the adjustment problem and its amenability to solution by a system of freely-flexible exchange rates is less than convincing.[30] The example that he uses as a basis for analysis is misleadingly simple. The argument relies upon speculators being blessed with 'correct foresight' and even at that, the argument can only contend that there is no reason to expect that the authorities will be capable of achieving 'a more nearly optimum pace and timing of adjustment'. One source of inefficiency that Friedman's analysis ignores is the possibility that the needs of the 'real system' will require a different (longer) period of decision than that on which private speculators will base their decisions. The need for financing during a period of a reversible basic adjustment may be quite long and to suggest that private, short-term speculators would support a currency over a long period borders upon an act of faith. Johnson assumes that exchange rates will change gradually because of the large currency-blocs that would evolve in a system of flexible rates. This assumption eliminates the problem of tempering the speed of adjustment but does not countenance the problem of a

---

[29] The need of the period-analysis framework for discrete changes has been dropped here in order to simplify the exposition.

[30] Friedman, *Readings in International Economics*, pp. 433–5.

reversal of C_T^* over a period of, say, two years. The government could, according to Johnson, establish its own exchange-stabilisation agency if it felt the performance of the private sector to be inadequate. However, the possibility of a divergence in goals between public and private speculation seems to be ignored. No mention is made of the possibility of reduction of transitional cost or of the desire of a nation to exercise some control over its international net worth. Rather the emphasis is placed upon the undeniable political weaknesses of governmental intervention whereby the system could retrogress into a *de facto* adjustable peg.[31]

A system of freely-flexible rates would provide an optimum solution for payments adjustment problems when the disturbances that affected the system were purely monetary. Equally flexible rates would be ideal if real disturbances generated a monotonic trend in C_T^*. The system would impose upon national governments a passivity with reference to their reserve positions and their international net worths and would allow private traders to determine the appropriate mix of adjustment and saving (or dissaving) during the course of a reversing disturbance. The greater the relative importance of monetary disturbances and of gradual, non-reversing real disturbances and the more passive the attitudes of national economic authorities, the greater is the advantage of a system of flexible rates. The greater the concern of governments with the direction and rate of change in the international net worths of their nations and the more prevalent and the stronger reversing disturbances, the more desirable is intelligent government intervention in the foreign exchange market likely to be – whether this be accomplished through government intervention in a system of floating rates or through an adjustable peg. The desirability of authoritative intervention depends directly upon the wisdom of that intervention. Some compromise of the virtues of the automaticity of a freely-flexible system with intelligent intervention – a sort of 'managed currency' – would seem to be optimal,[32] but it is most important that under such a system the authorities would recognise a non-reversing disturbance and not delay adjustment in order to try 'to kick against the pricks'.

There is a contention that controls and other impediments to trade thrive under a system of fixed exchange rates since they substitute

---

[31] Johnson, *Hobart Papers*, No. 46.
[32] Cf. Keynes, *A Tract on Monetary Reform*, Ch. V.

for a depreciation and that adoption of a system of freely-flexible rates would improve international resource allocation. The argument rests upon the greater recognition of the direct link of the damage to export industries and the benefit to the import substitute industry that would derive from a tariff. While this may be a valid contention, it is also possible that the institution of a system of flexible rates in a world in which governments wanted to increase their reserve positions or achieve a surplus on current account, would generate an equivalent amount of mercantilistic intervention in the capital account.[33]

SUMMARY

The competitive ratio, period analysis framework releases balance-of-payments theory from its cumbersome, equilibrium mould – stationary or dynamic – and instead allows balance-of-payments analysis to be conducted in a setting in which disturbances of differing kinds and intensities are in the natural order of things and can occur at haphazard intervals.

The theory is based upon the fact that the terms of trade necessary for payments balance and those actually prevailing may not be equal and the both C_T^* and C_P are capable of independent variation through time. Equality between the two can be restored by the sacrifice of domestic goals, by temporary measures or by basic adjustments of the real income and resource allocation in the focus country and abroad. Given the modern primacy of high employment in the set of domestic target variables, certain aspects of the classical medicine are excluded from the policy alternatives that are available to the authorities. Since different disturbances can engender different time-paths for C_T^*, the transitional costs of adjustment can vary with the disturbance. As a consequence, it becomes possible to conceptualise criteria under which different policy packages would be selected for different disturbances.

Finally, the different kinds of policies that can be instituted affect both the active (or focus) country and its trading partners. It is quite possible for the trading partner to prefer the original situation to the alternative situation that the focus nation seeks to achieve. In that

[33] See Chapter 6 below for a discussion of the lack of sensitivity of the capital account to basic adjustments with the result that the flow of international investment will probably dominate the flow of international saving, pp. 125–8.

case, mutual frustration of policies can occur. The policy implications of the theory are clearly that nations should begin to anticipate the need for international policy action and for the elimination of any conflict in much the same way as the authorities currently try to anticipate disturbances that will sacrifice domestic targets.

6 The Capital Account Introduced

The introduction of the capital and unilateral transfer accounts into a theory of balance-of-payments analysis increases the complexity of the frame of reference by a great deal. When the framework of analysis built around the use of a competitive ratio and period-analysis was limited to transactions in current goods and services and a means of payment, there was only limited scope for variation in the target balance, and both the data-effects and the adjustments (both quasi- and basic adjustments) took their effects on transactions in goods and services and, therefore, in what might be called 'the same dimension'. The introduction of unilateral transfers and flows of international investments increases the number of dimensions. As a result, the selection of the target variable is made more complex, the range of quasi-adjustments is enlarged and the variability of data-effects can achieve a new order of magnitude.

THE ADDED COMPLEXITIES

The additional intricacies will be considered in sequence as affecting (1) target variables, (2) instrument variables and (3) data effects.

(1) The actual target for international payments policy can now relate to three different goals. The dominant goal among the three will be the effective target variable for policy purposes. The variable can change from period to period as the general interest function assumes a different optimal value in response to perceived changes in the data, or as the function itself changes over time. The target can be defined in terms of the basic balance (B_B) which gives the change in the net liquid reserve position, of the current balance (B_C) which denotes the change in the nation's international net worth, and in terms of the balance of trade (B_T) which measures, in currency units, the direct contribution of the international sector to domestic

employment. Under normal conditions, a country will define its
target in terms of the basic balance with the tacit accumption that
capital movements and unilateral transfers are not constrained by
balance-of-payments considerations. The target will then be that
$B_B = \Delta R^*$ and, for simplicity of exposition in this chapter, ΔR^* can
continue to be assumed to be zero (see pp. 65–6). Once that datum
is given, the equality of international saving and international investment is merely an equivalent way of describing the target. Given the
balance on unilateral transfers and assuming the magnitude of
international investment to be known, the target value of B_T is also
determined.

(2) The range of instrument variables has increased to the limits
imposed by the creativity of bureaucratic minds. Controls over
capital flows are now quasi-adjustments. These can be instituted in a
wide variety of forms for many different types of capital flow. In
addition to controls, there is a range of tax alternatives whereby
domestic investment can be made more profitable relative to foreign
investment or inward investment by foreigners more attractive to
them – although it is important to differentiate between permanent
tax measures designed to favour domestic investment and temporary
measures imposed because of a balance-of-payments deficit. The
reason for the greater scope for bureaucratic ingenuity is the traditionally greater willingness of nations to tolerate impediments to
international capital transactions. The most decisive statement of
this tolerance is to be found in the Articles of Agreement of the
International Monetary Fund and finds it forbears in Keynes' concern with national freedom to use the weapon of monetary policy for
domestic employment policies.[1] There is a probable tendency on the
part of national authorities to regard any misallocation costs
incurred as a result of quasi-adjustments on capital transactions as
generating less disutility per unit of foreign exchange saved than
equivalent current-account measures. A quasi-adjustment on capital
transactions may also be preferred because of the smaller probability
of retaliation.

In addition to measures affecting private international capital
movements, quasi-adjustments can be applied to government loans
and expenditures. These could include a decrease in foreign aid or

[1] It is possible for a key- or vehicle-currency nation to enjoy a trend monetary
flow. This trend is assumed to be zero in Part II. It is considered briefly in
Chapter 11.

loans made to developing nations, the imposition of an export-content requirement on aid and on loans (tying), a reduction in contributions to international bodies and/or a reduction in foreign exchange costs of military commitments abroad.[2] Finally, there are various types of controls that can be imposed upon private unilateral transfers. Most important of these are measures designed to increase the rate of profit repatriation of foreign subsidiaries of international corporations based in the deficit nation, or to retard profit repatriation by subsidiaries of foreign corporations located in the deficit nation.

The definition of a basic adjustment has not been changed by the introduction of capital movements and unilateral transfers. A basic adjustment is still defined as a measure that will alter the competitive ratio and, in that way, effect a change in resource allocation in both countries. Note, however, that quasi-adjustments on unilateral transfers can affect the flow of international saving that can be achieved with any given value for the competitive ratio.

(3) The component items in capital account and unilateral transfers are subject to wider year-to-year variability than are aggregate trade flows. The more important these accounts are as a proportion of total transactions, the larger and more irregular can data-effects be expected to be and the larger the period-to-period variation that will occur in the value of the competitive ratio required for full basic balance (C_B^*). As a consequence, the growth of capital and transfer accounts will tend to increase the adaptability to change that is required of policymakers, national economic systems and international institutions. The introduction of capital movements and unilateral transfers does not necessarily imply any cyclical or short-term reversibility of C_B^* but it does negate the idea of relative constancy of the ratio.

Before considering the causes underlying the (contended) increase in the variability of the component items in capital account and unilateral transfers, reference needs to be made to Johnson's recognition of 'stock' and 'flow' deficits or surpluses in the balance of payments in so far as they apply to the capital account.[3] A 'stock' deficit on capital account reflects a decision on the part of the residents

[2] Military commitments abroad could comprise both goods-and-services and transfer account items. A reduction in military commitments for balance-of-payments purposes is not considered in this study on the assumption that military commitments are made rationally.

[3] See Harry G. Johnson, 'Towards a General Theory', pp. 158–60.

or citizens of the focus country to shift out of domestic money into foreign assets.[4] A 'flow' deficit is symptomatic of a decision to have total planned investment greater than total planned saving – that is to have planned international investment greater than planned international saving. The main distinctions between the two lie in the expected duration of the deficit and therefore in the legitimacy of financing as a means of meeting the deficit. Since a stock disturbance on capital account does involve asset acquisition, the total net worth of the nation does not deteriorate but neither does the international net worth improve unless the deficit is partially met by increased international saving. A flow deficit on capital (or on current) account cannot be permanently financed.

When analysis was limited to current transactions in goods and services, and in the absence of realignments of important trading nations in trading blocs, the effect of economic growth, together with any concomitant changes in income distribution, was likely to dwarf other data-effects in times of normalcy – with the possible exception of stock disturbances. The effect of growth on a nation's C_T^* will vary in both magnitude and direction in the long run, but in the medium or short run, the effect of fully-employed growth will be fairly steady and will change only gradually over time. Three reasons suggest that flows of unilateral transfers and international investment are more subject to violent changes than transactions in goods and services in the absence of political and economic upheaval. However, some component items in the unilateral transfer account are more similar to goods-and-services transactions in the stability of their behaviour. These can be referred to as 'flow transfers' (as opposed to 'stock transfers'): they will maintain through time a fairly well-defined volume and a fairly constant distribution among nations. Flow transfers comprise dividend and interest payments and receipts (subject to the impact of any quasi-adjustments), government pension and personal unilateral remittances. Institutional unilateral remittances may tend to vary in both volume and in geographic distribution slightly more than the items cited above but can also be more usefully included in flow transfers. Stock transfers include such

[4] One of the problems of analysis that springs from the inclusion of the capital account is the distinction between residents and citizens. International net worth is a national concept and would seem to call for a definition of citizenship. However, the current account has been traditionally analysed in terms of residents. For present purposes, the concept of 'permanent residence' seems to be optimal. Strictly it is a currency and not a nation that has a balance of payments.

items as foreign aid, reparations and other transfers that involve large amounts in each payment, and are subject to political review at frequent intervals and which, in consequence, can change significantly from year to year in both volume and geographic distribution.

Government loans, stock transfers and private capital transactions are likely to exhibit greater year-to-year changes because of (1) the larger size of the individual transaction; (2) the possibility of interdependence of decisions because similar decision models are used, and because private investors communicate their views and general feelings with each other; and (3) the greater sensitivity of all of these decisions to political variables coupled with the greater susceptibility of political variables to sudden change. Political considerations can also augment the likelihood that economic disturbances will bring about changes in the composition of capital flows by kind of asset and by geographic mix. Since the feedback on the current account from capital exports is highly sensitive to changes in both the mix by asset-type and the mix by country, variation in composition can cause large data-effects without any noticeable change in the aggregate volume of transactions.[5] Finally, inward investment is determined by yet a further set of considerations and economic variables, and changes in the inward flow are as likely to reinforce changes in outward investment as they are to offset them and their effects. The size of data-effects in the expanded frame of reference can therefore be expected to be potentially greater, particularly if the data-effects resulting from investments and transfers reinforce those resulting from goods-and-services transactions.

It is no longer possible to use a single definition of the trading conditions that must prevail in the world if international goals are to be achieved. The value of the competitive ratio, C_T^*, is that required for balance to be achieved on trade account given the absence of quasi-adjustments and full employment in all nations. But, C_T^* is no longer uniquely defined since the demand for the exports of the focus country will be influenced by the net outflow of foreign investment. There are counterpart sets of trading conditions for current account balance, C_C^*, and for basic balance, C_B^*. Which of the ratios represents the conditions that must apply in the world if no corrective policy is to be instituted, will depend upon which target is dominant. If all transfers (including capital exports) are undereffected in the period in which they are made, it follows that $C_B^* > C_C^* > C_T^*$ for a

[5] See Chapter 7 below for an analysis of variation in feedback.

country with deficits on both capital and unilateral-transfers accounts. As before, the asterisk is meant to denote full employment and the absence of quasi-adjustments. The absence of an asterisk from a particular ratio does not mean that the quasi-adjustment has been applied to items in that account, merely that the focus country has some quasi-adjustment in force at some level of international economic transaction.[6]

TRANSFER PAYMENTS

The influence of unilateral transfer payments on the rate of international saving cannot, of course, be positive. However, for some kinds of payments very high rates of feedback on the trade account follow almost automatically so that the diminution of international saving per unit of transfer payment of this kind will be quite small. Certainly the high ratio of induced saving to payments is likely to apply to direct government loans and government foreign aid programmes.[7] Aid contributions to international institutions will tend to have lower feedback ratios if only because of the impossibility of tying such aid to domestic exports.

Flows of interest and dividend payments present a different set of problems. The relation between a dollar of net payment and the rate of international saving will depend not only upon trading patterns but also upon the stage of development of the recipient country. As a general rule the more developed the recipient country, the bigger will be the reduction in international saving. The reverse also holds true: receipts of dividends and interest will increase saving by more if it comes from a rich country than from a poor country because of the higher marginal propensity to import out of net foreign-exchange receipts that characterises poor countries.

The proportionate importance of net flows of dividends and interest receipts in the current account will significantly affect the sensitivity of the flow of international saving to changes in the competitive ratio.[8] To examine this relationship it is necessary to

[6] Anne Krueger, *Journal of Economic Literature* (March 1969) pp. 12–14, fails to differentiate among quasi-adjustments that act on current and capital accounts presumably on the grounds that a capital export or an increase in imports will have an identical effect on the domestic and foreign absorption/production patterns. Such an assumption is only realistic, if at all, in a static model.

[7] The question of feedback is discussed in Chapter 7 below.

[8] For a detailed analysis of the proposition that dividend and interest transactions tend to have a different sensitivity to depreciation than goods sold in

distinguish three types of goods in the current account: ordinary goods that maintain their price in domestic currency after devaluation or depreciation; α-exports (credits) that maintain their price (unit value) in foreign currency after devaluation, and β-imports (debits) that maintain their price (unit value) in domestic currency after devaluation. Dividend and interest receipts are α-credits when the assets that give rise to them are denominated in foreign currency and dividend and interest payments are β-debits when the assets that give rise to them are denominated in the depreciated, domestic currency. Strictly, assets denominated in domestic currency and liabilities in foreign currency both generate 'ordinary goods' but the existence of either tends to *reduce* the sensitivity of the current account balance to currency depreciation because the flows of dividends and interest do not respond to change in the price levels as goods do. Effectively these ordinary goods are in perfectly inelastic supply and they represent 'windfall losses' in the same way that α-credits and β-debits represent 'windfall gains'.[9]

Portfolio, fixed-value assets and liabilities can be denominated in either foreign or domestic currency. Equities and direct investments are both necessarily specified in the currency of the host country of the enterprise. Equities and direct investments will generate α- credits.[10] Any nation with a sizeable net asset position in direct investment can expect to find that devaluation or depreciation of its currency will prove to be a sensitive instrument with which to influence the current account. *Per contra*, a nation with a sizeable adverse position in fixed-value securities denominated in foreign currency will find a large part of its current account immune to currency depreciation. When a depreciation is required because of a higher rate of domestic than of foreign inflation, the depreciation merely restores the *status quo ante* and the owner of assets denomi-

---

competitive industrial markets, see my 'Imperfect Markets and the Effectiveness of Devaluation', *Kyklos* (Fasc. 3, 1965) pp. 512–30. In the text all goods are assumed to have perfectly elastic supply schedules so that prices are determined by administrative decisions and institutional peculiarities and not by output considerations.

[9] The United Kingdom considered its 'ordinary credits' in refusing to devalue sterling in the early twenties: See *Winch, Economics and Policy: A Historical Study*, p. 88.

[10] Enclave industries supplying the investing country with primary products could be exceptions as could foreign-based manufacturing facilities that feed the home market almost exclusively.

nated in foreign currency will have benefited from the lower foreign rate of inflation if his assets are defined in money and will receive an increase in dividends measured in domestic currency, on his equity holdings. If the depreciation were caused by an adverse real disturbance owners of assets denominated in foreign currency enjoy a partial immunity to the adverse shift. The immunity to the adverse shift in the terms of trade is reflected in the national as well as in personal fortunes. A nation that is a substantial net creditor on assets denominated in foreign currency will experience a smaller income effect as a result of depreciation than it would for the same real disturbance in the absence of its overseas assets. Given the importance of debt-servicing in the international accounts of developing countries, any appreciation of their currencies due to favourable real disturbances would furnish a disproportionately large income effect.

CAPITAL FLOWS

Apart from government long-term loans (net of repayments) which are usually motivated as much by political as by economic variables, international capital transactions are undertaken by private entities that seek either gain or risk reduction. For non-monetary capital movements, investment flows will indicate the availability in another nation of a higher total rate of return on capital but the general, monetary rate of return paid to capital in different countries is not the sole criterion. For portfolio investments diversification gains can outweigh small differences in marginal money rates of return: for large bond issues, borrowers will be sensitive to total costs so that floatation cost differentials, the technical ability of the source market to absorb an issue of the planned size and the absence of foreign-exchange controls can overpower rate differences. Direct investments will take place in response to a wide variety of incentives that may range from variation in international cost conditions in certain products to a defensive decision to protect an export-serviced market from competition from local manufacture. It is apparent that the variables that underlie the aggregate of international investment are large in number and are subject to frequent changes.

The complexity of the determinants of international investment flows and their variability suggests that the questions of cost and benefit of international investment and the correct adjustment process do not lend themselves to analysis defined in terms of optima.

Johnson is wrong when he contends that, in order to solve the problem of a flow deficit on capital account, it is necessary to 'determine the level of current account surplus or deficit, capital export or capital import at which economic policy should aim'.[11] This would clearly constitute a valuable piece of knowledge, but it is not a problem in the theory of payments adjustment any more than the optimum volume of trade in goods and services is germane to payments adjustment theory. What matters is not the optimum flow of international investment nor for that matter, the composition of the flow, but rather the actual flow, its variability and its responsiveness to balance-of-payments policies. Nor is 'the degree to which it is desirable to discriminate in favor of investment at home and against investment abroad' a problem for the analyst of payments adjustment,[12] that degree of discrimination is analogous to the 'normal' level of tariff protection afforded to goods.

Distinguishing between stock-adjustments and flow disturbances on capital account is considerably more difficult than distinguishing between their current-account equivalents. One of the main difficulties is the more ponderous mechanism involved in the direct-investment process because of the time-consuming character of the establishment of a foreign subsidiary operation and because of the greater exposure of direct investments to foreign uncertainties. Portfolio adjustments can be effected relatively quickly, although the per-period flow of portfolio capital will tend to be highly variable because of both its ability to adjust quickly and its sensitivity to quite small changes in short-term yields. Even though portfolio adjustment is, by its very nature, a stock-adjustment process, it can be incorporated into the analysis quite effectively as a flow phenomenon. The flow can be expected to show quite considerable variation around some trend that is attributable to a combination of wealth and diversification effects. Direct investments respond to larger numbers of variables and can suffer from a larger stock-disequilibrium. Conceptualisation of the determinants of flows of direct investments is not easy but can be approached most usefully in three stages: the stock-flow distinction; the role of different types of industries; and the type of subsidiary created.

A flow of direct investment abroad will involve the continuing transmission of funds to foreign countries for the creation, acquisition or expansion of foreign productive capacity in response to normal

[11] Harry G. Johnson, 'Towards a General Theory', p. 168.   [12] *Ibid.*

patterns of growth in the world economy. Such a flow will comprise a very large number of individual investment decisions and will therefore have some inherent element of variability over time. A flow of international investment will exist when foreign investment opportunities are more attractive (and therefore more productive and profitable) than the marginal available domestic investment opportunity. It is unlikely that such a flow will have a zero trend over time but the trend itself would be expected to vary only slowly from period to period. However, there could be a significant amount of variation around that trend because of temporary factors affecting investment decisions and their timing. It is also possible that shifts in the trend will occur if the volume of direct investment is sensitive to threshold levels of economic variables or to other phenomena that experience discrete changes.

A stock-adjustment process involves, as a matter of definition, a non-instantaneous reaction to a difference between what is wanted and what is. The existing distribution of the global stock of reproducible capital can be compared with an 'ideal' distribution or with a target or second-best distribution. Ideally capital would be distributed so that the marginal efficiency of capital (or investment) would be equal in all industries in all countries. This is a theorist's elysium which, it is hoped, the second-best distribution may slowly approach. The second-best distribution is one which, given the stock of capital in each country, those investors with the power to raise funds conceive of as ideal subject to their expectations about economic and political uncertainties. Given the other parameters of the system, it is the size of the difference between the target or second-best distribution and actuality that will determine the flows of direct international investment. The target distribution will respond to profit expectations, industrial structure,[13] technological and managerial gaps and the ability of the host country labour force to absorb the type of technology that the investor deems suitable. These variables are subject to quite dramatic changes so that the time-pattern of the volume of direct investment flows will not necessarily resemble the usual mathematical formulation of stock-adjustment whereby each succeeding stage involves a smaller adjustment. It is posssible for the target distribution to change more quickly than the actual so that the perceived 'flow' is quite erratic.

[13] See Richard E. Caves, 'International Corporations: The Industrial Economics of Foreign Investment', *Economica* (February 1971) pp. 1–27.

The surge of direct investment that has taken place since 1958 may well be the result of the potentially large stock disequilibrium that had been building up in the world economy since 1913. The forty-five-year period from 1913 to 1958 was one of international economic chaos of varying degrees such that direct international investments were seriously discouraged. When post-Second World War normalcy was restored in the late fifties – signalled by the mass of convertibility decisions[14] – the large gap between the target distribution and actuality could begin to be closed. The gap was accentuated by the simultaneous creation of the European Economic Community and, to a lesser degree, by the formation of the European Free Trade Association.

Direct investment flows take place in order to serve different markets with different kinds of goods. As a consequence, the volume of investment in each of the sub-aggregate areas can respond to different sets of underlying forces and will be sensitive to different political hazards. The types of investment can best be classified by the characteristics of the products that they are destined to furnish: non-competitive goods; competitive homogeneous goods and differentiated goods.

Non-competitive goods are those imported by a nation because that nation lacks the resources necessary to satisfy its own domestic needs. Ignoring such unrealistic possibilities as the United States becoming self-sufficient in bananas or in coffee, or Scotland in wine or in grapes through a combination of tariffs and hot-house cultivation, non-competitive goods are those which require a specific factor of production which is not available in the consuming country. The category of non-competitive goods can be broadened to include those goods which are produced in small quantities domestically but in which the country cannot, for lack of adequate supplies of the specific factors, be self-sufficient at or near the going price for imports. The crucial aspect of this type of good is that the specific factor is neither mobile between nations nor reproducible, so that the nation is dependent upon foreign production. Goods in this category usually require mineral deposits, a particular kind of soil or a particular climate for their production. It is possible to include in this category goods requiring very advanced technology but usually the nations unable to produce such goods are unable to devote foreign exchange to direct investment abroad. The purpose underlying such

[14] See Triffin, *Gold and the Dollar Crisis*, p. 17.

investments is to acquire a reliable source of supply – either to serve as an input for a domestic production organisation or as an input for a sales organisation. The bulk of this type of investment will be located in primary-producing countries and mostly in poor countries. The volume of investment will depend upon the change in self-sufficiency of the investing country in minerals or upon changes in the horizons of the corporations. Investment of this type will be very sensitive to the atmosphere that exists in poor nations toward foreign investments – particularly toward investment in depletable resources – and to the recent history of nationalisations and expropriations.

Competitive goods are homogeneous goods that are sold in general markets. They can be made with general factors of production such as unspecialised land, labour and capital. Whether or not they are produced in a country or imported depends upon the relative price of the different inputs at home and abroad. Relatively little direct investment can be expected to take place in competitive-goods industries unless there is some means of linking the products up with a distributional organisation in the investing country or unless there are economies of production that are internal to the firm.[15] In the absence of any Coase-economies, supplies of homogeneous goods will be imported from the most efficient producer and, since any foreign investor will be at some disadvantage relative to indigenous producers because of a lack of familiarity with local customs and laws and because of the danger of unfavourable political attention by the host governments, indigenous entrepreneurs can be expected to supply all the capacity that exports require. Multinational corporations can arrange for international trade in intermediate goods that is internal to the firm. Investment is unlikely to take place in order to accomplish these transactions unless the Coase-economies outweigh the advantage enjoyed by indigenous entrepreneurs.

Differentiated goods comprise mainly durable manufactured goods sold in imperfect markets. Each particular good is, or is made to appear, different from its competitors through slight variations in design or specification. Any differences that do exist will be magnified by sales promotion and advertising. The sale of goods of this type

---

[15] See R. H. Coase, 'The Nature of the Firm', *Economics*, n.s. IV (1937) pp. 386–405, reprinted in *Readings in Price Theory*, ed. G. J. Stigler and K. E. Boulding (Homewood, Ill.: Richard D. Irwin, Inc., 1952) pp. 331–51.

requires a marketing organisation. The possession of an established marketing organisation constitutes an asset on which a return can be earned since would-be competitors must surmount the barrier to market entry that the organisation constitutes. Foreign investment can take place to protect the value of an existing marketing organisation, particularly when its existence is threatened by a competitor willing to undertake local manufacture. Differentiated goods are also likely to induce direct foreign investment abroad because of the return of knowledge that is freely available to foreign manufacture from design experience and research and development expenditures made by the parent corporation. Investments in productive capacity for differentiated goods will take place as local demand for the goods grows once entry into the market has been established – this investment will involve either the expansion of existing capacity or the creation of capacity to replace export sales. An original investment in a nation will be made when the mraket is deemed large enough to be able to support local manufacture or will shortly be expected to achieve that status.

The primary determinants of direct foreign investment flows will be different for each of the three categories of products. Investment in non-competitive goods capacity will respond to anticipated changes in the demand for the end products in the home market and will be most directly influenced by the expected growth of domestic income. Differentiated-goods capacity will grow with foreign income and particularly as certain semi-developed nations attain threshold levels of *per capita* national income. Foreign investment in capacity in competitive goods will respond to technological innovations that enable processes to be developed that use unskilled labour intensively, to the spread of international corporations able to achieve Coase-economies and to changes in the marginal, homogeneous export or import. The latter influence will stem from favourable changes in the terms of trade (C_B^*) as goods that were once produced domestically can be produced abroad more efficiently given Coase-economies are large enough to outweigh the advantages of indigenous firms.

The *type of subsidiary* created by the foreign investment has its most important influence upon the balance of payments as a whole through the variation in the repercussions of different subsidiary types upon the demand for the goods and services (exports) of the investing country. However, the type of subsidiary created abroad may exert some influence upon the magnitude of the capital outflow. There are three different types of direct-investment subsidiary: an *ab ovo* or 'green field' venture in which a corporation or manufacturing concern is started from scratch; an expansion of capacity inian existing subsidiary;[16] or the acquisition (take-over) of an indigenous and on going firm. The advantage of the latter form of subsidiary is that the investing corporation acquires a share of and entry into the local market as well as productive capacity.

Because the purchase of an ongoing subsidiary includes payment for the value of the market share, investment in the type of subsidiary per unit of potential sales is likely to be greater than in an expansion or a green field venture. On the other hand, a green field investment is likely to commit the parent corporation to additional outlays of investment funds in future years.[17] The main influence exerted by the type of subsidiary upon the volume of investment funds committed derives from variation in the ratio of exported capital (both equity and debt) to the value of the overseas asset. The difference can be made up by partners' equity, by minority interests' equity and by debt financed in the host country. If the subsidiary is less than wholly owned, the transfer of investment funds is likely to be smaller and the possibility of local debt-finance greater. To the extent that acquisitions are more likely to involve partnerships or minority interests and are likely to be seen as more credit-worthy by the local financial sector because of their ongoing quality, takeovers can have a low ratio of funds exported to the asset value of the subsidiary. The question of local creditworthiness may also affect the degree to which local debt finance is available for wholly-owned subsidiaries – expansions being more creditworthy than green field ventures. Take-overs will occur almost exclusively in developed nations where barriers to entry in imperfect markets can be important and where firms suitable for acquisition are more plentiful. Since credit markets are also likely to be better developed in these countries, the ratio of exported funds to total assets may be lower for take-overs. However, these general indications can be overwhelmed by host country

---

[16] When a manufacturing unit is created to service an existing sales subsidiary, this should be considered as a green field investment.

[17] J. David Richardson, 'Theoretical Considerations in the Analysis of Foreign Direct Investment', *Western Economic Journal*, IX (March 1971) pp. 87–98, distinguishes between young firms and mature firms. The virtual necessity of further investment funds emanating from the parent is a characteristic of the young firm. See also Chapter 8 below.

regulations governing foreign direct investments and their financing. These regulations can vary substantially among countries and, sometimes, even from year to year within the same country.

The multiplicity of kinds of direct investments and the varying responses of different categories to particular economic variables reinforce the contention that there is considerable potential year-to-year variability in the outflow of direct investment funds – both net of inward direct investment and gross. This contention derives further support from a theoretical analysis designed to question the legitimacy of the application of models suitable for diagnosis of domestic expenditures on plant and equipment, to the aggregate of foreign investment flows.[18] The first danger in this practice is self-evident since direct capital exports can cover either a larger or a narrower range of expenditures than expenditures on plant and equipment. Capital exports can cover the whole range of financial commitments of a subsidiary or plant and equipment expenditures by subsidiaries can be financed, at least in part, by debt. Equally dangerous is the failure to distinguish between different types of foreign subsidiaries in the way in which their parent corporations are likely to supply them with funds – young firms being supported as proves necessary in the process of establishing themselves in markets and old firms being expected to obey more orthodox criteria of generating a profit and financing their own expansion. Thus, any system of analysis that attempted to relate the flow of investment to orthodox macro-economic indicators could prove seriously at fault if the population of foreign subsidiaries contained a large number of young firms. This source of error will be compounded to the degree that new ventures constitute a significant proportion of total direct investments since new ventures will be subject to a third, different set of criteria for investment decisions than those governing expansions of capacity in young or mature existing subsidiaries. Another factor that can contribute to errors in the estimation of capital exports is the degree to which the investment plans of foreign subsidiaries are decided locally or multinationally. If the subsidiary is 'independent', the decision will be made in accordance with conditions in the host country. If the subsidiary is 'international' investment decisions will be made jointly for all subsidiaries and will depend upon conditions in all the countries which host elements of the international corporation. Analyses of investment decisions based on conditions in the

[18] See Richardson *Western Economic Journal*, ix, p. 87.

host countries will be in error if international subsidiaries are quantitatively important.[19]

The rapid growth of the multinational form of corporate organisation could tend to concentrate the decision-making power over a large proportion of direct investment flows into the hands of a relatively small number of organisations. In addition the growth of a form of enterprise that owes its existence to direct international investment is likely to increase the volume of direct investment flows and possibly its rate of growth. It is not possible to deduce *a priori* whether this concentration of power will increase the variability of direct investment flows or will tend to stabilise them. Certainly the potential for greater variability will exist and, if the decision-making bodies are in close communication with each other, use the same raw data and are unmindful of the consequences of massive flows of direct investment, quite large swings could be inflicted on the international system from time to time. However, an awareness of the interdependencies should be forced upon the decision-makers by the national monetary authorities and the growth of multinational corporations could even prove to have a slight stabilising effect overall.

The difficulty of analysing direct-investment flows by means of historic data confirms the notion that the introduction of the capital and transfer accounts will tend to enlarge the potential size of data-effects. But that does not mean that forecasting direct-investment flows is impossible since survey techniques should be able to generate quite accurate forecasts for periods of one or two years into the future.

INTERNATIONAL INVESTMENT AND BASIC ADJUSTMENT

The aggregate of net international investment is an important element in the determination of a nation's deficit or surplus at any given prevailing ratio or of the value of C_B^* needed to achieve full balance. Basic adjustment that reallocates resources in the two countries is recognised as the most efficient (and therefore as the most desirable)

[19] See *ibid.*, p. 94. The term 'independent' overlaps quite closely with Perlmutter's concept of 'polycentric', but describing a subsidiary as 'international' could mean, in Perlmutter's classification, either extreme internationalism (geocentricity) or domination by the parent company (ethnocentricity). See Howard V. Perlmutter, 'The Tortuous Evolution of the Multinational Corporation', *Columbia Journal of World Business* (January–February 1969) pp. 9–18.

means of adjusting the economic system to permanent change. The relative sensitivity of the net flow of international investment to basic adjustments will determine (in a world free from impediments to trade and capital movements) how the process of adjustment will be divided between a reduction in capital flows and a reallocation of resources.

The demand on the part of the government to make loans (net) is unlikely to be affected by a change in C_P except perhaps by the wealth effect that must inevitably follow from a change in the international trading conditions required for full balance. Any decrease in demand of the government would probably be attributable to a form of disguised quasi-adjustment that reduced the necessary basic adjustment.

The demand for portfolio investment in fixed-value assets will depend upon the real rates of return expected at home and abroad given the available set of yields. Unless the change in C_B^* has caused expectations of further changes, there would seem to be no reason to assume that the basic adjustment, in itself, would have any permanent effect on flows of portfolio investment. This conclusion does not preclude some stock adjustment taking place if yields in the two countries had been made unequal by the disturbance. Equity portfolio investments will also be immune to basic adjustments on average, although some adjustment may take place as equities in both countries have their profit expectations altered by the disturbance and the consequent adjustment.

Direct investments may respond to the adjustment in certain industries. If the disturbance was adverse to the focus country, direct foreign investments in homogeneous goods capacity are likely to diminish because of the change in trading conditions, and some inflow of this type of investment may occur. The net effect in differentiated-goods industries is less clear. Exports of differentiated goods will have become more competitive, and this will tend to reduce the incentive to create manufacturing capacity abroad, but the wealth effect may accentuate the need to expand capacity in the foreign country to prevent other firms from doing so.

For practical purposes the flow of international investment can be considered immune to basic adjustments. This insensitivity has policy implications. First, the capital account cannot be relied upon to help absorb the shock (and reallocation cost) of any disturbance regardless of its source. Sooner or later, income levels must be adjusted and resources reallocated to fit the new conditions. Secondly, international investment must dominate international saving, and nations wishing to increase exports of capital must reduce either their consumption levels or their rate of domestic investments. If a nation wishes to reduce its rate of international investment, it must do so by discriminatory means and not by a basic adjustment. Thirdly, the argument in favour of using quasi-adjustments on capital account items to counter any disturbances originating in the capital account is strengthened. On the assumption that resource reallocation involves a real cost, there is an argument for failing to use a basic adjustment for any disturbance that is known to be temporary in nature. The argument for the imposition of a quasi-adjustment is the stronger, the more closely the quasi-adjustment can be tailored to fit the source of the disturbance. For disturbances arising in the capital account, the probability that a well-fitting quasi-adjustment is available, must be high.[20]

It is possible to use the rate of interest as a macropolicy instrument to affect the flow of international investment. Unfortunately government lending and direct investment are unlikely to be influenced by changes in relative interest rates of the order of magnitude which major credit markets can achieve. Portfolio investments will respond to changes in relative long-rates but the response will be a stock adjustment response that will vary with the length of time the differential has been in effect.

The insensitivity of government loans is self-explanatory. Direct investments will not be sensitive to change in interest-rate differentials because the rate of return needed to induce business expansion or creation in a foreign country so greatly exceeds any marginal rate of return required by the flow of domestic investment in the host country. Similarly high, and therefore intramarginal, rates of return will be required for take-overs. Direct investment is dominated by large corporations, and the investment plans of these businesses are not sensitive to marginal changes in interest rates – particularly when the risk of exposure to foreign governments is present. Any inflow of direct investments will also be intramarginal with respect to interest rates so that there is the risk of the net flow of direct investment appearing to have a perverse relationship with relative interest rates.

[20] Harry G. Johnson has made this point in 'Towards a General Theory', pp. 159–60.

It is possible, in unrestricted and uninhibited national financial markets, that the volume of direct and portfolio investment needed for foreign subsidiaries could be jointly responsive to interest-rate differentials. The mechanisms involved would require either that the ratio of equity investment to debt investment on the part of the parent corporation be sensitive to lower rates of interest prevailing in the host country or that the source of debt-financing can be shifted from the investing country to the host. This procedure will not generate as much aggregate sensitivity to interest-rate differentials as might be supposed because of the practice of inhibiting too great extensions of credit to foreign-controlled firms and because the internationalisation of capital markets has reduced the scope for rate differentials for large loans.

The aggregate demand for foreign assets is likely to show little sensitivity to changes in the competitive ratio or to interest-rate differentials. Some minor sensitivity will exist, but so little as to make the instrument variables inefficient means (high cost tools in terms of domestic goals) of influencing the net flow of international investment. The degree of sensitivity that exists will be affected by the composition of the aggregate. The demand for international investment in a fully-employed world is then primarily determined by forces which are data to any policy made. The most influential variables are wealth, technological gaps, expected growth and profit rates in different nations, the scope for Coase-type economies, and the political climate for direct investments. In terms of any available instrument variables, the schedule has low elasticity and is subject to large period-to-period shifts.[21]

CAPITAL ACCOUNT AND INTERNATIONAL SAVING

The introduction of capital transactions can affect the relationship between the volume of international saving that will be achieved for any value of the competitive position in a given structural setting. These effects derive from the impact of non-zero international net worths on current account and the influence of past international

[21] Cf. *The General Theory*, p. 164: 'For my own part I am now somewhat sceptical of the success of a merely monetary policy directed towards influencing the rate of interest ... since it seems likely that the fluctuations in the market estimation of the marginal efficiency of different types of capital ... will be too great to be offset by any practicable changes in the rate of interest.'

investment upon the resource endowments of nations and upon trade patterns.

The act of foreign investment matched by international saving, will increase the international net worth of the focus nation and, with it, the annual flow of international saving that will be achieved with any prevailing competitive ratio. In the simplest terms, a positive international net worth will shift the *TT* schedule in Figure 5-3 upward by an amount equal to net receipts of dividends and interest. The speed with which the flow of earnings will appear after the act of investment will vary according to the type of asset acquired but can normally be assumed to be delayed by at least one period. Ordinarily the flow of investment income can be expected to vary positively with international net worth and to be about zero when international net worth is zero. But, because yields on different sorts of assets and liabilities can vary substantially, it is quite possible for compositional factors to affect both the position and the slope of the schedule and for changes in the spectrum of yields to cause the schedule to shift even when the asset and liability mixes remain unchanged. If the average yield on assets exceeds that paid on liabilities, the net return on international net worth will be quite high. This situation is quite likely to occur in a key-currency nation which has acquired a large volume of highly liquid liabilities at quite low yields and has offset these liabilities with high-yielding direct investments in other countries (rather than with gold). Empirical studies of the yields obtained on the direct-investment assets encounter the often insuperable problem of determining the true (as opposed to the book) value of the assets and, for this reason, measures of international net worth are frequently suspect.

In addition to their contributions to net receipts of dividends and interest, international capital movements matched by international saving will alter the resource endowments of nations and, through this, leave their imprint upon the value of the competitive position needed for balance (C_B^*). Unilateral transfers that generate capital formation in the recipient country and that are matched by a trade surplus in the transferring nation can also affect resource endowments and C_B^*. Both portfolio and direct investment can contribute to capital formation in the recipient or host country. In so far as the decrease in domestic absorption in the investing country reduces the rates of capital formation there, the host country will increase its stock of capital both relatively and absolutely. In addition, direct investment flows facilitate the transfer of technological knowhow to the host country.[22] Both of these phenomena will exert their influence upon the pattern of trade. Finally, the existence of foreign subsidiary firms will influence the pattern of trade by replacing exports of finished products previously made by the investing country to the host country, but at the same time, opening up a market for intermediate goods exported to the subsidiary.

The net effect of the latter four items on the terms of trade cannot be judged *a priori*, nor indeed are they readily susceptible to empirical verification.[23] When the return flows of dividends and interest are included, C_C^* does seem to move in favour of the investing country, but even this does not determine that foreign investment is beneficial in total, since the acquisition of foreign assets required international saving on balance and a reduction of domestic absorption.

[22] See Cooper, *The Economics of Interdependence*, p. 105.

[23] Two large-scale studies have been performed in an attempt to assess the importance of foreign investment for the balance of payments. Both studies found the difficulties to be extreme and, while very competently performed, their results have been widely disputed because of the virtual impossibility of accurately assessing what would have happened in the absence of the foreign investment. This topic is considered in detail in the following chapter.

7 Induced International Saving

Induced international saving is to be distinguished from autonomous international saving. Induced saving is defined as the net flow of current credits that can be said to owe its existence to foreign investment made in the same or earlier periods. Autonomous international saving is the flow of saving that would be achieved in any given period in the absence of any capital transactions because C_P exceeded C_C^*.

If the induced international saving takes place in the same period as the international investment that gives rise to it, it is called concurrent induced saving and will partially offset the capital export. If the induced saving is generated by investments made in past periods – that is from inherited positive net worth – the impact of the credits will have been absorbed into the pattern of trade and the determination mechanism of the target competitive ratios. Any change in inherited induced saving from the previous period will enter the model as a data-effect. Inherited induced saving is a component of autonomous saving, concurrent saving is not. The distinction between the two can be more clearly drawn by reference to Figure 5-3 modified slightly so that the TT schedule represents the current account balance for a given balance on unilateral transfers. Autonomous saving is then the vertical distance between the TT schedule and the horizontal axis. Concurrent induced saving is the upward shift in the TT schedule that would result from a given volume and given mix of foreign investment. The proportionate rate of induced saving is clearly an important datum in assessing the desirability from the investing country's view of any capital export. The rate will indicate the degree to which a capital export will generate its own matching, concurrent saving without any adverse shift in the net barter terms of trade and to which the previous sacrifice of domestic absorption will yield a return in balance-of-payments terms.

For investments such as government loans and private portfolio assets, the process is relatively straightforward and adapts easily to period analysis: assuming no concurrent saving, the asset will start to generate a return in the period following the one in which the investment was made. This flow will continue until the asset is paid off or sold. In addition to the yields on the capital asset, the flow of inherited induced saving could be affected by changes in the rate of capital formation and growth that follow from the effected transfer. The mechanism is considerably more complex for direct investments since they can, in addition to yielding a return flow of dividends, affect both foreign demand for the exports of the focus country and the latter's demand for imports. In this way, they can change the value of C_i^*. The purpose of this chapter is to examine the mechanism whereby induced saving is generated in response to foreign investment, its impact upon payments balance and its implications for balance-of-payments policies.

No examination of the mechanism of induced saving and its implications could fail to consider the differential impacts of different kinds of investment in different host nations. Equally necessary is an analysis of the time-shape of the flow of induced saving that follows on different investments. The pioneering work in this area in both theory and empirical work consists of two large empirical studies undertaken to gauge the effect on the balance of payments and economic welfare of direct investments by the United Kingdom and the United States. These will be referred to, respectively, as the *Reddaway* and *Hufbauer-Adler Reports*.[1]

Both reports adopt what amounts to a period-analysis framework and conceive of the mechanism in very similar terms.[2] The repercussions on the international accounts of a single international investment will have different effects in the initial period when the investment is made (t_0) from the effects in the succeeding periods ($t_1, \ldots, t_n$). In t_0 there will be a debit in the capital account in the amount of funds transmitted – equal to the value of the foreign asset over which control is acquired less any financing obtained abroad. There will be an increase in the demand for the exports of the

[1] W. B. Reddaway in collaboration with J. O. N. Perkins, S. J. Potter and C. T. Taylor, *Effects of U.K. Direct Investment Overseas: An Interim Report* (Cambridge: Cambridge University Press, 1967) and Reddaway in collaboration with Potter and Taylor, *Effects of U.K. Direct Investment Overseas: Final Report* (Cambridge 1968), G. C. Hufbauer and F. M. Adler, *Overseas Manufacturing Investment and the Balance of Payments* (Washington, D.C.: U.S. Treasury Department, 1968).

[2] Appendix C in *The Reddaway Report*, pp. 167–75, gives a very lucid account of the theoretical approach.

investing (base) country as capital formation abroad increases the demand for capital goods. This increase in export demand will partially offset the capital debit. In the absence of a favourable data-effect, there will be a reduction in the liquid reserves or other assets of the nation equal to the difference between the capital debit and the value of induced exports.[3] All of these effects are one-period phenomena for any single act of direct investment. The consequences for periods t_1 into the future are continuing effects which may or may not vary systematically over time. These effects include the return of after-tax profits which will start in t_1. Since not all profits are usually repatriated, the net worth of the foreign subsidiary will increase over time with the result that the flow of profits should have a positive time-trend. Similarly the nation – presumably the national monetary authority – will receive less income from abroad on balance because of its reduced asset position. This series of debits (the 'notional financing charge' in Reddaway's terminology) may be conceived of as reducing over time as the flow of after-tax profits enables the authority to restore its reserve position. Finally, there will be two continuing effects which can be considered jointly. The establishment of a foreign subsidiary can alter trading patterns and the act of foreign investment can affect growth rates and patterns in the two countries. These two consequences will combine to have an effect upon the balance on goods and services that will be achieved in t_1 and after, given a constant prevailing competitive ratio.

The importance of the consequences of foreign investment for the trade balance revolves around the macroeconomic assumptions made about what would have happened in the absence of the foreign investment. In empirical studies, the state of affairs in the absence of foreign investment is referred to as 'the alternative position'. The assumptions made about the alternative position can greatly affect the quantitative significance of investment for the trade balance.[4]

The crux of the concern with capital formation is the effect of the resultant change in growth rates upon the trade balance at any given competitive ratio. If international investment accelerates growth in the host and retards it in the base country, then the growth effect will probably be to decrease the value of C_T^* for the investing country and

---

[3] There is a tacit assumption here that basic balance prevailed before the foreign investment.

[4] These are clearly brought out in the *Hufbauer-Adler Report*, pp. 67–8. For a description of the alternatives see also pp. 6–7.

improve its terms of trade. (This tendency toward improved terms of trade will be supplemented by the flow of dividends and countered by a wealth effect.) The improvement in the terms of trade can be seen as induced international saving. If nations are not fully employed and kept in a state of full employment, multiplier reactions could reinforce the growth effects. Finally, there is the possibility of a change in the underlying structure of international trade which will follow once the foreign subsidiary is in operation (t_1 and later).[5] The crucial questions here are whether the establishment of a foreign subsidiary (manufacturing, sales, or extractive) will increase or decrease the total demand for exports of the base country, and whether the existence of a foreign subsidiary will affect the value of imports into the base country. There are five main ways in which the trade-effects can be brought about. First, the displacement of exports of finished goods into the host country by the output of the subsidiary will have an adverse effect upon the trade balance of the investing nation. However, the loss may be illusory. It is quite possible that if the subsidiary had not been established, another competitor would have set up local manufacturing facilities and endangered the existence of base-country exports and their attendant organisation. The competitor could be indigenous, from a third country or even from the investing country.[6] If exports of finished goods were in danger, the establishment of the subsidiary could be described as 'defensive'. Second, the subsidiary's output might displace home output in third markets. Third, exports of intermediate products by the parent to the subsidiary will offset, wholly or partially, the loss of exports of finished goods. A fourth possible effect on the trade balance is the opportunity presented for the promotion of associated exports. This argument is a somewhat tenuous one since it can reasonably only be applied to green field ventures and not to expansions or to the introduction of manufacturing capacity in support of an existing sales organisation.[7] Exports made to a sales subsidiary should not be wholly attributed to the existence of that subsidiary since a series of local agents or factors would achieve some sales. Finally, extractive subsidiaries may yield primary products to the parent corporation at lower than world prices. In this way, the subsidiary would have a

[5] The assumption is always made that an investment in t_0 will become productive in t_1.
[6] The latter possibility is not considered in the text.
[7] See the *Hufbauer-Adler Report*, p. 30.

favourable effect upon the balance of trade even though it furnished imports. The same analysis could apply to manufacturing subsidiaries that supply competitive-goods imports to the parent corporation.[8]

Just as for the growth effect which it supplements, no strong *a priori* judgement can be made about the direction of any change in the trade balance that follows from a direct investment.

While the choice among macroeconomic assumptions most directly influences the flow of continuing induced international saving, the volume of concurrent induced saving is also influenced by them. If it is assumed that in the absence of foreign investment by the focus country no substitute investment takes place in the host nation, the rate of concurrent saving will be larger than if substitute capital formation is assumed to take place. The difference in the induced saving would be the demand for base-country exports in t_0 by the substitute enterprise.

However unavoidable the use of a general set of macroeconomic assumptions may be for a broad-based empirical study, the variability among direct investments is such that the procedure cannot be optimal. The most obvious example of the need for different assumptions for different direct investments is the lack of consistency in the goals, efficiency and conduct of macrostabilisation policies that exists between developed and developing or poor nations. While it could be reasonable to assume that in developed countries the rate of domestic investment is independent of the inflow of direct foreign investment matched by foreign saving, it is ordinarily not a reasonable assumption for poor nations. Take-overs are likely to generate different capital-formation effects than expansions or new ventures. The behaviour of competitors can also affect the validity of any set of macroeconomic assumptions since the rate of capital formation in the host country is less likely to be affected if the investment is in differentiated goods than in either of the other two categories. But, that assumption might well be invalidated by an oligopolistic market structure in the relevant industry if this type of market structure led an investment to be followed immediately by a competitor's entry.[9]

[8] Manufacturing subsidiaries of American firms are important sources of imports; subsidiaries of U.K. corporations are not – see the *Reddaway Report*, p. 298. The fact that imports may benefit the trade balance does not mean that labour is not adversely affected – see my *The Economics of Business Investment Abroad* (London: Macmillan, 1972) Ch. 7.

[9] John H. Dunning, *Studies in International Investment* (London: George Allen & Unwin, 1970) Appendix B, pp. 107–17, makes these points.

The only difference in principle between the frame of reference needed for direct investments and other kinds of capital flows is that trade-structure changes will be caused only by direct investments. Government loans and private portfolio investments can give rise to concurrent saving although, for the latter particularly, the connection between the international investment and induced saving may be less clearly seen. Foreign aid and other transfer payments can cause concurrent saving as the funds are spent on exports of the transferring country but, since no asset is acquired, growth effects are the only potential source of continuing induced saving.

Flows of induced saving and the time shapes of these flows are fundamental to the period-analysis model. For purposes of expositional ease, it is worth eliminating any further reference to the interrelation between international investments, growth rates and induced saving. Hereafter, growth will be considered as exogenous to the frame of reference. Since high-employment is assumed to be a primary concern of developed countries, multiplier effects will also be ignored. Flows of inherited induced saving serve to interrelate the international net worth and the value of C_C^*. These flows comprise both dividend and interest receipts (net) and the impact of any change in trade patterns. Flows of concurrent induced saving relate current international investments to current deficits (given C_P and C_T^*) or will reduce the basic adjustment needed to maintain full balance. The combination of the two types of induced saving will influence the optimum degree of preference to be accorded to domestic over foreign investment, and is a determinant of the general efficacy that can be expected from quasi-adjustments on capital account.[10] Finally, the rate of induced saving will determine the 'payback' or 'recoupment' period of a foreign investment. This is a cash-flow concept which measures the length of time required for a foreign investment to generate enough cash receipts to be able to restore any reductions in the authorities' international reserves. The concept of induced saving does not, since it involves the export of goods and services attributable to the existence of the foreign subsidiary, measure a real rate of return on the foreign asset.

Rates of Induced Saving

So wide is the range of alternative forms of foreign investment and unilateral transfers that the potential for wide variation in rates of

---

[10] These points are discussed in the following chapter.

induced saving is self-evident. The main differences in induced saving rates will probably occur among the four main categories of capital-account and transfer-account debits; direct investment, private portfolio investment, government loans and foreign aid. All forms of transfers have an induced saving rate in the sense that they increase the potential absorption of the recipient nation but it makes more sense to include flow transfers and their effects in the normal patterns of growth and payments.

Private portfolio investment is capable of very high or very negative rates of return when the investment involves highly speculative ventures on some foreign *bourse*. However, the bulk of portfolio investment is less spectacular and is made in fixed-value securities or in equities that will be held for a protracted period of time. There is therefore likely to be little or no concurrent induced saving from portfolio investment, and the continuing saving will be a fairly constant stream of payments per unit invested until the asset is sold or repatriated, at which time any capital gain or loss will be realised. Portfolio investment can have an effect on the rate of capital formation in the recipient nation if the asset is sold by a resident to release funds for investment in fixed assets. Portfolio investment can give rise to concurrent saving when new issues are sold in a foreign market to finance a large undertaking for which the foreign exchange component is a necessary part of the needed finance. The outflow of foreign exchange then does generate a return flow in the form of demand for exports, but this is an unreliable relationship for two reasons. There is no reason to expect that the imports that require the foreign-exchange component in the financing will be purchased from the nation in which the funds are raised and, secondly, it is highly probable that the funds will be repatriated to the borrowing nation prior to their actual expenditure on imports so that the feedback effect will show up as a data-effect for some future period rather than as concurrent saving.

The possible confusion between concurrent saving and later data-effects can also apply to government loans made to poor countries. These loans are frequently ear-marked for specific projects. However, both loan receipts and aid funds will tend to be spent quickly by developing economies so that feedback from these transfers can be thought of as concurrent saving – even more so if the government supplying the funds will only disburse them on receipt of notification of expenditures. Despite the common practice of tying aid and loans, there can be no assurance that the rate of concurrent saving will be high because of the ability of recipient countries to switch their available foreign exchange among goods. However, most attempts to measure the rate of induced saving or its complement, the proportionate foreign-exchange leakage, find rates of induced saving to be high.[11] There will be negligible continuing induced saving (apart from any possible growth effects) since interest rate payments on government loans are usually set at quite low rates and because payments on interest have a high cost in terms of imports demanded by the paying country – thus, the interest-receiving nation will only benefit by interest receipts less the exports it would have made. Amortization of outstanding loans has the same effect and, for this reason, loans should be considered net of repayments. The combination of the ability of the recipient nations to switch funds and the high rate of expenditure of new loans or aid will allow increases in aid or loans by third countries to provide the focus country with a favourable data-effect.

Direct investments can generate a wide range of concurrent and continuing induced saving. Variability of induced saving rates and time-shapes will derive from the different combinations of features that direct investments can assume. Some of the possible combinations are shown in Chart 7-1. Variations in feedback rates by industry and by country and differences in the proportion of foreign financing will provide additional sources of variation. It is to be expected, *a priori*, that rates of concurrent induced saving will be higher for investments that are located in countries with (i) close trade ties to the investing country and (ii) no domestic capital goods industries – and therefore primarily in poor and/or primary-producing nations. Concurrent saving rates will also be higher in industries for which the investing country has a capital goods industry and for investments that result in actual capital formation abroad and not merely the take-over of existing assets. Rates of continuing induced saving will be higher for investments in differentiated industries in which exports are displaced by local manufacture designed to supply a local market.

[11] See, for the United States, David E. Bell's statement before the U.S. Senate Banking and Currency Committee (89th Congress), *Hearings: Balance of Payments, 1965* (Washington, D.C., 1965) pp. 67–73: reprinted as 'Foreign Aid and the Balance of Payments', in my *The Dollar Deficit: Causes and Cures* (Boston: D. C. Heath, 1967) pp. 69–76. For the United Kingdom see B. Hopkin and Associates, 'Aid and the Balance of Payments', *Economic Journal* (March 1970) pp. 1–23.

CHART 7-1

Some Possible Combinations of Characteristics of Direct Investments

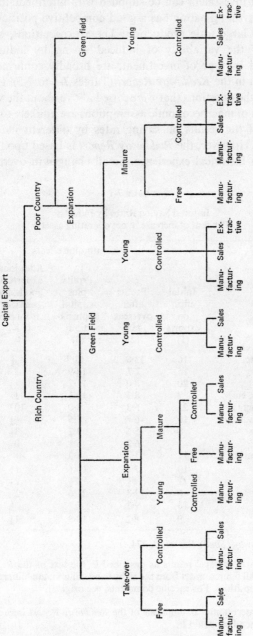

Notes: Some permutations have not been shown on the grounds that the probability of their occurrence was too small (e.g. no take-overs were considered to take place in poor nations).

Variations in rates of induced saving would be increased if variation in industry within sectors and variations in countries within the income-classification had been included.

This type of investment can be supplied with intermediate goods in which the investing nation has a good competitive position because of ongoing, large-scale production. These expectations, as well as evidence of the variability of induced saving by industry, host country and by type of investment, are broadly confirmed by the results given in the *Reddaway Report* (Tables 7-1 to 7-5). It is worth noting that the questions that were raised above about the validity of a general set of macroeconomic assumptions are unlikely to affect the reliability of the results on saving rates by different industries or countries.[12] However, the *Reddaway Report* is based upon a sample drawn from historical experience. Small changes in overall invest-

TABLE 7-1

Induced Saving Rates by Industry
(Per cent of increase in net operating assets)

Industry	Initial effect on exports (1)	Continuing effects			9-year addition to net operating assets 1956–64 (£ million)
		Profits after overseas tax (2)	Profits plus capital appreciation (3)	Additional exports of goods and services from the U.K. (4)	
Building materials, etc.	16	13·8	18·7	$-\frac{1}{2}$	49·0
Chemicals	15	7·7	14·9	-2	128·2
Textiles	20	8·0	11·7	$-\frac{1}{2}$	37·1
Food, drink, tobacco, etc.	7	8·5	10·1	1	197·0
Vehicles and components	21	5·3	8·0	$10\frac{1}{4}$	90·4
Metals and metal products	10	6·8	7·5	$-\frac{1}{2}$	174·4
Electrical engineering	3	5·6	7·2	$3\frac{1}{2}$	44·2
Paper	1	6·2	6·1	0	124·2
Non-electrical engineering	11	5·3	4·9	18	11·0
Total manufacturing	10	7·7	10·1	$1\frac{1}{2}$	855·5
Ditto, adjusted	*11*	$5\frac{1}{2}$	$7\frac{1}{2}$	$1\frac{1}{2}$	*755*
Mining	6	12·3	21·6	2	154·3
Plantations	18	9·3	7·7	$\frac{1}{2}$	22·1
Total	9	8·2	10·8	$1\frac{1}{2}$	1031·9

Source: The *Reddaway (Final) Report*, p. 374.

Note. All figures are 'average' results as described in the text of the *Report* and relate to the period 1955–64. All figures, apart from the right-hand column, are 'differences as compared with the alternative position'. For specific comments, see original.

[12] The macroeconomic assumptions of the *Reddaway Report* were as good as any single, general set could be.

TABLE 7-2

Purchases of Input Items from the United Kingdom by Subsidiaries in the Fifteen Specified Countries
(Annual Averages)

(a) *By industry*

	Vehicles and components	Non-electrical engineering	Building materials etc.	Electrical engineering	Textiles	Metals and metal products	Chemicals	Food, drink, tobacco, etc.	Paper	Total manufacturing	Mining	Plantations	Total
Purchases from U.K. (£ million)	19·2	3·5	3·9	3·8	3·0	6·3	4·2	6·5	0·1	50·5	1·0	1·2	52·7
Net operating assets (£ million)	104	20	47	51	67	160	148	345	133	1075	111	95	1281
Purchases from U.K. as % of net operating assets	*18·5*	*17·2*	*8·4*	*7·6*	*4·5*	*3·9*	*2·8*	*1·9*	*0·1*	*4·7*	*0·9*	*1·2*	*4·1*
Value of production (£ million)	149·7	34·2	40·1	93·9	69·2	256·7	145·3	728·1	81·7	1598·8	92·5	84·1	1775·4
Purchases from U.K. as % of value of production	*12·8*	*10·2*	*9·8*	*4·1*	*4·3*	*2·5*	*2·9*	*0·9*	*0·2*	*3·2*	*1·1*	*1·4*	*3·0*

(b) *By country*

	South Africa	Jamaica	Australia	Malaysia	Ghana	India	W. Germany	Nigeria	Argentina	Denmark	Canada	Italy	Brazil	France	USA	Total 15 countries
Purchases from U.K. (£ million)	12·7	1·0	16·1	3·3	1·5	7·0	1·2	2·0	0·5	0·1	5·4	0·1	0·3	0·1	1·4	52·7
Net operating assets (£ million)	97	8	202	55	25	156	30	51	15	5	295	8	27	23	284	1281
Purchases from U.K. as % of net operating assets	*13·0*	*12·1*	*8·0*	*6·0*	*6·0*	*4·5*	*4·1*	*4·0*	*3·2*	*2·6*	*1·8*	*1·4*	*1·1*	*0·6*	*0·5*	*4·1*

Source: The *Reddaway Report*, p. 365.   For specific comments, see original.

Note: For purchases and value of production the annual average is for the year 1955–64; for net operating assets the annual average is for the years 1955–63.

ment do reflect the mix of the sample by industry, country and type of concern. Data by country therefore are subject to bias because of the industry-mix in the individual countries and data by industry because of the country-mix in individual industries.

Table 7-1 shows the distribution by industry of the concurrent induced saving in column (1) and of continuing saving in columns (2), (3), and (4). The variance of column (1) is clearly large. Profit rates vary little with the exception of building materials and mining, but the trade-effects, column (4), do show an extreme difference of 20 per cent. Table 7-2 gives some limited evidential support to the hypothesis that input-sales to foreign subsidiaries are more important for differentiated goods subsidiaries serving local markets. The hypothesis regarding inputs probably needs qualifying by the

TABLE 7-3

Induced Saving Rates by Host Country

		Continuing effects			
Country	Initial effect on exports (1)	Profits after overseas tax (2)	Profits plus capital appreciation (3)	Additional exports of goods and services from the U.K. (4)	9-year addition to net operating assets 1956–64 (£ million)
Jamaica	27	7·9	6·2	9½	7·0
Ghana	– a	12·9	12·3	8½	3·5
South Africa	18	10·0	19·0	7	53·0
Nigeria	39	4·5	5·6	5	14·6
Malaysia	35	18·8	26·9	4	27·5
Denmark	15	4·8	4·5	4	6·3
India	20	7·9	7·9	3½	84·2
W. Germany	2	22·6	34·3	3½	44·8
Argentina	14	2·0	6·2	1½	14·9
Australia	8	8·5	16·0	1	201·2
Canada	4	5·3	4·7	½	267·7
U.S.A.	1	9·0	11·6	–1	133·3
Brazil	11	6·1	10·5	–1	8·9
France	1	3·0	–1·3	–5	17·3
Italy	10	15·1	20·0	–9	8·0
Total, 15 countries	9	8·4	11·4	1½	892·3

Source: *The Reddaway Report*, p. 216: (the sample includes all investments).
a There were technical problems in computing the initial effect on exports from Ghana but it was clearly 'large'. For details, see the original.

proportion of differentiated-goods subsidiaries that are located in nations well equipped to supply parts and by the age-distribution of subsidiaries since the older a subsidiary, the more likely is it to have developed local sources of supply. The sales of input items in Table 7-2 represent (with invisibles) the positive aspects of the trade effects.

Table 7-3 provides the data on concurrent and continuing rates of induced saving by host country. It is equivalent in its format to Table 7-1. The variance in column (1) is again quite large but the country variation in the after-tax profit rate is much larger than that shown by the industry breakdown. The extremes of the trade-effects are again very large. These data generally support the hypothesis that the poorer is the host, the higher will be the concurrent saving rate. The five countries with the largest (positive) trade-effects were, at that time, all members of the Commonwealth, so that some

TABLE 7-4

Profitability of New Ventures

A. Take-overs owned for at least five years (11 cases)

	Year of operation (as subsidiary of UK company)				
	0	1	2	3	4
Net operating assets at year end (£'000)	49,016	53,516	55,971	59,153	70,818
Pre-tax profits (£'000)	2,921	6,340	6,927	6,149	9,771
Profitability (% of average net assets for year)	11·9	12·4	12·7	10·7	15·0

B. Green Field ventures in existence for at least five years

	Year of operation				
	0	1	2	3	4
Developed countries (21 cases)					
Net operating assets at year end (£'000)	5,164	24,229	44,533	54,893	53,487
Pre-tax profits (£'000)	−36	201	140	−782	435
Profitability (% of average net assets for year)	−1·4	1·4	0·4	−1·6	0·8
Underdeveloped countries (17 cases)					
Net operating assets at year-end (£'000)	4,044	5,078	6,188	8,106	9,313
Pre-tax profits (£'000)	168	43	−82	889	1,149
Profitability (% of average net assets for year)	8·3	0·9	−1·5	12·5	13·2

Source: *The Reddaway Report*, p. 226.

support is gained for the hypothesis that continuing saving rates are positively correlated with close trade ties, and the evidence for a positive relationship between trade ties and the concurrent saving rate is even stronger.

Table 7-4 shows the profit rates of new subsidiaries for the first five years of their existence as subsidiaries. Take-overs achieved satisfactory rates of profit almost immediately, being slightly below the rates recorded for the sample as a whole (16·3 per cent).[13] These rates could be expected to increase as the integration of subsidiary and parent proceeded. In almost complete contrast, green field ventures in developed countries showed net losses, on average, for the first five years of their existence. In underdeveloped countries, a much smaller sample of green field subsidiaries achieved satisfactory rates of performance in the fourth year of their existence.

Finally, Table 7-5 provides data that support the hypothesis that the rate of concurrent induced saving will vary substantially with the

TABLE 7-5

Capital Equipment Purchases from the United Kingdom by New Ventures as a Proportion of the Change in Net Operating Assets (per cent)

	0	1	2	3	4	Total
			Year of operation*			
Green field firms (38 concerns)	9·93	14·19	31·10	21·09	†	20·65
Take-overs (11 concerns)	0·55	18·82	29·74	17·63	7·90	4·75

Source: The *Reddaway Report*, tables XVII.2 and XVII.4 and additional data supplied by the Cambridge D.A.E.

* The table combines the results for a number of new subsidiaries, without regard to the actual year in which they were started, by treating as year 0 for each one, the year in which fixed assets first appear in the record.

† Total net operating assets decreased in the fourth year rendering the computation impossible.

type of subsidiary organisation. In contrast with an overall rate for manufacturing of 10 per cent, green field ventures in the first five years achieved a 20 per cent rate while take-overs averaged less than one-half of 1 per cent. Of course, in strict terms, purchases of capital goods and investments following the original year are 'expansions.' As might be expected, the big difference in the concurrent saving

[13] *Reddaway Report*, p. 219 – if the very profitable subsidiaries in West Germany are excluded the average rate of profit is reduced to 15·4 per cent.

rates of green field ventures and take-overs occurs in the first year when the rate of concurrent induced saving of take-overs amounted to little more than one-half of 1 per cent. In later years (expansions) there was no substantive difference between the two rates and both were well above average.

Other Influences on Induced Saving Rates

Change in the volume and the composition of either the direct investment or the total international investment outflow aside, the factors that will bring about changes in the rate of induced saving will be the same as those that affect a nation's trade balance – real disturbances, monetary disturbances, quasi-adjustments and unintentional variation in income levels. The most important of these effects will be a change in the competitiveness of the exports of the investing country due either to a real disturbance (C_T^* changes) or to a monetary disturbance (C_P changes).

Concurrent induced saving is completely attributable to outflows of government loans and aid and of direct investment. The sensitivity of the two kinds of concurrent saving to a change in competitiveness derives from the type of transaction. If the government loan or aid is tied to exports of the transferrer, the ability of the recipient to escape the tying provisions depends upon its ability to switch. A change in competitiveness will increase the desirability of switching, but, not necessarily the ability to switch, though some slippage will undoubtedly occur as the goods of the transferrer become less and less competitive. When the aid is not tied – when, for example, it is distributed through international institutions such as the World Bank – the rate of induced concurrent saving out of contributions will be quite sensitive to the competitiveness of the donor nation. Concurrent saving out of direct investment will tend to respond to changes in competitiveness according to the premium that executives in a firm put upon starting a green field venture with equipment that has been tried and tested. If previous experience with the capital goods is considered important, then the rate of concurrent saving will not be very sensitive to changes in competitiveness. The relative insensitivity will also apply if a new venture is equipped with renovated used machinery from a plant in the investing country. Expansions of mature and independent subsidiaries will be more sensitive to competitiveness but, to the extent that new equipment must be married with the existing stock, these flows will have a bias in favour of the products of the investing nation. In summary the rate of concurrent induced saving will exhibit some sensitivity to the level of competitiveness. However, there are constraints operative that will tend to make this part of the flow of exports of capital goods less sensitive to change in competitiveness than are exports of capital goods in general.

The flow of intermediate products that comprise the bulk of continuing induced saving, will also tend to be less sensitive to change in the competitiveness of the investing country than exports of intermediate goods in general. Coase-economies may mitigate the loss of competitiveness somewhat and there is always a bias in favour of continuing an existing supplier relationship. However, this bias is likely to weaken over time if the deterioration in competitiveness is not quickly eliminated. Subsidiaries will have the natural impetus to seek sources of input supplies in the host country reinforced.

The rate of induced saving will reflect variation in income levels in the investing and in the host nation. Excess aggregate demand in the investing country will probably lead to pressure on the capacity of the capital goods industry and will reduce the rate of concurrent induced saving.[14] A recession in the host nation will reduce the demand for inputs into production by subsidiary firms in approximately the same way that total import demand is reduced. A shortage of capacity in the capital goods industry is not likely to follow from a surge of direct investments unless it is accompanied by an increase in planned domestic investment since a surge of direct investment outflows will normally tend to reduce planned domestic capital formation. Any reduction in exports of intermediate goods will be likely to have its effect on the rate of induced saving supplemented by lower rates of profit that are earned by subsidiaries located abroad.

Provided that the rate of induced saving is computed on the basis of net operating assets under the control of corporations located in the investing country, as the Reddaway data do, the rate of saving will be sensitive to the ratio of parent's equity to assets controlled (see Chapter 6). Variation in the rate of foreign financing will therefore affect the rate of induced saving achieved quite apart from any compositional or price-competitiveness influences. The role of leverage of this kind is likely to be greater in theory than in practice

---

[14] Hopkin, *Economic Journal* (March 1970), estimates that leakage from U.K. aid may rise from 33 per cent to 40 per cent when pressure on capacity exists in the relevant industries.

since nearly all nations either discourage or set limits to the amount of financing that foreign corporations may acquire locally. Certainly the leverage obtained would never be so great as to allow a foreign investment to achieve a rate of concurrent saving of unity. At the same time corporations have historically borrowed as much as they could obtain from local sources in order to reduce the risk of foreign operations.[15] It is quite likely that the emergence of international financial markets will provide foreign subsidiaries and international companies generally with the opportunity of reducing the ratio of equity to net operating assets without recourse to the host country's financial system.

The reverse half of this same coin is the investment by the parent corporation of additional funds in a subsidiary over which it already exerts operational control. The most memorable example of this took place in 1960 when Ford Motor Company bought out the minority shareholders of its English subsidiary. While this move did allow Ford to integrate its European production without fear of complaints from minority shareholders, the net result of the move, in the short-run at least, was to reduce the rate of continuing induced saving and to include in the category of direct investment outlays, $371 million of funds that were to all intents, portfolio investments.

Summary

Induced international saving takes two forms. Concurrent saving occurs only in the same period as the foreign investment that gives rise to it. Continuing saving takes place in periods subsequent to the act of investment, will endure for as long as the foreign asset exists and, in the case of direct investment, is capable of both secular and cyclical variation over time.

Continuing saving merges with the other ongoing influences of tastes, prices, incomes and data in the international economy so that it contributes to the determination of C_f^*. Changes in continuing saving can derive either from changes in saving rates or from changes in the nation's international net worth. The changes will appear as data-effects. It will be difficult to distinguish the data-effects caused by changes in the flow of continuing saving from data-effects consequent upon other disturbances.

For the purposes of analysis of payments adjustment, concurrent induced saving is a more immediate force. Concurrent induced

[15] The *Hufbauer-Adler Report*, pp. 14–18.

saving partially offsets the debit on capital account that gives rise to it. As a consequence, the rate of concurrent induced saving determines the net reserve loss that follows from a given international investment. It therefore directly affects the magnitude of the adjustment $(C_B^* - C_C^*)$ needed to establish balance. The rate of concurrent induced saving will vary widely for different investments. The reserve loss for a flow of international investment that comprises many different individual projects, is the product of the volume of investment and the average proportionate foreign exchange leakage. The latter is the complement of the average rate of concurrent induced saving which can be written as:

$$(7\text{-}1) \qquad k = (a_j K_j)/\sum_m K \qquad j = 1, 2, \ldots, m$$

where k is the average rate of concurrent saving, K_j is the individual foreign investment which, in this case, serves as a weight for a_j the concurrent rate of saving for investment j. Given that $0 \leqslant a_j < 1$, k will also be positive and less than unity.[16]

The leakage from any flow of international investment $(I_I = \sum_m K)$ is $I_I(1 - k)$. The variability of a_j is so great that k cannot be relied upon not to shift sharply from period to period. There is no built-in mechanism that will cause variations in k to tend to offset the balance-of-payments effects of any variability in the outflow of international investment. The combination of changes in I_I and k is as likely to be mutually-reinforcing as it is to be counteracting. Nor is there any classical medicine on which the adjustment process can rely if high employment levels are maintained in both nations. The inclusion of concurrent saving in the analysis of the impact of capital account on payments balance serves only to add emphasis to the need for continuing flexibility on the part of the national monetary authority.

The problem of period-to-period adjustment is not necessarily reduced in magnitude when the possibility of simultaneous flows of capital in both directions is included in the analysis. The need for adjustment derives from changes in the volume of the flows and in their immediate and automatic offsets. Variations in the volume of the two flows are certainly as capable of reinforcing each other as of having an overall stabilising effect. Compositional changes in the

---

[16] The upper limit of unity for a_j could in theory be exceeded by a large ratio of foreign finance to equity. Host country discouragement of excessive financing will preclude this possibility.

two flows can give rise to destabilising net effects as the average rates of concurrent saving aggravate changes in the two rates of investment, as well as to producing stabilising net effects. There can be no presumption that the set of a_j for inflows of capital is in any way a counterpart of the set of a_j for outflows.

8 Capital Controls as Quasi-Adjustments

A basic deficit can be reduced by restricting debits on capital and transfer accounts provided that these measures do not automatically engender fully offsetting feedback mechanisms. Since restrictions of this kind do not directly cause resource reallocation and changes in relative real incomes through their effect upon the competitive ratio, the restrictions are quasi-adjustments. However, these quasi-adjustments are less likely to suffer from retaliatory offsets than their current-account equivalents. Not all restrictions on the export of capital owe their existence to balance-of-payments strains, and some policies biasing the direction of investment can, like tariffs and quotas, exist purely in the national interest.

Capital controls are considered in this chapter to consist of a bureaucratic screening device imposed upon a set of applications to export capital in any form. This device has its most direct application to planned direct investment but can be extended to portfolio investment quite simply. The flow of portfolio investment responds to measures affecting its rate of return, and is therefore amenable to control through taxation. Direct investment is relatively insensitive to short-run factors or to marginal changes in rates of return. Thus, in practice, tax measures tend to be applied to portfolio investments and quota-screening devices to direct investments.[1] Given some volume of funds available for total foreign investments in any single period, the tax rate under a joint system can be applied to portfolio investments in order that capital exports for these purposes will equal the volume of funds available. Deciding upon what proportion of total funds should be made available for portfolio investment must be a bureaucratic, screening decision. Thus, for analytic purposes, the whole process of capital controls can be looked upon as a system of screening applications to export capital.

[1] A screening device can be imposed by a formula which the investment project does or does not satisfy as well as by discretionary screening.

The case for imposing controls over international capital movements for balance-of-payments reasons is equivalent to that which argues for the restriction of investment in a closed economy. In a closed economy at full employment, saving governs investment so that, unless the authorities are prepared to vary the rate of saving, any excess of investment over full-employment saving must be siphoned off. Interest-rate and credit availability effects, fiscal disincentives and functional finance are the orthodox instruments in a free-enterprise society. Internationally, unless the authorities are prepared to vary the rate of international saving or sacrifice some domestic goal by means of a basic or quasi-adjustment, the flow of international investment must be delimited to the available flow of international saving if full balance is to be attained. To the extent that the flow of international investment is not sensitive to domestic instrument variables (or to the degree that the variables are needed for domestic purposes), capital controls are the only available instrument.[2]

Capital controls have one characteristic that radically distinguishes them from other quasi-adjustments or from a basic adjustment. Interference with the freedom of residents to exchange domestic currency for foreign assets at the official or going rate of exchange will tend to reduce international net worth below what it would otherwise have been. Other types of adjustment operate on the current account and tend to increase international saving. If the frustrated exports would have engendered concurrent saving, international saving is actually reduced by capital controls. Because a basic adjustment (or a quasi-adjustment operating on the goods and services balance) directly affects the rate of domestic absorption, it adjusts the rate of international saving to match planned international investment. There is one aspect of capital controls that can vary the rate of international saving. That aspect is the requirement that foreign subsidiaries repatriate to their parent corporations in the focus country some percentage of profits that is higher than traditional proportions, international saving can be increased in a cash-flow sense of the term.[3] If the requirement is merely that historic proportions be maintained, the controls prevent the

[2] Harry G. Johnson notes the need for capital controls under certain circumstances in 'Towards a General Theory', pp. 159–60.
[3] If the I.M.F. procedure whereby all subsidiary profits are included in investment income receipts is followed, no increase in international saving is achieved: see Ch. 4, fn. 10.

substitution of a reduction in the rate of repatriation for an enforced curtailment of capital exports. Measures affecting foreign subsidiary behaviour are likely to prove unpopular with host governments and are, therefore, vulnerable to retaliation.

This chapter has two sections. The first develops a criterion by which the authorities in the focus nation can, given perfect knowledge, both decide upon the total allocation of funds for capital exports and apportion those funds among competing applications. The second section considers the implication of the system of controls for the flow parameters of the aggregate model. Throughout this chapter it is assumed that direct investments are only permitted by the host country if they are deemed beneficial, so that the responsibility of the authorities in the investing nation is limited to considerations of self-interest. It is also assumed that investment income cannot be usefully increased by fiat but that some means of preventing the substitution of retained profits for frustrated capital exports can be put into force.

A CRITERION

The purpose of imposing a set of capital controls is to reduce the net flow of international investment and thereby to reduce the *ex ante* deficit in the basic balance of payments. The degree to which foreign exchange will be husbanded is of paramount importance. At the same time, the general interest of the national economy presumably benefits from having its free choice interfered with as little as possible for balance-of-payments reasons. A straightforward criterion for a system of capital controls is, therefore, the maximisation of foreign-exchange saving per dollar of capital export frustrated.[4] Conceptually such a criterion would require that all applications for capital export be ranked in order of their rate of concurrent induced saving (a_j). Those with the lowest leakage rates would be approved. Some cut-off rate of concurrent saving would be determined from the combination of applications and leakage rates and from the volume of foreign exchange available in the target balance for international investment.

[4] In what follows, the real cost of administering and setting up a system of controls is not considered. This does not mean that in the decision of what package of balance-of-payments policies to use, real cost elements should not be seriously considered and means that a *new* system of capital controls would be reckoned as a costly quasi-adjustment.

This criterion would not offer any indication of what was the optimal rate of foreign investment.

The difficulties of measuring concurrent induced saving rates both in advance and after the fact, are well known. It would be possible for the authorities to impose a rough-and-ready control device that would rely upon the argument that different categories of capital export have quite different rates of concurrent saving and that the control device would distinguish among applications on the basis of this general relationship. Portfolio and equity investments and monetary transactions would have the smallest rates of concurrent saving and would be very severely restricted. Direct investments in developing nations would be allowed to go unhindered because of their high feedback rate, but direct investments in rich nations would only be permitted when they promised particularly high rates of concurrent saving.[5]

But, even if the leakage rate for each investment project were known in advance, such a simple criterion would neglect two important aspects of the problem. The first aspect is the time period over which the concurrent saving rate is to be computed. The second dimension that should be considered is the general interest of the focus nation. A quasi-adjustment is a national policy and is one of the arsenal of instrument variables that can be involved in the maximisation of the national interest. As such, a screening device should take the national interest explicitly into account and could, within limits, discriminate among projects by their conformity with national goals as well as by their cash-flow attributes.

The normal basis for computing a rate of concurrent saving is the accounting period for the balance of payments and is ordinarily one year. This was the explicit assumption made in the previous chapter about the timing of induced saving flows after the investment has been made. If there is a target date for the eradication of the deficit (other than the actual accounting period), then it is the target period that should serve as the basis for computation of concurrent saving rates. It is quite possible that the purpose of the quasi-adjustment is to reduce a payments deficit rather than to eliminate it immediately, and the target date for payments balance is some years into the future. Such a policy would follow if the tactic were to adapt gradually to a real disturbance. If the target date for the elimination of the deficit

---

[5] The distinction between developed and developing nations as hosts was a feature of the Foreign Direct Investment Program in the United States in 1968.

were, say, three years into the future, then all saving generated within the three-year period would be considered as concurrent. The ranking of projects could well change drastically as a result of the new definition of 'concurrent' and it is quite possible that certain projects would have rates of concurrent saving in excess of 100 per cent.

In addition to the complication of the saving-rate criterion that follows from a multi-year horizon, the possible interdependence of export sales of commodities and credit terms can affect both the meaning of concurrent saving and the validity of the rough-and-ready device. When a loan is made to a foreigner in order to facilitate a current export, the transactions must be allowed to be freely negotiated. Usually international trade credit of this kind will be categorised as monetary flows and will not be included in the concept of international investment. But the term or maturity of trade credit can exceed the short-run and, in such cases, this type of portfolio investment should be considered to have a very high rate of what is a variant of concurrent saving. In this way, some essentially portfolio transactions must take a high priority.

The interdependence of capital controls and national goals should allow for the simple saving-rate criterion to be amended so that projects that run counter to national goals in a political or qualitative sense are discriminated against, and so that there is a bias in favour of projects that reinforce those goals.[6] These distinctions might be made on the basis of the identity or the level of development of the host country or upon the type of industry involved – a highly cartelised industry being less acceptable than a more competitive industry and an investment that supplements domestic shortages would be preferable to one that threatens domestic employment levels in a specialised industry or in a concentrated geographical area.

The final emendation to the simple criterion is the need to consider the purely economic objectives of national policy. The simple criterion has a superficial suitability for balance-of-payments considerations because it emphasises cash-flow concepts. Such a policy puts emphasis upon the speed with which funds are generated and repatriated to the focus nation. This emphasis might conflict with the longer-run national interest. The use of cash-flows as the unique determinant of a capital-rationing device will be similar in its effect to the use of the (inverse of) capital intensity in an invest-

[6] See Tinbergen, *On the Theory of Economic Policy*, p. 2, for a definition of 'qualitative'.

ment criterion in a developing nation. The capital-intensity criterion does not generate an optimal strategy because it puts too much emphasis upon the capital-turnover rate.[7]

The distinction between the long-run and short-run benefits that will accrue from an export of capital can be analysed together with the distinction drawn between the incremental and organic approaches to the theory of foreign investment. Implicit in a straightforward criterion based on concurrent saving rates is the assumption that the rate of return on existing foreign assets and the demand for the exports of the focus country are independent of any reduction in the rate of international investment. This assumption underlies both the *Reddaway* and the *Hufbauer-Adler Reports* and is called the incremental approach. It rests upon the belief that any investment is merely a separable addition to the previous stock of assets and that, if capital exports were reduced, the nation (and the company) would sacrifice only the earnings of the frustrated capital export (less any return on domestic utilisation). Provided that the analysis is concerned only with temporary and small or marginal reductions in the flow of international investment or that the capital controls merely switch subsidiary financing from sources in the investing to sources in the host nation, the assumption is legitimate. In contrast, there is a body of opinion that stresses the interdependence of the profitability of existing foreign assets and the continuing flow of funds from parent to subsidiary – the organic approach.[8] The relevance of this theory is presumably limited to subsidiaries producing or marketing differentiated goods in a foreign, oligopolistic setting. The long-run (and, *in extremis*, the short-run) profitability of extant subsidiaries may require additional infusions of capital to preserve their market share against innovations of competing firms. This need for the international corporation to be able to succour ailing or threatened subsidiaries is probably limited to young firms, except in very unusual circumstances.[9] Mature subsidiaries, except for the possibility that the proportionate rate of repatriation of profits cannot be reduced and the potential rate of reinvestment of earnings increased, will ordinarily be immune to capital controls. If the organic concept of

[7] Alfred E. Kahn, 'Investment Criteria in Development Programs', *Quarterly Journal of Economics* (February 1951) pp. 38–61.

[8] This approach was originally expounded in Judd Polk *et al.*, *U.S. Production Abroad and the Balance of Payments* (New York: National Industrial Conference Board, 1966) pp. 132–6.

[9] See Richardson, *Western Economic Journal* (March 1971).

the theory of the international firm is accepted, a particular investment could have a very high rate of concurrent saving since the return would be equal to the sum of any concurrent exports of capital goods or of services and the differences in the subsidiary's (repatriated) profit when the investment was and was not made. If the failure to make an investment lowered the rate of return obtained on existing assets, the decline in the absolute profit would be an element in concurrent saving attributable to the investment.

The organic approach can apply to the creation or to the expansion of both sales and manufacturing subsidiaries concerned with differentiated goods. The sales organisation might be necessary to preserve a market share obtained by a distribution network of local agents, and the manufacturing subsidiary might be necessary to counter competitive investments and to enable an existing sales subsidiary to maintain its market share. The relevance of the approach is likely to be limited to subsidiaries in developed nations The incremental approach will apply almost without reservation to investments in non-competitive goods and in production facilities for competitive goods designed to serve markets in the investing nation.

The criterion for an efficient screening device will, ideally, combine the organic and incremental approaches by assessing the desirability of an investment through its effect upon the nation's international net worth. This can be done by determining the expected present value for the future stock of international assets at some appropriate rate of discount. In this way, any deterioration in the competitive position of a subsidiary in an oligopolistic market as a result of inability to transfer capital could be included in the criterion. A more useful way in which to express the criterion is by a series of internal rates of return for different capital exports.[10] The criterion must also allow for the effects of any concurrent or future change in the demand for a nation's exports as well as considering the domestic social costs of diverting resources to foreign nations.

The problem can be posed in the following way: assuming that the authorities have decided upon a set of policies that will determine

[10] This analysis differs from that given by Peter H. Lindert, 'The Payments Impact of Foreign Investment Controls', *Journal of Finance* (December 1971) pp. 1083–99, mainly in that it distinguishes between returns on capital and increased demand for exports and considers the marginal cost of financing rather than some unchanging average cost. However, the approach here was helped by Lindert's insights.

the flow of autonomous international saving and face an *ex ante* deficit, should capital controls be imposed and, if so, how stringently and how should the authorities discriminate among competing applications?

The criterion will authorise those capital exports that are deemed beneficial to the investing nation. Thus, the internal rate of return on the project must exceed some measure of national cost. If all projects were to be ranked by their private internal rates of return, it would be possible to create a schedule of national investment opportunities as a function of the internal rate of return. A cut-off point would therefore allow the highly profitable investments to take place. However, in addition to the private rate of return, it is also necessary to compute a social rate of return that will allow for any balance-of-payments effects (other than investment income) that the individual projects may generate. Against this schedule of estimated social rates of return, there is a cost schedule.

Figure 8-1 shows schematically how a system of capital controls would work under conditions of full knowledge. This idealised system can also be used to indicate the criterion for using capital controls as a quasi-adjustment, how to separate socially worthwhile from extra-marginal investment projects and how to allocate the funding of international investment between international saving and reserve reduction.

Illiquid foreign assets can be acquired either through international saving or through a reduction of the net liquid reserve position. Each of these methods involves a cost. The cost of foreign investment achieved without impairment of the reserve position is the opportunity cost of the resources required to generate the appropriate flow of international saving. The cost will increase with the flow of international investment because of the diminishing marginal efficiency of domestic investment and because of the increasingly adverse terms of trade needed to generate the larger flow of international saving. Thus, provided the authorities are willing and able to effect an adjustment and to increase the rate of international saving, the opportunity cost schedule will be similar to that shown by the schedule SS' in the figure. When the flow of international saving cannot be increased, either through unwillingness on the part of the authorities or some institutional rigidities, the schedule becomes inelastic at the specified flow of international saving. Similarly when a reversing disturbance takes place, the opportunity cost of

158   *The Aggregate Theory*

increasing international saving for a single period or small number
of periods becomes quite high as a result of the imputed real costs of
the double adjustment. The opportunity cost will be very inelastic,
and a very high rate of return to international saving will have to be
generated before those costs will be incurred. These conditions are
shown by the opportunity cost schedule *SFS''*.

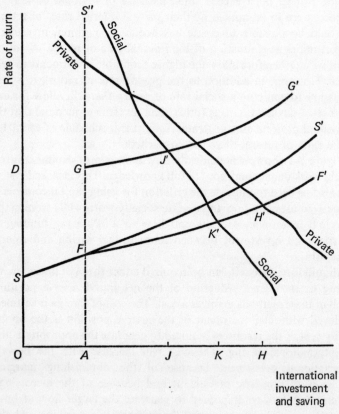

FIGURE 8-1

Capital Controls Criterion

Note: The investment project shown where the two rate of return schedules
intersect has, on balance, no international effect.

The cost of international investment achieved by a reduction in the
national net reserve position is the sum of the actual cost of borrowing funds abroad (the notional financing charge in the *Reddaway*

Report) and the disutility incurred as a result of the reduction in the net liquid reserve position. The financing cost comprises the combination of these two costs. Both the borrowing costs and the 'illiquidity premium' can be deemed measurable in terms of a rate of return per unit change in net reserves,[11] and this cost will presumably be minimised by the authorities by the correct mixture of asset reduction and liability increase. The financing cost will increase with the rate of reduction of net reserves. The actual cost will depend upon the cost of borrowing and the size of the illiquidity premium. The latter will depend upon the difference between the actual net liquid reserve position of the focus country and some position that is considered a target by the national authorities. The cost of borrowing will depend upon foreign interest rates, foreign assessments of the ultimate strength of the currency, upon the existing institutional arrangements and on the strategy of the authorities of the focus country. The financing cost is shown by FF' in the figure.

The total cost schedule is SFF' which comprises international saving until the opportunity cost equals the minimum financing cost (AF). Any additional international investment will be achieved through a reduction in the net reserve position.

The demand for international investment is represented by the schedules of private and social internal rates of return. The social internal rate of return schedule is derived from the private schedule by allowing for the balance-of-payments effects of the individual projects and reranking them where necessary. These balance-of-payments effects will be affected by the cost of foreign exchange since the larger is the premium that attaches to foreign exchange (either through the illiquidity premium or the terms-of-trade effect of increased international saving), the greater is the value to be attributed to any induced saving.[12] Except for those projects for which the discounted present value of induced saving equals the capital export, the social internal rate of return will be less than the private internal rate of return. Thus the social internal rate of return schedule will be below the private rate of return schedule because corporations will not take the externalities of balance-of-payments effects into their private calculations. Variations in the rate of

[11] The illiquidity premium is similar to a concept developed by Grubel in 'The Optimum Stability of Exchange Rates'.
[12] The greater is the cost of financing, the bigger the gap between the social and private internal rate of return schedules.

induced saving among investment projects is only one factor affecting the social desirability of the project and can be outweighed by variation in expected profitability.

In an unconstrained world in which basic adjustments can be made freely, international investment will equal *OH*. This will be funded by international saving of *OA* and reserve reduction of *AH*. Optimal policy would allow for international investment of only *OK* but the bureaucratic cost of inefficiency is considered greater than the social good that would derive from the restriction of capital outflows. Because some of the international investment has been funded by reserve reduction, the financing cost will increase in the subsequent period. As *FF'* shifts upward with reductions in the net reserve position, international investment can only be funded by international saving since continued financing of international investment must inevitably encounter the absolute constraint. If the cost of financing were equal to *OD*, the utility derived from an increase in the reserve position exceeds the opportunity cost of international saving, and basic adjustments will be made to allow full balance to exist with a positive increase in reserves as well as unconstrained investment.

When the flow of international saving cannot be easily adjusted and the opportunity cost schedule is *SFS''* and if the cost of financing exceeds the inefficiencies attendant upon capital controls, capital controls will be instituted. Under these circumstances, the total cost schedule would be *SFGG'*, international investment would be *OJ* and only those projects with a social rate of return greater than *JJ'* would be authorised. The *GG'* schedule would shift upward in the ensuing period and, in the absence of any change in the flow of international saving, the capital controls would become even more severe. In this way, projects that are clearly profitable are precluded by the capital controls because of the rigidities in the system of international adjustment.

THE IMPLICATIONS FOR THE FLOW MODEL

The existence of a system of capital controls must, if the controls constitute an effective force, affect the composition and the magnitude of the flow of international investment. The influence of the capital controls on the flow model can best be considered in relation to the flows that would have taken place in the absence of any capital controls, but given some package of balance-of-payments policies that would increase the rate of international saving and produce full balance. There are three aspects that deserve consideration: (1) the sensitivity of the optimum flow of international investment to the institutional arrangements that exist and to the degree to which the authorities in the investing nation are prepared to make use of any channels available to finance deficits; (2) the interrelationship between the effectiveness of capital controls and the length of time that they have been in force; and (3) the discriminatory impact of controls and their influence upon the parameters of the model.

(1) The optimum flow of capital exports is sensitive not only to such exogenously determined factors as private and social internal rates of return but also to the value of the illiquidity premium and the marginal borrowing costs. These costs are directly influenced by the national general interest function and by the institutional arrangements that exist. The illiquidity premium will depend upon the availability of international credit from international institutions and through pre-arranged international agreements as well as upon actual international reserve positions. The marginal borrowing cost depends upon whether or not the authorities can and will float loans abroad, whether there is a built-in tendency for financing to take place automatically or whether any financing must be achieved by attracting funds into the domestic capital market from abroad by raising the spectrum of interest rates in the investing country.

If the authorities are prepared and able to negotiate loans of foreign exchange, whether they be denominated in domestic or foreign currency and presumably of a maturity that exceeds the expected period of strain on international payments, then the supply of foreign exchange is likely to be quite elastic to the cost of funds. It is true that the supply schedule of funds obtained by these means will slope upward or will shift upward in discrete steps as functions of both the reserve position of the nation or of the rate at which the foreign exchange needs to be acquired. But, foreign exchange obtained in this way will not be subject to the very high marginal cost that funds obtained through market forces can incur.[13]

It is possible that financing will be acquired without any positive action on the part of the authorities in the investing nation. Such an occurrence would result either from a deliberate policy of 'counter-investment' by the authorities in the host nation or because of

[13] See Thomas D. Willett, 'Official Versus Market Financing of International Deficits', *Kyklos* (Fasc. 3, 1968) pp. 514–23.

institutional arrangements. A strategy of counter-investment is worthy of consideration by host-nation authorities because the policy deliberately tempers any reduction in international net worth that follows from the establishment of a subsidiary enterprise in or a portfolio inflow into the nation. Counter-investment requires that funds that are transmitted to the host nation – that is the investment less any concurrent induced saving – be neutralised by the domestic authorities and the funds reinvested abroad. In this way, foreign-exchange earnings are generated to be set against the potential out-flow of dividends and interest that result from the original investment. Financing by liquid claims can occur almost automatically if the investing country is a key-currency nation. However, there is a clear danger in relying upon a process that involves lending long and borrowing short, and one example of this dangerous policy culmi-nated in the demise of the Bretton Woods era in August 1971 (see Chapter 11). While it has been assumed that host governments did not oppose the foreign investments (or they would have denied their entry), there are varying degrees of enthusiasm with which foreign investments are welcomed and the degree of enthusiasm may affect the willingness of the authorities in the host nation to temper the burden of financing. To the extent that capital controls discriminate against portfolio and equity investment outflows and in favour of direct investments with high rates of concurrent saving, and to the extent that direct investments arouse antagonism in some host countries, the imposition of capital controls could contain self-defeating elements.

(2) As with all quasi-adjustments, the effectiveness of capital controls can be expected to diminish over time. Any arbitrary screening device and system of prohibitions will contain short-comings or loopholes that permit the regulations to be evaded. The greater is the familiarity with the system, the greater are illicit capital exports likely to be. One obvious means of circumvention is to keep the repatriation of funds to some minimum rate required so that a pool of assets is developed abroad. Another means of evading the restrictions would be to transfer funds from subsidiaries in less developed nations (or some other preferred area) to subsidiaries located in developed nations. To the extent that the ease of circum-vention is greater for firms with subsidiaries located in several different nations, the growth of the multinational corporation as an organisational form may weaken the effectiveness of capital controls.

These weaknesses in capital control programmes are self-evident and are compatible with the avowed purpose of quasi-adjustments to temper the speed of (basic) adjustment and to avoid unnecessary reversible adjustments in the face of temporary disturbances. But it is possible that capital controls suffer from an additional weakness that relates directly to the brevity of their effectiveness or imposition. It may well be that the release of the capital control programme will lead to a surge of capital exports as corporations strive to re-establish optimal portfolios and debt–equity ratios.

(3) Capital controls can be expected to reduce the total outflow of international investment and, in the process, will tend to discriminate most strongly against portfolio and equity investments. At the same time that the flow of international investment is constrained, the average rate of concurrent saving (k) will be increased. This will be accomplished in two ways. Firms wishing to export capital will be discouraged from applying for foreign exchange when funds are available from foreign sources. This bias will lower the ratio of funds exported to the asset value of the subsidiary. Given that the ratio of concurrent induced saving to asset values is independent of the source of financing, the ratio of concurrent saving to international investment will be increased. Secondly, the screening process will contain a bias toward projects with higher rates of concurrent saving. This bias is a function of the illiquidity premium and the marginal cost of financing. If the disturbance to be countered by a quasi-adjustment is a short-lived one, the authorities are likely to impose, arbitrarily, a high liquidity premium and to make the bias quite significant.

It is possible for a capital control programme to overemphasise the illiquidity premium and, effectively, to make the screening device equivalent to a saving-rate criterion. Such policies could damage existing foreign subsidiaries and, through them, the general interest. There is, however, no *a priori* reason why the administration of capital controls should be inept.

9 The Aggregate Theory Summarised

The model presented piecemeal in the preceding eight chapters will be more easily comprehended if the functional relationships and the conditions necessary for payments balance are assimilated into a formal, *ex post*, flow model. However, the creation of such a model with its apparent generation of steady-state solutions runs the danger of de-emphasising the inevitability of period-to-period variation in the flows. This potential variability in the flows is fundamental to the theory. Professor Joan Robinson has pointed out the damage done to Keynes' concepts by formal models:[1]

> Out of [the complete collapse of the market economy in the thirties] emerged what has become known as the Keynesian revolution. After the war, Keynes became orthodox in his turn. Unfortunately, the Keynesian orthodoxy, as it became established, left out the point . . . Consider what was the point of the Keynesian revolution on the plane of theory and on the plane of policy. On the plane of theory, the main point of the General Theory was to break out of the cocoon of equilibrium and consider the nature of life lived in time – the difference between yesterday and tomorrow. Here and now, the past is irrevocable and the future is unknown.
>
> This was too great a shock. Orthodoxy managed to wind it up in a cocoon again.
>
> The very essence of the problem was uncertainty. . . . In the new macro–micro theory, this point is lost. By one simple device, the whole of Keynes' argument is put to sleep. Work out what saving would be at full employment in the present short-period situation, with the present distribution of wealth and the present hierarchy of rates of earnings for different occupations, and arrange to have enough investment to absorb the level of saving that this distribution of income brings about. Then hey presto! We are back in the world of equilibrium where saving governs investment and micro theory can clip into the old grooves again.

[1] Robinson, *The American Economic Review* (May 1972) pp. 3–4.

Translate the terms from Keynes' domestic model to the international frame of reference, and the indictment of current orthodoxy serves as a burning *caveat* against the dangers of interpreting the flow model that follows as anything more than a simple expository device.

The assumptions are delineated first. Then follows the set of *ex post* relationships that comprise the model in the absence of quasi-adjustments. Quasi-adjustments and the simple mechanics of period-to-period changes are integrated into the *ex post* relationships; and the final section briefly reviews the implications of the model for balance-of-payments policy and anticipates the concluding part of the study.

THE BASIC ASSUMPTIONS

Some assumptions involve the simplification of behavioural macro-economic relationships and these are given in the following sections. The fundamental assumptions are:

1. The world consists of a focus country and 'the rest of the world'.
2. The discrete timing sequences of changes appropriate to period analysis does not affect the validity of the model.
3. Both countries have defined balance-of-payments targets for any given period. These targets reflect both the options considered feasible by the authorities and existing national tastes, institutional framework and resource endowments. All variables are subject to change between periods.
4. The primary national target is a given trade-off between unemployment and inflation. The balance-of-payments target is subservient to that goal subject to the realisation that a nation must 'pay its way' over a period of years or suffer severe dislocation of its economy. Price levels in the domestic economy do not change within a single period.
5. Factors of production are mobile internationally. The international movements of labour and technology are deemed to affect the resource endowments and growth rates and biases of nations as data-effects but have no direct impact upon the balance of payments. Flows of migrants remittances and royalties are generated by 'stocks' and not by current flows of factor migration and technological transfer and consequently, are included in the payments data as 'flow transfers'. Changes

in the flows are considered data effects. Capital movements and stock unilateral transfers do have direct balance-of-payments implications in addition to their effects upon growth.

6. Any transfer is undereffected.

7. An increase in a nation's competitive ratio will improve its balance of trade and its balance on current account, assuming appropriate expenditure switching policies are put into effect. The full effect of an improvement in the competitive ratio is spread over several periods.

8. An increase in the competitive ratio made to reduce a basic deficit will reduce the real income of the nation through an adverse shift in the net barter terms of trade, *ceteris paribus*.

9. An increase in international saving will reduce the potential rate of domestic absorption.

10. A depreciation of the national currency or a change in the domestic price level will not be so affected by changes in relative prices that it can have a perverse effect on the relationship between the competitive ratio and the trade balance.

11. Capital account and transfer debits incurred by the central government are rationally determined and are seen as an element of overall foreign policy. As such, these expenditures are seen as givens to which balance-of-payments flows must adjust and are not considered sensitive to policy variables. However, current account debits on government account are subject to the effects of quasi-adjustments.[2]

12. Autonomous monetary flows made in order to acquire foreign currencies or foreign short-term assets are excluded from the model.

THE FUNDAMENTAL RELATIONSHIPS

The condition for fully balanced payments is that, *ex post*, actual acquisitions of international assets shall be equal to the actual, autonomous change in international net worth over the prescribed period of time without either the imposition of quasi-adjustments or the sacrifice of domestic goals.

$$I_I^* + \Delta R^* = S_I^* \qquad (9\text{-}1)$$

[2] See, for example, Harry G. Johnson, 'An Overview of Price Levels, Employment and the Balance of Payments', *Journal of Business* (July 1963) pp. 279–89.

where asterisks denote the value of the flows that will occur in the absence of special policy measures, where I, S, R^* and the subscript I all have the meanings ascribed to them in equation (4-1) (see p. 65).

While it is most simple to assume that ΔR^* is equal to zero, there is no reason to expect this to be so in the normal state of events. Each nation will have some concept of what it considers to be an appropriate reserve position and will have some actual stock of net reserves. Any discrepancy between these two quantities will lead to some desired change in reserves which will affect the overall balance-of-payments target. A decision deliberately to reduce reserves in order to finance an expected deficit may be a legitimate policy but it is not a position of full balance. For expositional ease, it is assumed that ΔR^* is zero for the rest of this chapter so that basic balance is consonant with full balance.

International investment comprises three different flows, each of which can constitute both an inflow and an outflow in any single period. It is assumed that capital only flows out of the focus country. Each of the three types of capital has a different set of determinants which are not necessarily steady flows through time for any given set of values for instrument variables and the two categories of private investment are subject to the disturbing effects of changes in investor expectations (see Chapter 6). In the absence of capital controls of some form, the variability of the component flows of international investment is such that the total flow must be seen as a given in any single period.

$$I_I^* = I_{I0}^* \tag{9-2}$$

Under conditions compatible with full balance, the left-hand side of equation (9-1) is determined independently of payments policies – foreign policy, planned acquisition of foreign assets by the private sector and national reserve policy are all independent of the usual instrument variables. If full balance is to exist, the flow of international saving must be capable of adjustment.

The determinants of international saving are numerous. Like international investment it is the sum of several distinct flows. For simplicity it is assumed that the flow of stock transfers and the rate of concurrent induced saving out of those transfers are given.[3] This

[3] It may prove useful to distinguish between net and gross international saving. Gross international saving is the difference between net domestic product and absorption. Net international saving is gross saving less net transfer outpayments. This distinction permits the expansionary effects of the balance on

assumption is necessary if the relationship between the flow of autonomous saving and the competitive position is to be assumed to be given. International saving is defined as the change in international net worth achieved during a period. It consists of the sum of feedback or concurrent saving (S_F), inherited saving (S_W) and autonomous saving (S_A). While the effect on exports and imports of goods and services of existing foreign subsidiaries should be included in S_W, it is clearer if S_W is limited to net receipts of dividends, interest and related fees and royalties and if the trade effects of foreign subsidiaries are included in autonomous saving.

$$S_I^* = S_F^* + S_W^* + S_A^* = k.I_{I0} + y.(INW) + S_T^* \qquad (9\text{-}3)$$

where y is the average yield of investment income (broadly defined) on international net worth (INW) and S_T is autonomous saving on goods and services. As before, k is the average rate of concurrent induced saving on capital exports.

If payments are measured in domestic currency, all three flows will respond positively to changes in the competitive position: the concurrent saving through $\partial k/\partial C > 0$; investment income will contain some proportion that is defined in foreign currency; and S_T^* responds positively to changes in C by definition. Inherited and autonomous saving can be jointly expressed as a simple linear function of the competitive ratio:

$$S_W^* + S_A^* = A(C_P - C_C^*) \qquad (9\text{-}4)$$

where A is measured in currency units per unit change in either competitive ratio.

The condition for full balance can be expressed quite simply by recasting equation (9-3) and, assuming $\partial k/\partial C = 0$, by setting $S_I^* = I_{I0}^*$.

$$I_{I0}^* = k.I_{I0}^* + A(C_P - C_C^*) \qquad (9\text{-}5)$$

Full balance exists when C_B^* is equal to C_P where C_B^* is the value of the competitive ratio that is necessary for full balance to obtain. If international investment is equal to zero, then full balance will

---

goods and services to be seen separately from the balance on current account which measures net international saving. Gross international saving includes the concurrent saving and dissaving induced by unilateral transfers. The distinction is made in my 'A Keynesian Framework for the International Accounts', *Weltwirtschaftliches Archiv*, Band 103, Heft 1, pp. 10–11. All references in the text refer to net international saving.

obtain when $C_P = C_C^*$. The increase in C necessary to offset a given capital outflow is a function of both k and A. Setting $C_P = C_B^*$,

$$C_B^* - C_C^* = I_{I0}^* \cdot \frac{(1-k)}{A} \qquad (9\text{-}6)$$

A is an indicator of the sensitivity of the current balance to a basic adjustment and must be divided into the leakage from the investment to give the magnitude needed to requite a given flow of investment: the larger are A and k, the smaller is the depreciation required to offset any increase in the flow of international investment and the smaller is the terms-of-trade cost of a given (increase in the) flow of international investment.[4] Alternatively, the larger is k, the larger is the volume of investment that can be financed by a given flow of autonomous saving.

Note that if C_C^* exceeds C_P, autonomous and inherited saving are negative. While total international saving can be made positive by a sufficient volume of international investment and concurrent induced saving, balance can never be obtained without a target decrease in the stock of international reserves.

THE RELATIONSHIPS WITH QUASI-ADJUSTMENTS

Quasi-adjustments are substitutes for basic adjustments and are most clearly analysed in a situation of payments deficit and equation (9-5) can be recast in terms of an inequality. Assuming that the flow of international investment exceeds the (positive) sum of inherited and autonomous saving, $C_B^* > C_P > C_C^*$:

$$I_{I0}^* > k \cdot I_{I0}^* + A(C_P - C_C^*) \qquad (9\text{-}5a)$$

A quasi-adjustment will be signified by qualifying a variable or a coefficient with a prime and, necessarily, dropping the asterisk where applicable. Thus, I_{I0}' indicates the existence of a programme of capital controls. The authorities have three broad categories of quasi-adjustment to consider as alternatives to financing and to basic adjustment: capital controls, domestic deflation or barriers to trade.

The intent of capital controls, if zero financing is contemplated, is to reduce the leakage from foreign investment and to bring it into equality with the flow of autonomous saving. Capital controls

---

[4] The value of k for the marginal investment is assumed to equal its value for the average investment.

reduce C_B^* so that C_B' is equal to C_P. Capital controls can both reduce I_{I0} to I_I' and, at the same time, increase k to k'.

Domestic deflation will increase the flow of international saving by reducing the demand for imports. The social costs of such a policy are obvious. Assume that deflation of the focus country does not affect the level (or composition) of aggregate demand in the rest of the world and, therefore, does not reduce foreign demand for exports of the focus country. The quasi-adjustment of deflation seeks to reduce import demand by the excess of investment leakage over autonomous saving. Equations (9-6a) and (9-6b) show how payments balance can be reached by domestic deflation. In the equations, Y^* and Y' represent the values of full-employment and deflated national income respectively and m stands for the marginal propensity to import.

$$I_{I0}^* = k.I_{I0}^* + A(C_P - C_C^*) + m(Y^* - Y') \qquad (9\text{-}6a)$$

$$A(C_P - C_C^*) = I_{I0}^*.(1 - k) - m(Y^* - Y') \qquad (9\text{-}6b)$$

What has happened as a result of the domestic deflation is that C_C' has been reduced below C_C^*. The fact that the flow of international investment is presumably unaffected means that C_B' is reduced by the same amount as C_C' and C_B' is brought into equality with C_P. (Essentially, $(C_B^* - C_B') = (C_C^* - C_C')$.)

The final quasi-adjustment is an impediment to imports of current goods and services unmatched by offsetting measures by the rest of the world. This device attempts to reduce imports, increase autonomous international saving, by the same amount as was achieved by deflation in equation (9-6a): $m(Y^* - Y')$. The difference between impediments to trade and deflation is that impediments to trade attempt to reduce imports by substituting home goods for exports and therefore involve virtually no decrease in domestic absorption, while deflation attempts to reduce imports by reducing domestic absorption. The effect of both deflation and impediments is to reduce C_C' below C_C^* and in this way to reduce C_B'. This mechanism contrasts with that of capital controls which is to reduce C_B' without affecting C_C^*.

The conditions for balance set forth in equation (9-5) contain the seeds of their own destruction since current international investment will, except in very unusual circumstances, increase the flow of autonomous saving in subsequent years. Letting i stand for the effect of international investment in year t $({}_tI_I)$ on the balance on current account in later years and assuming i to be constant over time, it can be shown that the amount of international investment that can be made with the same C_B^* and, in the absence of data-effects, will increase annually.[5] Alternatively the currency can be appreciated slowly without reducing the flow of foreign investment.[6]

$$_{t+1}C_C^* = {}_tC_C^* - \frac{{}_tI_I}{A} \quad (i) \tag{9-7}$$

$$_{t+1}S_I^* = A(C_P - {}_{t+1}C_C^*) + k \cdot {}_{t+1}I_{I0}^* \tag{9-8}$$

Assuming k and C_P not to change from year to year, the increase in the flow of international investment needed in successive years to generate full payments balance, amounts to a multiple of the increase in autonomous and inherited saving:

$$_{t+1}I_I - {}_tI_I = \frac{1}{1-k}(i \cdot {}_tI_I) \tag{9-9}$$

THE CAST OF THE THEORY

Despite the tendency of the formal interrelations presented in the preceding two sections to suggest that balance is something of a natural state, the main distinguishing stamp of the aggregate theory is its emphasis on the probable instability of international payments flows over time. This emphasis is inherent in the use of a period analysis framework and derives from Johnson who, when he introduced stock decisions as an important category of international disturbances, set the stage for a disequilibrium theory of international payments adjustment.[7] The concept of stock disturbances was almost prerequisite to any introduction to the theory of balance of payments of autonomous international capital flows. Any body of analysis that claims relevance to real-world policy problems must countenance the disequilibrium characteristic of frequently shifting schedules that are represented in the aggregate theory by data-effects. While the sources of data-effects are not limited to capital-account transactions and to

[5] Note that $i \gtrless y$ depending on whether or not the effect of investment on the demand for exports and imports is positive or negative.

[6] This concept is clearly analogous to the original Harrodian growth model: R. F. Harrod, 'An Essay in Dynamic Theory', *Economic Journal* (March 1939) pp. 14–33.

[7] 'Towards a General Theory', pp. 158–60.

current-account transactions consequent upon them, and while the capital account and its repercussions do provide the most frequent causes of ongoing disturbances to the existing payments flows, growth effects and structural changes in trading conditions are important in their own right. Disturbances can also intrude from changes in government policies, from the monetary sector and from the greater interdependence among developed nations. In particular, the capital and transfer accounts and their repercussions are likely to be important sources of *temporary* fluctuations in the value of the competitive ratio needed for payments balance. This increased likelihood of reversing disturbances has important implications for the approach to the use of quasi-adjustments as legitimate policy measures and for the optimality of a system of freely-flexible rates of exchange even when the absence of destabilising speculation is assumed.

An important attribute of the aggregate theory is the possibility that the classical medicine can be overpowered by deliberate policy actions for quite long periods of time. The subservience of international payments considerations to the achievement of domestic goals, except in extreme circumstances, combines with the prevalence of disturbances in the international sector itself to let C_P and C_B^* lead almost independent existences. The classical medicine under a system of fixed rates of exchange relies essentially upon the existence of some sort of price–specie-flow mechanism – possibly implemented through or made more effective by income effects induced by changes in the trade balance – to equalise C_P and C_B^*. However, the classical medicine can be thwarted as C_P responds to changes in domestic price levels and C_B^* to the inevitable disturbances that stem from growth and shifts in other schedules. Under these conditions, any proposal for a system of fixed rates of exchange or for one in which exchange rates were changed only under duress, must be an exercise in Panglossian optimism.

One analytic approach that attempts to incorporate capital flows into the theory of balance-of-payments adjustment is Machlup's attempt to explain the United States payments deficit from 1950 to 1967 in terms of the transfer mechanism.[8] Machlup's diagnosis uses an implicit model that is not dissimilar to the aggregate theory. His hypothesis is that the transfer mechanism would ultimately work to

[8] Fritz Machlup, 'The Transfer Gap of the United States', Banca Nazionale del Lavoro *Quarterly Review* (September 1968) pp. 195–238.

eliminate the payments deficit but that it has been frustrated by the authorities' overridding concern with domestic goals. Machlup contrasts what he calls the 'net real transfer' (the balance on goods and services) with the 'net financial transfer' consisting of net unilateral transfers including investment income plus net long-term investments. If the transfer mechanism works, an excess of financial over real transfers will eliminate itself. In fact, Machlup is relying upon the classical medicine rather than on the transfer mechanism by allowing the terms of trade to change and to supplement the international saving induced by the international investment flows. There is a question of doctrinal accuracy in applying transfer theory to that period since the transfer problem, as usually defined, is concerned directly with the need to adjust or not to adjust the net barter terms of trade in response to some constant flow of transfers in an equilibrium frame of reference. Using a simple regression of real upon financial transfers (in the same year), Machlup finds that the rate of offset is 80 per cent or more. From this he argues that to restrain financial transfers will not prove to be an effective means of eliminating payments imbalance. No role is assigned, except indirectly, to changes in competitiveness or to trend or to shift disturbances and the analysis does not distinguish between the different kinds of transfer in so far as differences in their rate of concurrent induced saving is concerned. Since the composition of the flow of financial transfers varies considerably over the period, this is a serious shortcoming.[9] In his interpretation of his findings, Machlup makes two pertinent observations: (1) that the authorities seem to have as their prime objective that target variable that has been least successfully pursued in the recent past; and (2) that a rich nation should expect to have positive net financial transfers that will amount to about 1.4 or 1.5 per cent of gross national product. Machlup prescribes a small depreciation of the U.S. dollar.

Machlup's prescription of a basic adjustment implies that the foreign investments are socially desirable and are therefore integrated in some overall – domestic and international – set of policy goals. Provided that the host country does welcome the foreign investments, this assumption would seem to require qualification only to the effect that investment without an offsetting transmission of real resources is not likely to provide as much assistance to the host nation as it might envisage and that an awareness of the transitional costs of

---

[9] *Ibid.*, p. 225.

adjustment requires investing nations to consider the costs of any irregularity in the outflow of capital. The first qualification requires that international saving be equal to international investment and the second that adjustments should be kept to a minimum and should be performed gradually. These concepts should influence authorities in their conduct of international economic policy.

In addition to laying stress upon the need to integrate domestic and international goals in a general macropolicy stance, the aggregate theory has several implications for policy, namely that:

(1) Disturbances can occur frequently and can have a cumulative effect.

(2) National policy towards payments balance should be positive and anticipatory rather than passive. Thus forecasts of shortrun payments problems and distinguishing different categories of disturbance so that some trends in C_B^* which can be determined are fruitful areas for research.

(3) The automatic adjustment mechanism is no longer reliable, so that C_P and C_B^* can diverge for quite long periods of time.

(4) Transitional costs of adjustment require greater recognition of the possibility of reversing disturbances, broaden the range of legitimate policy instruments and emphasise the desirability of gradual adjustments.

(5) The optimum institutional framework for payments adjustment will depend upon the weighted frequency of different types of disturbances and upon the intelligence and skill with which the economic authorities conduct a discretionary or interventionist payments policy.[10]

(6) Non-zero basic balances are legitimate short-run national targets so that the possibility exists of a mercantilistic incompatibility of international targets and the frustration of unilateral interventionist payments policy.

[10] If intelligent intervention by the different national authorities, supplemented by adequate financing, is a pragmatic solution to the problem of adjustment in international payments positions, the 'Keynes of it all' is clearly visible, albeit chronologically inverted. The aggregate theory has taken the conceptual approach of *The General Theory*, has applied it to the model in *The Treatise* and has derived a policy solution conceived originally in *The Tract*.

Part Three

The Implications for the Institutional Setting

10 Target Compatibility and International Co-operation

The aggregate theory of international payments adjustment allows for the possibility that nations will deliberately strive to have non-zero basic balances. The concept of a payments goal that is either positive or negative can derive from the desire of a nation to finance a deficit considered temporary or to avoid adjustment in the face of a surplus that will not last. Another reason for having a non-zero payments target is that national authorities are deliberately using the international sector to help in the achievement of domestic, macroeconomic goals (see Chapter 4, pp. 64–8). The short-run theory requires that nations be prepared to adjust their balance-of-payments policies to meet many different kinds of disturbance – real or monetary and shift, trend or reversing – of varying magnitudes at irregular intervals. National authorities will be always trying to reconcile any differences between forecast and target international balances.

In a world prone to trend and shift disturbances and in which the classical medicine is not allowed to work effectively, a regime of fixed rates of exchange would not be an efficient system for the resolution of payments imbalances. Such a system would merely cover up the imbalances by facilitating the financing of the debits, until national concern with the international net worth induced a crisis. At the opposite extreme, a world of freely-flexible rates of exchange, while it would ensure adjustment, would not be completely efficient because of the continuous and continuing equality of international investment and saving, in the absence of any disturbances originating in the monetary account. This could involve an excessive amount of adjustment by the productive sectors of trading economies. There remains some system of controlled adjustment whereby governments effect adjustments as the efficient functioning of the system requires.

Governments do not have sole control over their balance of payments. International instruments (except for capital controls) involve changes in ratios (relative prices or exchange rates) of which only one element is under the control of the authorities, or they involve impositions of commercial policies of absolute magnitudes which can be counteracted by trading partners. Thus the success of a balance-of-payments policy depends upon a passive reaction by trading partner nations. The clearest example of this interdependence of instruments is the phenomenon of offsetting devaluations of national currencies precluding depreciation and restoring the *status quo ante*. International interdependence of instrument variables derives from an incompatibility of short-run targets.

If the inefficiencies of a system of freely-flexible rates of exchange are not to be surpassed by the inefficiencies of a system of discretionary adjustment, mutual offsetting of policies must be avoided, and this can only be done if international targets are compatible.

The task of this chapter is to conceive of an institutional system that will both permit the policy flexibility needed by a disequilibrium system and will eliminate the possibility of abortive attempts at adjustment. Chapter 11 will examine briefly the institutional monetary arrangements that would be necessary to enable the system to avoid disturbances originating in the monetary balance and affecting the real sectors.

THE LIKELIHOOD OF TARGET INCOMPATIBILITY

If national payments targets are not mutually compatible, there exists at the present time no set of political–economic institutions through which the incompatibility can be eliminated. Any target incompatibility can seriously impair the ability of national economic authorities to achieve their quantitative goals – domestic as well as international. In fact, the argument could be made that there is little scope remaining for improving the sheer mechanical efficiency of domestic macrostabilisation techniques because twenty-five years experience has garnered most of the spectacular accomplishments possible in that area. However, precisely because so little has been accomplished in the elimination of rigidities in the international payments system, international co-operation with regard to potential payments imbalances could yield substantial improvements in the technical efficiency of macropolicy instruments.

In the world economy there exists a series of constraints on international payments targets. Because each international transaction involves both a paying and a receiving country, the sum of national balances for any single category of transaction must be zero – accounting discrepancies aside. The implications of these constraints on the goods and services account and the transfer and capital accounts are very important for the efficiency of national policies. No nation can aim at achieving a surplus on goods and services account on a continuing basis unless the rest of the world is prepared to accept – as a target – a deficit of the same size. This is merely another way of saying that the world as a whole cannot export unemployment. Equally no nation can maintain a surplus on current account (save internationally) unless some nation is prepared to indulge in international *dis*saving by the same amount. The inexorability of these constraints requires that nations have compatible goals reached through serendipity or negotiation, that they fail to achieve their international targets, or that they indulge in mutually-frustrating international policies.

One aspect of incompatible targets has been the concern of economists for a long time. The system of adjustment that imposes the major part of the burden of adjustment on the deficit nation rather than on the family of surplus and deficit nations, has tended to give a deflationary bias to the world economy. This awareness of the need for a multinational attack upon imbalances is central to the concept of 'harmonisation' of macropolicies. However, 'harmonisation' does not confront the problem of target incompatibility and the distinction should be made explicit. According to Johnson, the need for harmonisation would be eliminated in a world of freely floating exchange rates.[1] Harmonisation must, therefore, be taken as accepting the pattern of flows on capital and current account that would evolve in a world in which national economic authorities remained passive in the international process. Any incompatibility of goals is solved by the intensities of demand and the pleasure-pain calculus that determine the ultimate pattern of international transactions. This passive acceptance of the virtues of the market mechanism would seem to reflect either the traditional neglect in balance-of-payments theory of the capital account (and direct investment in particular) or a complete faith in the benignity of direct and portfolio

[1] Harry G. Johnson, Paul Wonnacott and Hirofumi Shibata, *Harmonization of National Economic Policies Under Free Trade* (Toronto: Private Planning Association of Canada, 1969) pp. 33–5.

capital flows – a faith which is rejected in many nations at the present time.

Contrast the passive attitude which harmonisation seems to betoken,[2] with a system of adjustment that recognises the importance that nations can attach to achieving specific values for their international target variables. First conceive of an ideal situation in which international targets obey the constraint. Each nation's aggregate goals will be met by suitable adjustments involving something of a *tâtonnement*. No balance-of-payments policy undertaken by one nation will be offset by another for quantitative purposes since the adjustment instigated by one country will assist the trading partner in achieving its own goals. (It is possible that quasi-adjustments will have qualitative effects that will engender mutually-frustrating policies.) But, provided that nations rely upon basic adjustments, international instruments will not conflict with domestic measures and nothing will prevent nations from reaching their feasible targets. If, however, targets were not compatible and nations were not willing passively to accept the slings and arrows of fortune, policy actions by one nation will interfere with the efforts of trading partners to achieve their own goals and will be wholly or partially offset. Adjustment will be stillborn and the efficiency of domestic policies must surely suffer. Target incompatibility is a broader concept than harmonisation since, while both policies allow for international co-operation in the adjustment process, target incompatibility allows for nations to exchange their views *ex ante* on their international targets. Anticipatory consultation would permit advance recognition of disturbance arising from unsympathetic aims and a serious barrier to effective harmonisation would be laid bare.

One of the fundamental tenets of the doctrine of mercantilism was its insistence upon the desirability of an export surplus. If all nations instigated policies to attain an export surplus, incompatibility of targets was a hallmark of the mercantilist era. Keynes' never-ending concern for the level of employment in the United Kingdom induced him to provide the mercantilist doctrine with a partial and conditional rehabilitation in *The General Theory*. Keynes saw virtue in the preoccupation of mercantilist thinkers with a positive or favourable balance on trade account. The positive balance made a direct contribution to aggregate demand and to employment levels and an indirect contribution through the effect of an influx of precious metals

[2] Harmonisation can have anticipatory features, see *ibid.*, pp. 35–6.

upon the level of interest rates. He also noted that protectionist measures could be justified as a means of precluding the abortion of a domestic expansion by preventing foreign leakage of aggregate demand. However, he did recognise that all of these devices were inferior to a simultaneous expansion of aggregate demand in all nations so that changes in trade balances would be of little account.[3]

As Keynes painted it, the policy implications of mercantilism could be described in the concepts presented in the preceding chapters, as involving the use of basic adjustments and/or quasi-adjustments to maintain a continuing surplus on the balance of trade. The problem of maintaining that surplus on a continuing basis was not solved by Keynes. No nation can maintain a continuing surplus and a continuing influx of precious metals unless other nations passively accept both the deficit and the efflux. Further, in the absence of a secular growth in the stock of precious metals absolutely as large as the desired trade surplus, the mercantilist policy would absorb greater and greater proportions of the world stock and must ultimately founder. Under modern conditions, a positive balance of trade can be maintained for much longer periods by the simple expedient of matching a continuing outflow of long-term capital with a surplus on trade account. This device requires that some nation be willing to accept the decrease in international net worth and, at the same time, negates the indirect effect of a monetary inflow upon the rate of interest. In the same way, a nation can achieve a positive balance of labour without international saving by a series of unilateral transfers. The latter method has the additional advantage of failing to generate a return flow of dividends and interest to reduce the balance obtainable on trade account.

In terms of the competitive ratio, seventeenth-century mercantilism advocated that C_P exceeds C_T^* and/or C_T' and the investment version of mercantilism would require that C_P equal C_B^* (C_C^*) which exceeds C_T^*. In more traditional terms, mercantilism advocates the establishment and maintenance of a slight undervaluation of the national currency.

Approximately thirty years after Keynes' partial rehabilitation, Professor Joan Robinson chose as the topic of her inaugural lecture, *The New Mercantilism*.[4]

---

[3] *The Means to Prosperity*, p. 24.
[4] Pages 9–10. The term 'new mercantilism' is also used by Kari Levitt but her view is firm-oriented (microeconomic rather than national (macroeco-

The great slump is now a half-forgotten nightmare. Ever since the war, partly by good luck, partly by good management and partly by the arms race, overall effective demand has been kept from serious relapses. Nowadays governments are concerned not just to maintain employment, but to make national income grow. Nevertheless, the capitalist world is still something of a buyer's market, in the sense that capacity to produce exceeds what can be sold at a profitable price. Some countries have experienced spells of excessive demand, but this corrects itself only too soon. The chronic condition for industrial enterprise is to be looking around anxiously for prospects of sales. Since the total market does not grow fast enough to make room for all, each government feels it a worthy and commendable aim to increase its own share in world activity for the benefit of its own people.

This is the new mercantilism.

. . .

For the rest, everyone is keen to sell and wary of buying. Every nation wants to have a surplus in its balance of trade. This is a game where the total scores add up to zero. Some can only win if others lose.

The new mercantilism whose concepts are followed by developed nations in the modern world, is not that defended or rationalised by Keynes. His partial rehabilitation depended upon the existence of depression in foreign countries and an inability on the part of the nations of the world to achieve high levels of employment through the effective use of macrostabilisation instruments. But the new mercantilism does have close ties to traditional mercantilism. Both have as their primary attirbutes a desire for an undervaluation of the currency and a willingness to manipulate international instrument variables in order to achieve national goals without any concern for the repercussions on trading partners' welfare, for global efficiency or for the repercussions of their goals on their own welfare in the longer-run. The main additions brought by the new to the traditional concept of mercantilism are the explicit inclusion of foreign investment as a national goal and the possibility that the undervaluation of a currency could be self-perpetuating.[5] Pursuit of mercantilist

nomic). The concept of mercantilism used here is traditional and Robinsonian.
See Kari Levitt, *Silent Surrender* (Toronto: Macmillan Company of Canada, 1970) p. 3 and pp. 157–85.
[5] Robinson, *The New Mercantilism*, pp. 16–17.

policies reinforces the deflationary bias that exists in the modern world. As each nation, pursuing its separate ends, attempts to avoid purchasing as much from foreigners as it sells to them, the deflationary bias is extended to resource allocation as well. Particularly in those nations that do not achieve their sought-after surplus on trade account, impediments to imports are erected. These spawn counter-measures in erstwhile surplus nations and the whole apparatus of protectionism is nurtured because the interdependence of national goals is disregarded in the process of policy formulation.

The advantages of having an undervalued currency consist of the impetus to employment, freedom for financiers and large firms to invest abroad, and the possibility that an unfavourable adjustment may be averted if it occurs when the currency is undervalued. The impetus to employment is only beneficial if the impetus can be expected to continue for some period of time, since a temporary surplus will lead to overinvestment in tradable goods industries.[6] Freedom to invest abroad is particularly important for direct investment in differentiated goods industries designed to serve host country markets. Competition to establish capacity in these industries and to establish a substantial market share in a fast-growing market can be severe and a temporal primacy invaluable. If focus-country concerns are free to invest abroad and their competitors in foreign countries are constrained by balance-of-payments considerations, the long-run advantage gained by national firms may be large. An undervalued currency may be self-sustaining but the hypothesis is unproven. According to Mrs Robinson, freedom from balance-of-payments constraints will permit domestic investment to proceed at the maximum desirable pace. This unimpeded flow of investment will add to productivity and diminish any tendency for wage increases to exceed the productivity gains and will thereby lessen the rate of inflation. In countries in which stop–go investment policies are enforced by balance-of-payments strains, increases in productivity will be less capable of offsetting cost-push pressure. Implicit in this hypothesis is the assumption of passiveness by the deficit nation. Finally, the possibility that adjustments to favourable and unfavourable disturbances do not have symmetric real cost patterns can make a sustainable degree of currency undervaluation advantageous. If the cost of adjustment per unit change in the competitive ratio needed for balance is greater for unfavourable than for favourable

[6] See Nicholas Kaldor, *The Economic Journal*, 81 (March 1971).

disturbances, there is a clear argument for maintaining a slight under-valuation of the currency. This apparent advantage could be negated if the asymmetry in costs of adjustment were matched by an asymmetry in the probable 'sign' of the disturbance – that is if an under-valuation of the currency increased the probability that an adverse disturbance would occur.

The interdependence between the gains to be enjoyed from currency undervaluation and the probability that these gains will be thwarted is the essence of target incompatibility. The problem involves a kind of externality that is very reminiscent of the paradox of thrift. Attempts to achieve a target that is inconsistent with the goals of trading partners run a significant risk of being frustrated by the classical medicine or by overt or covert policy decisions on the part of trading partners. Since the benefits of undervaluation are positively related by the length of time over which the undervaluation can be maintained consistent with the achievement of domestic goals, the costs of pursuing mercantilist policies will be likely to exceed the national as well as the global benefits.

In a multination world, it is quite possible that some nations will be defining their international targets in different dimensions. In this way, nations could get misleading signals from other nations as they impose policies on different subaccounts. The less apparent the incompatibility of targets, the greater are the potential costs.

Consider a nation, the investor, that defines its targets in terms of a zero basic balance but has a surplus on current account that is less than its deficit on capital account. The basic balance will be negative. Assume that the unilateral transfer balance is zero and that the volume of international saving that would be achieved in the absence of concurrent feedback saving be negative. Let the rest of the world, the host, define its target in terms of the current account and aim at balance. The targets are defined in different dimensions. The host may be willing to accept that its basic balance be zero so that it is possible for the targets to be compatible in terms of the basic balance but incompatible in terms of the current balance. If the investing nation attempts to increase its rate of international saving by basic or by quasi-adjustments, it will work directly counter to the host who will also be attempting to improve its current account. Mutual frustration is unavoidable. The dilemma here can be traced to the fact that the investor's rate of autonomous saving is negative and the host that has positive autonomous saving, sees itself as having an overvalued currency. What is a fairly apparent source of inefficiency when couched in a two-country framework, will be less so in a multi-nation world. Had the investing nation realised that it was seeking to invest more quickly than its trading partner was willing to allow and had it, accordingly, restricted its capital outflow, there would have been no conflict in the balance-of-payments policies. When the negative autonomous saving of the investing nation manifested itself as concurrent feedback saving diminished, both nations would be willing to adjust their current balances.

There are two other kinds of target incompatibility that deserve mention. Both of these revolve around the mix of debits and credits in the capital account and in the monetary account – the latter being assumed to include transactions in short-term assets. A nation wishing to acquire real foreign assets through direct investment may have no basic deficit because of an inflow of portfolio capital or because monetary liabilities may flow in to eliminate any imbalance on autonomous transactions. While compositional factors in goods and services account have no place in balance-of-payments theory, compositional factors in the capital account can be an important source of target incompatibility. If direct investments earn a higher rate of return than portfolio investments or are repugnant to the host on nationalistic grounds, the host may attempt to delimit the ability of the investing nation to acquire real assets within its boundaries. If attempts to reduce the rate of acquisition of real assets in the host lead to the host attempting to force the investing nation into a current or base deficit (by achieving a surplus on current account) the incompatibility of international targets will generate inefficiency.[7] When the acquisition of real assets is semi-automatically financed by counter flows of liquid funds, similar dangers of incompatibility arise.[8]

Differences in time horizons over which adjustments are to be achieved can make otherwise compatible goals incompatible. This possibility is particularly relevant when nations envisage undergoing a temporary deficit that will be self-eliminating such as a plan to accelerate growth involving a temporary deficit pending the in-corporation of the additional productive capacity and technology. If trading partners are not made aware of and/or do not fully condone

[7] The classic example of this kind of policy recently was the French policy during the last years of the presidency of General de Gaulle.

[8] A rough estimate shows that from 1950 to 1970, the United States acquired long-term foreign assets worth $96 billion while saving internationally only $49 billion. See my *The Economics of Business Investment Abroad*, p. 24.

the temporary deficit, incompatibility may occur because of timing problems rather than because of any long-run incompatibility of targets.

The possibility of target incompatibility has been considered as though nations had specific values for their international targets. Given the greater emphasis that tends to be placed upon the achievement of domestic economic goals, it is quite possible that international targets are specified as ranges of acceptable imbalances in the dominant dimension. In such circumstances, targets only become incompatible when the sum of the lower limits of, say, the balances on goods and services exceeds zero. The greater the range of targets, the smaller would the risk of incompatibility seem to be. Any comfort drawn from this fact is likely to be short-lived. Having a range for a target merely specifies a maximum rate of deficit-financing that will be condoned. Unless the situation is temporary and will reverse itself without any positive policy action – in which case financing is likely to be a very acceptable policy – international reserves will be depleted and some positive policy action will ultimately be inevitable.

There is a paucity of official pronouncements about international payments targets but both the United Kingdom and the United States have gone on record as wanting to achieve surpluses on current account. Target deficits are not to be found for developed nations. In the real world, then, the possibility of incompatibility of payments targets can be considered to be sufficiently probable and of sufficient importance to warrant considering means for its elimination.[9]

ANTICIPATORY CONSULTATION AND FACILITATED ADJUSTMENT

To eliminate or prevent the inefficiencies in macro-policies that will result from the existence of incompatible payments targets will require co-operation among nations. This co-operation will be an

---

[9] For the United Kingdom, see the Radcliffe Report, *Committee on the Working of the Monetary System Report* (Cmnd. 827: London, 1959) pp. 22–3. For the United States see the statements attributed to Secretary of the Treasury John Connally in *The Washington Post*, 16 September 1971, p. 1, and later validated in the *Economic Report of the President, 1972*, (Washington: U.S. Government Printing Office, 1972) pp. 154–5. According to these pronouncements, the United States required a $9 billion surplus on current account less government grants and a $13 billion increase in the current account. Employment aspects were not absent from this stated need.

ongoing process since there is no reason to believe that targets, once made compatible, will not revert into conflict. Thus, if a forum for the reconciliation of target incompatibility were to be instituted, it must be seen as a permanent addition to the network of international institutions devoted to economic co-operation. The permanency of these arrangements will derive from the greater magnitude and the increased frequency of disturbances that characterise the modern world. In addition to their direct effect through changes in composition and direction, the large flows of international investment may also help to engender uncertainty and cautiousness in the minds of the economic authorities so that targets are more likely to be incompatible. This section considers (1) how target incompatibility might be reduced by regular, anticipatory consultation and negotiation by the national authorities, (2) what would be required of the participants in such a conference, and (3) how such consultation would naturally expand to serve as a means of facilitating accommodation to balance-of-payments strains.

There is nothing novel in the suggestion that national economic authorities consult on balance-of-payments problems. Consultation has taken place informally among members of the O.E.C.D. nations to consider their secretariat's forecast of the balances of payments of member nations. However, approaching the consultation in a formal way and making a declaration of targets prerequisite to that consultation would provide a novel aspect to the process. Essentially what is being added is discipline. J. J. Polak has cited four conditions that are necessary for the successful international co-ordination of economic policies in addition to the need for clearly-formulated sets of goals.[10] These are:

(1) A commitment on the part of participating nations to observe certain rules.
(2) The presence of objective tests to determine the fulfilment of an undertaking.
(3) Negotiations should be specified in terms of concrete government measures rather than in terms of the effects of such measures.
(4) The effects on other countries of any measures taken should be obvious and specific.

It would be necessary for participating nations to agree to announce

[10] J. J. Polak, I.M.F. *Staff Papers*, IX (July 1962) pp. 163–4.

composite targets giving all three target balances or ranges and identifying the dominant balance. The announcement of targets would inevitably involve a degree of forecasting since it makes little sense to announce a target rate of international saving unless the expected flows of international investment and of international transfers are known. To the extent that the forecasting of component parts of the balance of payments is a prerequisite to the consultative process, the basis for negotiation may be more rough-hewn than shaped. Machlup has cautioned the profession about the dangers of forecasting the 'market balance' and the art of forecasting international payments is still in its infancy.[11] However, there is no reason not to suppose that a good measure of improvement is attainable in international fore-casting in much the same way that improvements have made in forecasting domestic performances. The announcement of targets would also require that estimates be furnished of domestic targets for the ensuing period and the prospect of compatibility could be tested against both full-employment targets and cyclically-adjusted balances.[12] It is certainly not necessary for international consultation on the question of target compatibility that forecasts be perfectly accurate or that a full global model of international payments and the supporting domestic flows be constructed. The need for forecasts derives from their use in formulating targets and in their potential value as bases for negotiation in the event that targets are incom-patible. Whatever the success of the process of international consulta-tion, the discipline imposed upon national economic authorities in the formulation of payments targets must almost inevitably benefit the overall efficiency of macrostabilisation techniques.

Given the enunciation of international targets and the expectations about the levels of domestic performance, the compatibility of international payments goals could be tested. If all nations in the world were represented, the first step would be a simple exercise in arithmetic.[13] In the absence, as is probable, of several nations, the

[11] Fritz Machlup, 'Three Concepts of the Balance of Payments and the So-called Dollar Shortage', *The Economic Journal*, LX (1950) pp. 26–48.

[12] See *The Economic Report of the President, 1972*, pp. 152–3.

[13] Mr Michael V. Posner, in his very valuable paper, 'The World Monetary System: A Minimal Program for Reform', *Essays in International Finance*, No. 96 (October 1972) pp. 3–4, suggests that only five nations are so interdependent as to prevent easy devaluation. The larger forum is suggesteed on the grounds that no important trading nation would want to feel it was not crucially involved and, that, while smaller nations may devalue to remove deficits, there might be resistance to deliberate achievement of surpluses.

net balance of the participating nations would have to be equal and opposite to the net target balance of the non-participating nations. This balance, or range of balances, could then be assessed as realistic or unrealistic. If, as is to be expected, the nations not represented would be predominantly developing nations, the reasonableness of the computed joint target would not be independent of the volume of transfer and investment credits that they were forecast to receive net from the participating nations. If the joint target for the non-participating nations was deemed to be reasonable, basic target compatibility could be said to exist. If the joint target were not realistic, it would be necessary for the participating nations to readjust their individual targets until basic compatibility were achieved. The final, negotiated targets would, like the original targets, have to be announced publicly so that nations submitted themselves to the discipline of an avowed position. Clearly this process of the elimination of target incompatibility would represent a complex bargaining phenomenon, perhaps of the magnitude of GATT negotiations in the early years, since alteration of a nation's avowed target would be likely to entail some change in its competitive position and its actual balance-of-payments performance. Once basic compatibility had been reached through negotiation, participating nations might consider the possibilities of bilateral incompatibilities with their more important trading partners since it is quite possible that compositional factors in bilateral relationships would be unacceptable. These factors might comprise the mix of direct and portfolio investments that were aimed at or forecast and/or the mix between international saving and financing that was foreseen on a bilateral basis even though the overall goals seemed acceptable. The solution of the compositional, bilateral incompatibility would be capable of disrupting the overall basic compatibility that had been obtained, and it is probable that both sorts of compatibility would, in practice, be negotiated simultaneously.

International negotiation on international payments targets and imbalances will require an ability to communicate with precision and without fear of misunderstanding. Delicate negotiations cannot be conducted when language is susceptible of ambiguity. It is necessary then as a precondition for the elimination of target incompatibility that there be some common frame of reference that would provide sets of common definitions, a common vocabulary and common approach to the interrelationships that exist among the various subsectors of the international accounts and the transactions that they embody. In the same way, the frame of reference must be couched in a short-run model since policies are formulated and conducted in terms of the short run.

Polak's first two requirements for successful international co-ordination of economic policies are that nations agree to observe certain rules of conduct and that their obedience or non-obedience to the agreed-upon code be clear from objective tests. A negotiated compatibility of international targets will not benefit the efficiency of global economic policies unless nations actually seek to realise their revised, and not their original targets. Thus the test of the elimination of target incompatibility is not in the avowal but in the practice of target revision. Negotiation on targets is meaningless until nations bargain in concrete terms on how the compatible targets will be achieved. The introduction of specific government measures – basic or quasi-adjustments – fulfills Polak's third and fourth requirements. The element of forecasting that was implicit in target formulation, now becomes *explicit and mandatory*. Ideally the process of negotiation becomes directly relevant to ongoing or anticipated payments imbalances and incorporates pre-agreement or simultaneous agreement of all participating nations on the necessary adjustments or on the necessary financing.

It should be immediately apparent that the precision of exact payments balance or the exact attainment of targets is not the goal of the negotiations. Rather the intent is to keep unforeseen imbalances in payments relatively small and to create machinery that will facilitate their elimination. In this way severe adjustments under crisis conditions and mutually-offsetting policies will be eliminated. The world of international payments is too complex and too subject to unforeseen disturbances to be an area in which fine-tuning virtuosi may exhibit their skills.

There remains the need for enforcement and discipline. Nations do not willingly adjust. The process of negotiation must be based on forecast balances as well as on target balances and it is possible that nations could attempt to subvert the process of adjustment by deliberate underestimation of their forecast balance of payments. In this way they might achieve their original rather than their revised target. Some discipline could be enforced by requiring that participating governments make available as interest-free loans for periods of up to five years, the proceeds of any untargeted surplus on basic balance. Such a measure would diminish the incentive to achieve a surplus that was not agreed upon. Of course, the original *Prosposals for an International Clearing Union*[14] would have had the surplus nation as well as the deficit nation pay interest on any imbalance over and above a certain specified amount. It remains to be proved that the world has yet come far enough to agree to such a proposal. However, some penalty for an untargeted surplus will help to keep the process of bargaining reasonably honest. Additionally national forecasts will automatically generate forecasts for other important trading nations and will serve as checks on inaccurate forecasts.

Another measure that would diminish the incentive to achieve a surplus that was not agreed upon would be an equivalent to the Scarce Currency Clause defined in Article VII of the I.M.F. Charter.[15] This would allow the group of consulting nations to introduce restrictions directed against any member of the group that persisted in running unplanned surpluses. Presumably the most important part of these restrictions would consist of measures of commercial policy against imports from that nation. Group action of this kind might be invoked if the surplus achieved by a nation (in excess of any planned surplus) were to amount to 5 per cent (or more) of imports of goods and services and investment income debits for two consecutive years. The offending nation might avoid the restrictive measures by negotiating a defiict of suitable size in the third year and taking appropriate (concrete) steps to attain such a deficit.

If the world continues to view impediments to international investment as less harmful than are quasi-adjustments on current account items, the participating nations could agree upon a limitation of capital flows out of deficit nations. There are obvious problems entailed in such an agreement. The restrictions should apply only to new investments and not to ongoing direct-investment subsidiaries since these operations might be vulnerable to reduced support from the parent organisation. More importantly the exercise of constraint on capital movements should not be left only to the authorities in the potentially-deficit country. Prospective host nations must refuse permission for new investments in their nations when the funds would originate from a potentially-deficit nation. In cases in which

[14] Cmnd. 6437 (London: H.M.S.O., 1943), reprinted in *World Monetary Reform – Plans and Issues*, ed. Herbert G. Grubel (Stanford: Stanford University Press, 1963) pp. 54–79.

[15] See Brian Tew, *International Monetary Cooperation, 1945–56* (London: Hutchinson University Library, 1958) pp. 91–3.

host nations particularly wanted the investment to take place, they should be constrained to finance the investment (less concurrent feedback saving) by a government-to-government loan. The purpose of such arrangements would be to preclude nations investing internationally without generating the necessary international saving except with the permission of the host government and to avoid attempts to reduce capital flows via impediments on current account items.

To the extent that the original set of international payments targets was incompatible, the revision of targets would require some negotiated adjustment. Clearly the economic and negotiating skills necesssary for such agreement do not now exist. Nor are governments, currently, likely to be willing to consign their payments targets to a group of economists – even expert economists. Like the forecasting skills, the expertise will need to evolve slowly. The most difficult part of the process from a technical viewpoint will be to distinguish between reversing and shift or trend disturbances – particularly where the reversal will take place well into the future. In the beginning, then, there will be a tendency to emphasise adjustment rather than financing, although the existence of short-run phenomena should make nations wary of too quick adjustments of the competitive ratio.

Negotiations of the type proposed here would need to be conducted in some international forum. The International Monetary Fund is the organisation best qualified to serve as the forum. However, because the process of adjustment is central to the proposed negotiation, the Fund would need to undergo a change in *Weltanschauung* before it could be expected to function effectively in the role of neutral mediator–arbiter. The Fund has a history of distaste for adjustment and, if this distaste has weakened over the years, it is not yet dead. Another possible forum is the GATT. The type of negotiations proposed are of the kind that have fallen within the experience of the GATT. Moreover if commercial policy measures are more and more involved in balance-of-payments negotiations, as seems possible, the GATT becomes an increasingly fitting forum.

It is possible to draw a clear analogy between the problem of target compatibility and international co-operation and the problem of macrostabilisation in a closed economy. In the latter, the task is to ensure that sectoral plans and targets are both mutually compatible and, at the same time, not in conflict with national economic goals.

Thus international co-ordination on payments imbalances is reminiscent of indicative planning among nations. However, there is
an argument to be made that international co-operation is more
important than is domestic internal planning of a formal variety. The
reason for the lesser need for domestic planning is the ability of the
authorities to substitute automatic stabilisers for planning at least
as far as the goal of high employment is concerned. But it is the very
success of domestic policies in achieving high levels of employment
in the post Second World War era that has destroyed what might be
called, the international payments stabiliser or the classical medicine.
In a world committed to high levels of employment, the international
market is not allowed to transmit its signals for correction. It is the
absence of automatic political or mechanical solutions to payments
imbalances that would make anticipatory consultation potentially
such a valuable addition to the international mechanism.

CONCLUSION

What has been proposed does smack of Erewhon, or perhaps it
constitutes an adjustment equivalent for Paretian optimum. But a
consideration of the alternatives makes the case for moving in the
direction of international co-operation stronger. The alternatives are
a choice between the experience of the recent past and a system of
flexibility of exchange rates. In the recent past, adjustment procedures can only be described as crisis-induced. Adjustments have
taken place long after the need for them arose and have usually been
much more severe than would have been needed under a system in
which adjustments were not delayed. Even a more responsive system
of *ex post* adjustment would be unsatisfactory in some absolute sense
and would not eliminate the possibility of target incompatibility. A
system of freely-flexible exchange rates will not, in the real world,
operate as efficiently as Milton Friedman would wish. In a world in
which nations have policy targets other than balance on autonomous
international transactions – be these targets explicit or implicit –
national economic authorities will interfere with the pure market
mechanism to achieve those goals. The market rates would reflect
the determination behind the interferences and mutually-offsetting
measures would be commonplace. To the extent that these measures
were restricted to monetary phenomena, no harm would be
done. But, once given a 'legitimate' reason for interfering in the

foreign exchange markets, national authorities would have the same opportunities for delaying adjustments that they enjoy under the so-called adjustable peg. To the extent that the authorities availed themselves of these opportunities, the value of a system of flexible rates would be severely impaired. (Note that even under international co-operation the possibility of delay exists but it requires explicit acknowledgement on the part of both debtor and surplus countries and the risk of losses to central banks.) It is quite possible that under a system of flexible rates of exchange that, contrary to Friedman's implications,[16] that exchange and trade controls would flourish as nations attempted to achieve a payments surplus.

The proposed system of anticipatory consultation and co-operation in adjustment does not determine the rate at which basic adjustments are made. The system is fully compatible with concept of gliding parities – particularly so as the anticipatory system would involve an ongoing process of consultation. At the same time, the mechanism for anticipatory consultation would reduce the probability that nations would fail to obey 'the presumptive rules'.[17]

[16] See Friedman's remarks in *The International Adjustment Mechanism*, p. 115.
[17] For a proposal for gliding parities and a critique of the mechanism, see Richard N. Cooper, 'Flexing the International Monetary System: The Case for Gliding Parities', and J. Marcus Fleming, 'Discussion', in *The International Adjustment Mechanism*, pp. 141–64.

11 The Monetary Background

The aggregate theory excluded from its compass autonomous international flows of convertible currencies whether they be held in interest-bearing short-term assets or in liquid funds. Questions of domestic monetary phenomena are subsumed in the macroeconomic aggregates that they generate and are incorporated into the question of international payments adjustment through these macroeconomic effects. The purpose of segregating international monetary elements from the so-called real elements of international payments was to permit separate analysis of the functioning of the real sector. The basic hypothesis is that, if the real sector can be kept in approximate balance through intelligent balance-of-payments policies, the real sector would not be a source of disturbances that would cause disruption in the monetary sector. These derivative monetary disturbances would be likely, in turn, to aggravate the malfunctioning in the real sector. It is, of course, equally important that the monetary system be sufficiently flexible that it does not generate within itself disturbances that it can transmit to the real sector. The purpose of this chapter is to consider what international monetary arrangements would be necessary for the sector to function smoothly in the absence of real disturbances.

Disturbances can be defined as originating in the international monetary sector when international movements of liquid funds force the competitive position of a nation to deviate from that value which is consonant with its balance-of-payments posture. Such a deviation would cause flows of exports and imports of goods and services and, possibly, flows of international long-term capital to be disrupted from their expected paths to the detriment of the system of resource allocation and the achievement of domestic goals. This problem has its analogue in the closed-economy model in which it is important to avoid bank failures, and fear of bank failures, that can disrupt the normal flows of spending.

The first problem is that which exists when there is a trend inflow of monetary assets into a nation over a lengthy period of time. Such a flow would tend to bias the policies of the recipient nation towards a deficit on basic balance that might be at odds with its national goals. The second characteristic which an efficient monetary system should enjoy is the ability to avoid having imposed upon the world, the set of exchange rates that appear to speculators to be warranted. What appears to the business community to be an appropriate set of exchange rates may be at variance with that set that best suits the economic goals of the family of nations. Finally, there is the question of the desirable amount of international liquidity that should be created for the monetary system to function smoothly.

THE PROBLEM OF A LASTING MONETARY FLOW

Since the industrial revolution, dominant national currencies have served as the main unit of account and medium of exchange for international transactions. These key currencies were deemed sufficiently strong that private corporations, commercial banks and central banks from other countries held working or transaction balances, and also precautionary balances in these key currencies. The acquisition of these balances represented a use to which international saving was devoted. These balances tended to grow over time with the world price level and the volume of international trade so that a key-currency nation was a recipient of an enduring inflow of liquid funds. This monetary inflow presented problems of policy for the key-currency nation and these problems were capable of undermining the strength of the international financial system.

A lasting monetary inflow presents a nation with three policies among which it must chose: to enjoy improved terms of trade and to reduce its international net worth by running a deficit on current and basic balances so that it accommodated the targets of the other nations; to run a deficit on capital account by investing in illiquid assets abroad and in this way to serve as an intermediary;[1] or to acquire with the proceeds of the monetary inflow, liquid foreign assets. The diminution of international net worth is likely to conflict with the national goals of a strong, rich nation. Further such a policy is likely to weaken, ultimately, the confidence in the key currency. To use the inflow of short-term funds to acquire illiquid

[1] See Emile Despres, Charles P. Kindleberger and Walter S. Salant, 'The Dollar and World Liquidity: A Minority View', *The Economist* (5 February 1966) pp. 526–9.

assets can strengthen net receipts of investment income, and particularly so if the key-currency nation is saving internationally at the same time, but the liquidity position of the nation will gradually deteriorate to such a stage that a crisis of confidence must sooner or later be induced. The third policy option prevents the key currency from becoming vulnerable but it is, at the same time, self-defeating since it does not permit foreign nations as a group to increase their international net worths and their transactions balances.

There is a fourth possible course of action that has never been tested. It involves a variant of the intermediation process originally conceived by Despres, Kindleberger and Salant. The acquisition of short-term liabilities in the key-currency nation would be offset by 'counter-investment' in long- or medium-term assets defined in the appropriate foreign currency. This would provide the non-key-currency nation with the liquidity that it requires but would not allow the acquisition of working balances to affect the international net worth of either party. What this would amount to is merely the creation of liquidity by deliberate international agreement, and bilaterally rather than indirectly in the way that Triffin originally recommended. The key-currency nation would acquire counterpart assets and would undertake to use them only when there were monetary withdrawals from its currency that might endanger the international system. Presumably the key currency would derive no benefit from such an undertaking and would be likely to incur a cost. This cost might well be smaller than the breakdown of the system when the ultimate crisis was encountered when intermediation was effected by the acquisition of direct investments and might well be less than that imposed by the inability to adjust that the unswerving maintenance of the parity of the key currency required. Under a system of counter-investment, the key currency would be allowed to change its parity since the gain from the counterpart assets could be used to repay the loss incurred in holding a depreciated key currency.

The potential basic conflict that is evident in the key currency arrangement is still greater in the modern world in which rich nations cannot allow the classical medicine to work its painful cure for currency overvaluation. The essential characteristic of a key currency is its ability to avoid inflicting an exchange-loss upon its holders. Only if they can be reasonably sure of such safety will foreigners be willing to hold the currency as an asset. In the modern era in which domestic deflation is not a feasible national policy, no national currency could continue to function as a key currency in the face of a long trend disturbance that was adverse. Sterling was able to function well as a key currency prior to 1914 because of its financial dominance, the absence of any serious adverse trend disturbance and because of London's indifference to depressions which tended to be more severe in the peripheral regions of its world. The dollar was able to function as a key currency because it started from a position of great strength and temporarily enjoyed financial dominance. However, the inflow of liquid funds was used to finance a basic deficit at a time when an adjustment would have been desirable had it not been for the key currency status of the dollar. The era of the key currency has passed. No longer can a national currency both assume the dominance and be assured of the requisite favourable or non-adverse trend disturbance. It is necessary to find some means, other than a national currency, to serve as the unit in which transactions balances can be held. For this, some international unit of account will be necessary and central banks will need to be able to hold assets designated in that numeraire.[2]

It is possible that there will be long-lasting monetary flows in the absence of a key currency but the probability of a protracted inflow on monetary account into a nation becomes much less probable. Any such flows would present the same set of problems as key currency status for the recipient nation. Provided that the monetary authorities could neutralise the inflow and use the funds to acquire some type of international asset – special drawing rights in the Krause plan – there would be no adverse consequences. Such flows can both result from and embarass domestic macrostabilisation policies. It may prove desirable for nations to have the acknowledged privilege to discriminate against foreign monetary inflows in much the same way that a nation will maintain its right to refuse to allow foreign direct investments that are not in the national interest, to take place.

Any monetary flows not connected with key currency status are unlikely to be long-lasting, although seemingly persistent flows could result from interest rate differentials or expectations of a change in parity. The interest rate differential will only give rise to a finite flow, although it could be uncomfortably large for small nations. The expectation of a change in a parity requires a separate system to

[2] For an insightful proposal incorporating such an arrangement see Lawrence B. Krause, *Sequel to Bretton Woods*, Ch. 4.

preclude the possibility that such flows do create disturbances that originate in the international monetary sector.

NEUTRALISING EXCHANGE-RATE SPECULATION

A system of international co-operation on balance-of-payments policies implies a system of managed rates of exchange as participating nations finance deficits as well as institute mutually agreed upon basic adjustments. It is quite possible that the group of economic authorities will rationally agree to allow a particular nation to run a basic deficit for a protracted period. If this policy has been adopted it is important that the set of exchange rates not be imperilled by waves of speculation in the foreign exchange market. Such speculation may easily occur if the duration of the deficit is thought to exceed the planning horizons of foreign exchange traders and fears for the tenability of the rate of exchange of the currency of the deficit nation appear.

One way of curtailing speculation is to increase the uncertainty that surrounds such an action. A means by which this could be achieved is to widen the band around the parity and to forbid support of currency within the centre of the band. A wider band has obvious attractions but it addresses itself almost completely to the task of the elimination of speculation in liquid funds and does not provide a means whereby a trend or a sizeable shift disturbance could be adjusted to. Further, to the extent that movements within the band allow adjustments to take place, they would act as a system of flexible rates of exchange and would, in a minor way, involve certain businesses in considerable uncertainty. Within the wider band, variation in exchange rates would ensure that basic balance were obtained in the absence of monetary flows.

A second means of preventing market expectations from disrupting an agreed upon rate of exchange is to influence those expectations to accept that the existing parity or parity band can and will prevail into the indefinite future. To create such a climate will be a complex task when adjustments are foreseen as frequent occurrences. Clearly the problem of small adjustments, such as might be made operative in a system of anticipatory co-operation, is that small adjustments would lead to anticipations of further adjustments in the same direction and therefore would offer speculators a 'one-way' bet. This problem may not be as serious at it at first appears since the volume of funds available to take advantage of such a situation is finite and the situation can be countered at the cost of giving up interest rate policy.[3] However, the recent experience with speculation is in large measure due to the obvious failure of the monetary authorities to set and to maintain a set of exchange rates that was sustainable and to the fact that the overvaluation of particular currencies became irrevocably clear before the authorities adjusted to it.[4] Given that periodic review of any extant set of rates is integral to the co-ordinating mechanism, whether the changes be brought about through formulae, presumptive rules or managed currencies, speculative flows must not be allowed to exert a disruptive effect upon foreign exchange rates.

Any acceptable international monetary system should enable people and businesses to insure against a foreign-exchange loss at a small cost. Insuring against a foreign-exchange loss is essentially a defensive speculation since it involves only changing the timing of a foreign-exchange transaction that would have taken place in the normal course of events as foreign-exchange is converted into the numeraire currency of the owner. Another way of defining defensive speculation is that such speculation does not cause the speculator to take a position in foreign currency. That position has come about in the normal course of operations. Defensive speculation affects the timing of conversions so as to minimise losses or maximise gains from the foreign exchange positions. The volume of funds that can be used for defensive speculation has grown inordinately in recent years as multinational corporations have begun to integrate production, sales and financing more closely. Defensive speculation is a legitimate commercial and financial endeavour. In contrast offensive speculation can be defined as consisting of taking a position in a foreign currency purely in the expectation of making a profit from changes in parities. It is probably inevitable that the system accommodate multinational corporations and, therefore, defensive speculation. But, a system that accepts defensive speculation as legitimate must also accommodate offensive speculation since the two cannot be distinguished. The task, then, is to create a mechanism or set of institutional arrangements whereby speculation will not be allowed to create a disturbance in the international monetary account.

[3] See Ralph C. Bryant, 'Discussion', in *The International Adjustment Mechanism*, pp. 185–6.
[4] See the remarks of Milton Friedman in *ibid.*, pp. 114–16.

To persuade a depositor to keep funds in a commercial bank requires that the depositor have confidence in the bank's ability to be able to pay out in full. The analogy between a commercial bank and the exchange rate has been lucidly drawn by Triffin in his essay on the meaning of convertibility.[5] The need to avoid disruptive switches of deposits among commercial banks in times of financial crisis was apparent in the United States prior to the introduction of deposit insurance by an agency of the Federal Government. Deposit insurance obviated the need for (small) depositors to protect themselves by guaranteeing a 'rate of exchange' on deposits in insured banks. The mechanism whereby speculation in foreign exchange can be defused, is analogous to deposit insurance since it involves the possibility that an agency of the government may make losses on an aspect of its operations. Historically central banks have been less than enthusiastic in their willingness to incur losses in the furtherance of domestic targets. Contracyclical monetary policy does involve the prospect of losses and Keynes envisaged the adequacy of assets as a limiting factor in the conduct of monetary policy *à l'outrance*.[6] This attitude may have changed with reference to domestic policy but there is little evidence, if any, to suggest that central banks would willingly contemplate losses on international account. This does not mean that they do not do so. Support of an untenable exchange rate involves the national authorities in losses when devaluation ultimately takes place.[7]

The impact of defensive speculation on a nation's competitive position can be reduced if the process can be made to bypass the foreign exchange market. This can be achieved by having the central bank in a country stand ready to accept deposits denominated in foreign currencies. The central bank will accept deposits in minimum units of any currency in exchange for the correct amount of its own (domestic) currency calculated at the rate of exchange prevailing in the spot market when the deposit is made. Deposits would be either call money or time deposits of varying maturities. Each deposit would earn interest at the rate prevailing in the main money market

[5] Triffin, *Gold and the Dollar Crisis*, pp. 21–30.
[6] *The Treatise*, II, pp. 334–7. Keynes also seems to have had reservations about the willingness of the Bank of England in the twenties to undertake 'loss operations' in pursuit of aggregate goals.
[7] Herbert G. Grubel provides an analysis of this policy question in 'Official Forward-Exchange Policy and Devaluation', *Weltwirtschaftliches Archiv*, Band 101 (2), 1968, pp. 297–304.

202   *The Implications for the Institutional Setting*

of the currency in which the deposit was defined. In practice it would probably be desirable to have each central bank post an authoritative list of going interest rates at noon, local time, each day. Thus a deposit made in New York in deutsche mark would earn the rate announced in Frankfurt on the same day and a deposit with the Bank of France in U.S. dollars would earn the appropriate rate announced in New York on the preceding day.

Call deposits could be encashed at any time at the existing spot rate. They would be paid out in the currency of the central bank which had accepted the deposit. Interest-rate considerations aside, the central bank would incur a loss by accepting the deposit if its currency had depreciated during the term of the deposit. If the interest rate paid on the 'strong' currency were lower than the central bank could earn on the domestic currency, if it chose to use the funds deposited, the central bank might make a profit on the operation. The bank would have enabled the depositor to take a position in foreign currency in order to offset any position in foreign exchange held commercially. By this means the international monetary system would allow firms to protect themselves against exchange-rate risks without creating any great pressures in the foreign exchange market against the currency that was presumed to be weak or overvalued. Time deposits would be held until term and encashed at the rate of exchange prevailing at noon on the day of maturity. Interest on all deposits would be earned in the currency in which the deposit was defined. It is quite possible that a secondary market would be created in time deposits. In practice there would need to be a minimum deposit size. Small amounts of protection would be obtained in the private and forward foreign exchange markets.

While it is possible that the central bank would accept deposits computed at the rate of exchange prevailing when the deposit was made, it is possible that the involvement of the central banks would be limited to positions in which the rate of exchange in the spot market were at the limit of the band. If deposits could be made at rates of exchange 'within the band', the limits of the band would be less likely to be reached. Maintaining a perfectly elastic demand curve for each currency at the going (or limit) rate of exchange would presumably ensure that the forward market was perfectly sensitive to any interest rate differential.

The existence of this mechanism would reassure speculators that a declared rate of exchange could be maintained because the position

taker takes a position only in its own currency. This possibility will
reduce speculative pressures in the foreign exchange market. However, the existence of foreign-exchange liabilities on the part of central
banks will be likely to affect not only their profit and loss statements
but their attitudes towards the desirability of having realistic rates of
exchange. Certainly there will be less of a tendency for monetary
authorities to intervene in the foreign-exchange markets to stabilise
spot rates within the band and thereby to reduce the uncertainty
facing the speculator. Equally banks in deficit nations will be more
prone to use interest-rate policy aggressively in domestic markets
since the greater the difference between foreign and domestic interest
rates, the smaller is the potential loss exposure on deposits denominated in foreign currency. It is quite possible under this scheme, for
central banks with apparently undervalued currencies to incur losses.
Depositors would be able to earn the higher yields available on a
weak currency by making deposits defined in that currency and, if no
depreciation took place, the central bank would be exposed to a loss
operation. In this way, central banks in surplus nations with undervalued currencies would be made vulnerable in a manner reminiscent
of the Proposals for an International Clearing Union. The potential
loss exposure on both counts, would be likely to act as a catalyst for
the authorities to avoid the unnecessary financing of deficits or any
postponement of currency depreciations that were known ultimately
to be inevitable. It may well be that the attachment of central bankers
and of economic authorities to loss avoidance may provide the
discipline necessary for the international payments co-ordination
mechanism to work with reasonable efficiency.

For this discipline to be imposed upon policy-makers, it would be
useful to require that profit and loss statements on foreign-currency
deposits be computed and published separately from the overall
accounts of the central bank. Presumably the sub-branch concerned
with foreign deposits would lend the domestic currency that it
received to the central bank proper at the going interest rate and
would be authorised to have unlimited access to the assets of the
central bank and central government.

If the authorities were willing to accept the possibility of loss
incurred by the provision of a service in the prevention of (too rapid)
a change in the rate of exchange, the need for a widening of the band
would be eliminated. The greater the width of the band, the smaller
would the loss exposure of the central bank be likely to be, but

variation within the band serves mainly to create uncertainty for speculators at the expense of inflicting uncertainty onto commercial enterprises. As such, it is not an ideal means of preventing speculation.

From the standpoint of monetary policy, the acceptance of foreign-exchange deposits by central banks is no different from the transfer of the funds abroad. Paying domestic currency into the central bank will reduce the money supply in exactly the same way that the purchase of foreign exchange would. The system of the acceptance of deposits in foreign exchange would have the advantage that profits would be known to the tax authorities directly and, to the extent that commercial banks were prone to speculate in foreign exchange, the operations of commercial banks would be visible to the central bank.

An alternative version of the same scheme would be for central banks to strengthen their abilities to withstand speculative pressures by arranging for greater powers of absorption of short-term funds in their own money markets and for unlimited swaps among central banks. Such swaps would carry an exchange-rate guarantee, being denominated in an international unit of account, and central banks would still incur exchange losses when their currency depreciated after a period of support. The main difference between the two systems is that the acceptance of foreign deposits can be more easily subjected to separate reporting of the profit and loss of operations, that the ability of the central banks to withstand speculative pressures is more apparent when the basic liability is defined in domestic currency, and that the acceptance of foreign-currency deposits requires less inter-bank co-operation. A final means of achieving the same end is to supply central banks with large amounts of liquidity in order that it may be able to tide itself over a prolonged period of deficit caused by a reversing disturbance.[8]

The more realistic the exchange-rate structure and the smaller the period-to-period changes in the sets of parities, the smaller is the exposure of central banks to loss under any of the systems. Foreign-currency deposits would be profitable if depreciations did not occur during the term of the deposit. If rates of inflation in all nations were approximately equal, exchange rates would adjust only for changes in real variables and adjustment would be relatively small. If different rates of inflation reinforced the changes in the underlying real variables, exchange rate adjustments would be that much larger. The

[8] See Grubel, 'The Optimum Stability of Exchange Rates'.

greater loss exposure that follows from higher rates of inflation, unless offset by interest-rate differentials, would bias the authorities towards maintaining low differential rates of inflation and this, in turn, might reduce the size of the necessary change in parity.

THE NEEDED GROWTH IN INTERNATIONAL RESERVE ASSETS

The stock of international liquidity and its rate of growth cannot be precisely defined in terms of optima. However, the need for reserves and for their growth are clearly related to the institutional setting in which payments imbalances are resolved. The greater the reliance upon financing and the greater the potential volume of destabilising speculation, the greater will the need for international reserves be. Contrariwise, the more prompt the adjustment procedures, the smaller is the needed volume of reserves likely to be – though it will never be zero, even with freely flexible rates as long as nations desire to retain some control over their international net worth.

Provided that the acquisition of reserves has some cost, there will always be some trade-off among reserve acquisition, international investment and absorption so that the concept of an optimal stock of international reserves has some value from a national policy-making point of view. Presumably it is possible to argue that the total need for reserves is equal to the sum of the needs for reserves of individual nations. Cooper is prepared to argue that the need for reserve growth should be passively decided by the declared need for reserves by the totality of nations.[9] This number would be known as a result of the declaration of payments targets, and special drawing rights would be created to fill this need. Grubel also specifies that the supply of international reserves should be that which fills the needs of the totality of nations and would allow nations to specify this volume in the light of a given cost per unit of reserves held. Grubel argues in favour of a high charge so that the total supply of reserves will be increased until their marginal social productivity is equal to the (low) cost of their creation.[10] Thus, two respected economists would support a generous rate of reserve creation.

To the extent that the creation of direct debt between surplus and deficit nations can replace international reserves, the system of anticipatory consultation and financing proposed in the preceding

[9] Cooper, *The International Adjustment Mechanism*, p. 152.
[10] Grubel, 'The Optimum Stability of Exchange Rates'.

chapter would reduce the need for such ample supplies of S.D.R.s. In the same way the elimination of strains upon the foreign exchange market by internalising speculation in foreign exchange would reduce the volume of reserves required. However, these devices do not necessarily preclude the generous creation of S.D.R.s as a substitute for direct debt. Certainly S.D.R.s have the advantage of being indirect and this quality might facilitate the bargaining about targets and any arrangements for financing deficits that would be involved in the process of anticipatory co-operation and consultation.

There is the question as to whether it is possible to err by arranging for the creation of too much international liquidity. The danger may exist but it is likely to be small and would be fairly easily contained if the changes in global liquidity per period were based on a formula that took target reductions in reserve holdings into account. If a group of nations wanted to run basic deficits ($\Delta R^* < 0$) equal to the sum of target basic surpluses of other nations ($\Delta R^* > 0$), no international liquidity would be created and nations would acquire reserves by running basic surpluses. Too great a stock of reserves could be dangerous if it would contribute to the likelihood that nations would collectively try to run basic deficits. Under such circumstances, a global inflationary situation would prevail although it might be countered by an increase in the rate paid on holdings of the liquidity instrument. The probability of a global inflation being caused by the totality of nations trying to reduce their reserve holdings must, considering the general desirability of current account or basic surpluses, be reckoned quite small.

There is a danger that too great a stock of international reserves could lead a nation to delay making an adjustment that, in the absence of so large a stock of reserves, would have been seen to be inevitable. This nation would ultimately incur the real costs of a failure to adjust and would probably inflict some of those costs on other nations. If the surplus nations are content with their target surplus, there will be no international pressure on the deficit nation to make an adjustment. No system can prevent mistaken analysis or an unwillingness of economic authorities to grasp the nettle firmly.[11]

Balance-of-payments policy formulation is an inexact art. This inexactness must be a strong argument in favour of having the creation of international liquidity err on the side of excess.

[11] More correctly, 'like a man of mettle'.

CONCLUSION

It is important that the international monetary sector be seen as a separate entity. Man cannot avoid real disturbance and must set, as a policy goal, the minimisation of transitional costs of adjustment. However, monetary matters deal with the fiat decisions, man-made international institutions and co-operation. There is no reason, other than human fallibility, for disturbances to begin in the monetary sector and to transmit themselves to the real sector with their attendant social costs of adjustment.

Central bankers and others in authority are those who must guard against human fallibility. They must, in the course of international co-operation, run the risk of appearing to sacrifice national good to global welfare. In this, they must realise that the narrow interests of profit and loss and national wealth must be subordinated to the need to maintain a smooth-running system by using the power of national governments to counterbalance and to offset the spontaneous excesses and shortcomings of the private sector.

12 Valedictory

The essence of the theoretical approach presented in this book is that a short-run approach to the problems of international payments adjustment is necessary because no other framework can allow for the impact of sequences of different types of disturbances to be imposed at irregular intervals. In addition the short-run framework releases nations from the theoretical need to seek payments balance as their international goal and can include national targets other than balance. The implications of the aggregate theory for policy are profound. The innovations require a flexibility in policy-making on the part of national monetary authorities that was not present in the Bretton Woods system.

The search for a successor to the system conceived at Bretton Woods must recognise the interdependence between the types of disturbance that will predominate in international transactions and the characteristics of the new international payments system. In a world committed to the maintenance of high levels of employment, there can be no substitute for adjustments effected through changes in the terms of trade:

> If induced changes in employment are prevented or greatly reduced, virtually the only method of balancing international accounts without resort to direct controls will be through changes in the terms of trade, i.e. through the price system . . . Even without general price and cost changes, the essential means of adjustment contemplated by the classical theory – a change in the terms of trade – can be accomplished through exchange rates . . . [1]

Yet the proper degree of price or exchange-rate flexibility is certainly not pre-ordained. The argument for freely-flexible rates seems to allow for nations to accept with passivity a target of balanced payments and such subordinate balances as the market system shall decree. In the modern world such passivity is not to be expected. A system of freely-flexible rates coupled with nations seeking to use the aggregate of their international transactions for the furtherance of their national 'general interest', cannot but result in 'a dirty

[1] Lloyd A. Metzler, 'The Theory of International Trade', in *A Survey of Contemporary Economics*, ed. Howard S. Ellis (Homewood, Ill.: Richard D. Irwin, 1948), I 220–1.

float'. Such a system would be characterised by the inefficiency that offsetting strategies would create. Further, the probability that reversing disturbances that will optimally require financing will be commonplace, would argue for intelligent intervention by the authorities in the foreign exchange markets.

Yet the greater the incidence of monetary disturbances, the more suitable will be a system of flexible rates of exchange (tailored so as to avoid any risk of destabilising speculation and equipped with a generous amount of international liquidity). The more important are real shift disturbances, the more suitable would be a system of the adjustable peg – provided always that the peg did adjust. The more effective and the smaller the social costs of the classical medicine, the more suitable may a system of fixed exchange rates prove. Finally, if trend disturbances are very prevalent, a gradual system of controlled adjustment (such as gliding parities married either with presumptive rules or international co-operation) is likely to prove the most acceptable format. Since the latter system can also absorb monetary and reversing disturbances, it would seem to be the most promising of all systems.

Not only must the replacement system of international payments be able to allow the world economy to adjust to three types of real disturbances, but it must also be able to absorb the shocks of changes in national targets. It is the likelihood that targets can be incompatible that emphasises the need for international co-operation on an aggregate basis. This co-operation, in turn, would require delicate negotiation and continuing surveillance of the international payments system and of the desires and prospects of its members. For these negotiations, a common frame of reference that is both pragmatic and general, is a necessity. This commonality of language can derive from the concepts incorporated in the aggregate theory.

International payments policy is a part of aggregate national policy. It is necessary that payments policy be set in the same cast as domestic aggregate policy-making and that it accepts as inevitable, short-run shifts in the magnitudes of some of the most important flows. International payments policy must, as must macrostabilisation analysis, avoid the rigidities that a general equilibrium approach can impose. Successful international adjustment requires both a set of international institutions that are capable of flexing to meet the needs of the times and a willingness on the part of national authorities to intervene in the system in concert when and if the need arises.

Index

DATE DUE

SEP 9 '76			
SEP 10 '79			
GAYLORD			PRINTED IN U.S.A.

GAYLORD · PRINTED IN U.S.A.